Prayer Altars

A STRATEGY THAT IS CHANGING NATIONS

JOHN MULINDE
MARK DANIEL

World Trumpet Mission Publishing
Orlando, FL (USA)

Prayer Altars: A Strategy That Is Changing Nations

To order additional copies of Prayer Altars: A Strategy That Is Changing Nations, write to World Trumpet Mission Publishing, PO Box 770447, Orlando, FL 32877; email media@ worldtrumpet.com; visit our website at www.worldtrumpet.com; or call (407)846-8300.

World Trumpet Mission Publishing
PO Box 770447
Orlando, FL 32877

CONTENTS

Acknowledgment

We would like to begin this book by thanking the Lord for His faithfulness and His presence in our lives. Several decades ago, as the nation of Uganda began to seek God and cry out to Him to transform their nation, they found that He was true to His Word. When He said in the Scriptures, "If you seek Me, you will find Me" (Jer 29:13), He truly meant what He said. As the nation pursued God, He began to unfold a strategy of building prayer altars all throughout their land that would touch every aspect of society. This strategy was the key that unlocked the nation of Uganda to the purposes of God.

This book was not developed by one individual receiving revelation from God. It came about because thousands of people started to grasp the concept that building prayer altars could change the course of their nation. These individuals then began to carry the concept of building altars into other nations to see those territories changed as well. This strategy has now been used in several nations, and each time has shown that it is a key to draw the presence of God and bring change.

We therefore want to specifically acknowledge the nation of Uganda, where this strategy that changes nations was birthed and nurtured. An altar of the Lord was first built in the hearts of the people and then in their families, which then spread and ignited in their congregations, workplaces, and communities, and eventually in their nation. Without their obedience to the Lord's direction, we would not have a witness to the power this strategy can have in individuals, families, churches, businesses, communities, and nations.

We want to thank June Perez for the hundreds of hours she spent pulling together teachings and sessions where we would share our hearts and the lessons we have learned. June began working on the book by compiling our messages, thoughts, and notes, putting them in order, working with us through several different drafts, and then continuously focusing on the book production until it was completed.

So many people helped in the production of this book that it is difficult to recognize each one by name. However, to every transcriber, proofreader, editor, researcher, reviewer, intercessor, and assistant—and to all those others whose support, encouragement, prayers, and help made this book possible—we appreciate you and thank the Lord for you. You are a blessing.

We would also like to thank the teams of missionaries we have in Uganda and the United States, who are helping to carry out the work of building altars in their own lives, ministries, and families. We have seen breakthroughs take place in these people and their families because of their altars; they are all living testimonies of what an active prayer altar looks like.

Our missionaries have gone to foreign lands all around the world—such as the Far East, Africa, Europe, and North America—helping to build prayer altars. Many of them have stayed months at a time, working with congregations and different people in the land. They also labor night and day at home to keep the altar going in the mission bases we have in Kampala, Uganda, and Orlando, Florida. Their desire is to share a powerful testimony that is current rather than one from years gone by, so the mission bases are places where they keep the heavens open and the presence of God is experienced continuously.

We want to give special acknowledgment and thanks to our families. Our wives and children have made great sacrifices by releasing us and blessing us to travel around the world to carry the message of awakening and revival. An act of their surrender

—— JOHN MULINDE AND MARK DANIEL ——

to the Lord is their sacrifice of not having husbands and fathers who are home all the time. We are so grateful and love each one of you.

We also must acknowledge our churches and ministries, which have allowed us to carry the message to the nations by sharing their pastoral leadership with the world. They have helped carry the work forward through encouragement, prayer, and even finances. Our churches and ministries have given us the love and support of a family and have also been our spiritual homes; places to belong, to be cared for, and to be refreshed and renewed.

Finally, we want to thank the people all across the world, whether in Asia, Africa, Europe, North America, or South America, who have allowed God to take them to a completely different place as they have built prayer altars in their lives and in their surroundings. We have heard thousands of testimonies from people who have reoriented their lives around seeking God and drawing His presence. These testimonies are a living witness to the world of how an active prayer altar can truly change society. Without their steps of faith, their sacrifice, and reprioritizing their lives, there would be no witness to the power of this strategy, so we want to acknowledge their sacrifice and their walk, and give praise to God for them.

> *And now we thank you, our God, and praise your glorious name.*
>
> 1 Chronicles 29:13

John Mulinde
Mark Daniel

FOREWORD

In 2005, the Lord graciously opened up to us a new era of ministry. As we began carrying out mission work in new fields, we encountered many people who had heard about Uganda's national transformation. Many of these people had a desire to understand the underlying principle that brought a tremendous Holy Spirit revival to our nation, which has become more and more evident since the early 1990s.

As people in the nations asked us about this move of God in Uganda, we began to realize that the first generation of young people who had been part of this movement—who had been with us as we prayed, preached, and brought the Lord's prophetic word to the nation—were no longer with us. Some have gone on to pursue the Lord's specific vision for their lives in their own or other ministries. Others have left the nation and are serving the Lord further afield, again pursuing their God-given destiny. And some have gone home to be with the Lord.

Most of those working with us now to continue the work are a new generation of the Body of Christ who were born out of the continuing revival. We recently recognized that they had less understanding of the strategy God had given us to steer Uganda toward Him. Because of this and the many people the Lord has raised up in the nations to join us in this work of awakening and transformation, we thought it necessary to revisit the very basic teachings given to us by the Lord. One particular topic rose up as the primary focus: the establishment of prayer altars.

On enquiring from the Lord whether this was a message that ought to be repeated to this generation of believers—this new generation of harvest workers who are so desperate to see His transforming revival in their lives, homes, and communities—we felt assured that indeed this message still holds true to this day.

God has not changed; neither has He changed the message He gave us all those years ago.

This book contains very basic teachings on prayer altars: what they are, what they do, and how to establish them. Anyone in the Body of Christ can apply these teachings on altars to their own lives, from the pre-teen to the most elderly person. These principles can also be used to establish altars in your family, church, business, community, region, or nation.

Altars are a place of light in the impenetrable darkness of sin, a doorway linking the physical realm to the spiritual realm. A network of altars dedicated to the Lord will create a spiritual atmosphere that gives the Lord God the opportunity to intervene in the affairs of men in a sin-darkened world.

God is seeking for righteous men and women to raise prayer altars to Him. He wants a net of effective fervent prayer all over the land, in every nation, all across the globe. This is a strategy that lays foundations for transformation of whole territories and even nations.

One purpose of this book is to ensure that everyone understands that as long as we are called by the name of the Lord Jesus Christ, we have an obligation to raise an altar to Him. We have tried to maintain the simplicity of the call of God to us in those years when we were very young spiritually, and believe that this book will help every reader comprehend the mandate of God to build an altar.

By the end of this book, you should be able to understand
- the basic purpose and power of a prayer altar,
- the basic purpose and power of the priesthood,

—— JOHN MULINDE AND MARK DANIEL ——

- the results of living a lifestyle at the altar,
- the different types of prayer altars, and
- how to raise a prayer altar to the Lord, from the most basic personal altar to more elaborate corporate altars, which can influence entire nations for the Lord.

I encourage you to read this book, raise altars to the Lord wherever you go, and then do what Jesus Christ commanded His disciples more than 2,000 years ago:

Stay dressed, ready for action and service, and keep your lamps burning. Make sure the master finds you awake and alert when he comes. You must be ready because the Son of Man will come at an hour when you do not expect him.
                                                    Luke 12:35,37,40

Rev Dr John W. Mulinde
Kampala, Uganda

SECTION 1
WHY AN ALTAR?

Section 1
Introduction

IMAGINE you have rejected Christianity your whole life because your husband says he is a Christian but he beats you. He often goes into fits of rage, physically and verbally abusing you. Therefore, everything he represents is repulsive to you.

You live in a Buddhist nation that is full of ancestral worship, so it is very easy to reject Christianity. You did that for over 60 years, but then your daughter became a Christian. She is very fervent in her faith, and tries for much of her Christian life to share with you about Jesus and the experiences she has had with God. But you don't want to hear anything she has to say because you have no regard whatsoever for Christianity. Any time your daughter brings it up, you just walk out of the room.

Your daughter and her family build a family prayer altar in their home. They desire to not just say prayers, but to create an atmosphere in their home that draws the presence of God. As a family, they seek God, worship Him, saturate in His Word, and cooperate with the Holy Spirit as He leads them in building an atmosphere that welcomes His presence. One of their major prayers is that the presence of God would become so tangible in their home that when you walk into the house, His presence would soften your heart and strip away what blinds you to spiritual things and keeps you from knowing Jesus Christ as Savior and Lord. You don't even know this is happening, but your daughter is building an altar in her home and praying specifically for you.

You go to her house and for some reason, you are softer, more open, and drawn to your family more than you have been in decades. Your daughter starts to cautiously share Christ with you, and you are more open than ever before to hear what she is saying. You find yourself asking questions and wanting to know more. Even as you go home, you continue to think about what your daughter shared about Jesus and what He can do in your life. A hope begins to rise up in you that He can make a difference in your heart.

After a few months pass, you find your heart strangely warming toward Christ. One day your daughter asks if you would like to yield the whole of your heart to Him. For some reason, which only God knows, your walls of rejection, hatred, and woundedness begin to crumble. You receive Christ into your life, and you experience yourself being born again, with new life, new love, and new hope.

Your husband, who has been so abusive and full of anger all these years, sees the change that has come into your life. He repents for all the years of abusive behavior and asks forgiveness from you and your entire family. Your marriage is being restored and the relationships in your whole family are being transformed.

IMAGINE you are a young man who grew up in a home filled with dysfunction, rage, and anger. Your father spends all the family's money on gambling and alcohol. Your mother is angry and full of bitterness. There is no love being expressed; there is no thought or concern for the other people in the home. Your parents are constantly at war, fighting with one another. You feel forgotten, unloved, and alone, and you go through your whole childhood with a sense of rejection and abandonment.

The situation with your family continues to worsen with each passing year; a time comes when it seems that your family is totally destroyed. Your father has tried to poison your mother and is sent to prison for attempted murder. Your mother feels justified and emboldened in her anger and bitterness for what your father has done. You have nowhere to go and no family taking care of you. You are filled with anger and hurt. A couple of years pass, and you are full of hopelessness and pain.

Then you begin to hear testimonies of prayer altars; families being changed, healed, and transformed as they build altars in their homes. The stories you hear are amazing, but what is even more compelling to you is that they are describing a type of prayer that is deeper than you have known. It gives you a glimmer of hope. Hundreds of people in your nation—even thousands—are testifying that as they establish their altars and pray, they are drawing the presence of God into their homes. As His presence is being drawn into the homes, He is doing things that only He can do: changing, restoring, healing, and transforming in ways that no human could do. This type of prayer is not just asking God for help. People are being equipped to see how to draw the Lord into the family.

You have absolutely no hope; your family is beyond repair. There is no solution. Your father is in prison, and your mother is in a prison of her own. Through hearing the multitude of testimonies being shared in your nation, you decide to begin a prayer altar in your broken home. You start reading the Scriptures, seeking God's presence.

It is slow going at first. Your heart is shut down and your faith is low. Over months, God's presence starts to come stronger and stronger before you. As you saturate in His Word, a greater reality of who God is begins to break through the darkness that surrounds you. Your heart begins to soften and your wounds begin to heal. He delivers you from the anger and hatred you have for your parents. You begin to cry for them, longing for them to be set free from all that holds them in such destruction. You see Christ's heart for them and how He longs to set them free. You too have a burden for them, not to make your life easier but out of compassion for them. Through that time, God raises your faith to be able to believe that His presence can come into your home and transform your family.

As you start walking out what God shows you, your father, who is still in prison, is moved by the change and love God has been depositing in your heart. He knows he does not deserve any love from you, but God is doing such a real thing in your heart that it deeply impacts the heart of your father. One day as you visit him in prison he repents of the destruction and damage he has done to your family. For the first time in your life, you see him cry. Over time he gives his heart to Christ as his Savior and Lord.

When he gets out of jail, he visits your home and repents to your mother. As your home grows stronger and stronger with the Lord's presence, the Lord softens your parents' hearts. They reconcile and your family is made whole. For the first time you can remember, your parents begin to notice you, wanting to love you and build a family that can protect you. Even though you are in your mid-20s, you experience for the first time in your life the love of your mom and dad.

IMAGINE you live in a nation that has been devastated by war and violence, dictators, and the AIDS epidemic. Families have been broken down and society has been torn apart. In fact, you are embarrassed to even tell people you live in that nation, Uganda. But as the church begins to follow the direction the Lord gives the nation, building a network of altars of prayer in their homes, workplaces, communities, and all across their nation, you see God draw near and intervene in every aspect of society. Dictators are cast down, the incidence of AIDS decreases drastically, the government declares Uganda a Christian nation, military conflicts are diminished, the business infrastructure and economy are restored and become stronger, and the church rises up to a place of authority and influence across the nation.

All these testimonies are true. They came about by building effective prayer altars, and they tell of the transforming power that prayer altars are having in nations around the world. Come join us on this journey as we look at a strategy God has given for changing nations.

—— JOHN MULINDE AND MARK DANIEL ——

Chapter 1.

Spreading the Net of Prayer

Many people are seeing the rise of darkness in the nations, sensing a desperate desire for God to move, and experiencing a strong need to cry out in prayer. They see laws being issued against the church or nations pressuring other nations to conform to standards that are unbiblical. They see the pressure from the darkness that is building up, and sense an urgency of prayer. But some are feeling helpless and powerless, asking themselves, "What can we do? How can we change anything?" They are feeling called to prayer, but know that the level of prayer we are currently at has no power to break through this degree of darkness. The depth of their own walk with the Lord doesn't feel strong enough to bring about change. They watch hopelessly as the darkness increases.

> The level of prayer we are currently at has no power to break through the darkness.

As we look at the level of darkness we are dealing with today, being compelled by God's Spirit to prayer, we also see people praying at degrees and levels unprecedented in the past several decades. People, both young and old, from all across the different denominations and ethnic groups, in nations from all over the world, are beginning to feel a desperate need to pray. Sadly, they also sense that their own spiritual walk with the Lord is not deep or solid enough to handle the warfare. They are aware that the unity among individuals and churches is not strong enough to push back the darkness in cities or cultures, and realize that their one church, one prayer group, or one denomination is not able by itself to stop the darkness that is coming in like a flood. They are aware that they have to go deeper in the Lord and connect with one another to see the darkness pushed back and God's kingdom advanced.

Many of us are aware that if we do not see a move of God, the devastation and consequences are unfathomable. We know that things cannot continue down the path they are going now. If they do, we cannot even imagine the world we will see years from now. We are filled with a growing sense of urgency. There is desperation to come together to fight for the nations, but no real direction or inspiration for how to go about this.

Even with our confidence in the Lord, with our knowledge that nothing is impossible for Him (Luke 1:37), that He can raise up valleys and tear down mountains (Is 40:4), and that He does answer prayer (1 John 5:14-15), when we see the state of darkness in the world, the mindsets of the people, the perversions in the land, the spread of pornography and addictions, the destruction in families, the violence in nations, the selfishness, greed, pride, and humanism, we may begin to think that this wave against the kingdom of God is so big that we cannot stand against it. However, God has been unfolding a plan that is changing cities and nations, a strategy He is using in the nations to stay His hand of judgment and to bring about an outpouring of His Spirit in families, churches, cities, and nations.

> God has been unfolding a strategy He is using in the nations to stay His hand of judgment and to bring about an outpouring of His Spirit in families, churches, cities, and nations.

The Strategy God Is Unfolding

This strategy, which we call "prayer altars," is changing entire nations. Birthed out of Uganda, it is being used in Asia, Europe, North America, Africa, and other parts of the world. We have seen the impact it has had in various countries and cultures, and are confident that it will have a strong impact everywhere it is put in place. A great benefit of establishing altars is that it builds unity in the Body of Christ and the spiritual depth needed to break the darkness that is so dramatically and pervasively spreading across the nations.

This strategy starts by taking prayer deep into the heart of individuals, where the fire in each heart ignites and begins to really catch ablaze. This fire is then ignited in families and churches, and then across cities and even nations, so that the Body of Christ can begin to rise up. This network of personal, family, church, marketplace, and corporate altars spreads across entire regions and countries, and even whole regions of the world, causing the spiritual atmosphere to change so that the forces of darkness covering whole territories can be pushed back and broken. The forces of darkness are not too much for the power of our God!

This is not just another book describing the wonders of prayer; it is an unfolding of the way God worked through Abraham, Moses, and the early church to begin to occupy territory, advance His kingdom, break the powers of darkness, and draw His presence. This book reveals lessons God taught the Ugandans about how to create an atmosphere that would draw His presence and they saw God move in transforming revival and change their nation. We have used these lessons in Asia, North America, Africa, Europe, and other parts of the world, and have seen God changing society again and again. That is the reason we call this book, "*Prayer Altars: A Strategy That Changes Nations.*"

The Effects of the Altar
One of the things that is inspiring about prayer altars and that makes them contagious is that we can apply them to our own personal lives. Prayer altars have implications in every single Christian family, and can be established in churches and

Christian businesses. As people catch the vision of prayer altars, they will see that we all have a role to play in building altars all across the territory. This means that God can use us to affect the big picture or to change the course of the way things are going in our homes and communities, even in our nation. We will see that impacting a territory is not done by a powerful speaker, a singing artist, or a big event, but by the power of the Holy Spirit through prayer, and therefore that we all have a role to play in changing our society.

> Impacting a territory is not done by a powerful speaker, a singing artist, or a big event, but by the power of the Holy Spirit through prayer.

Once an altar is established, people realize that their family prayer altar is not just for their family; it is for their nation. They will see that as more and more people begin to seek God together, they are creating a place—an environment—where the presence of God will be drawn, not just for their own well-being or for their own family's protection, but so they can see the darkness being broken over their territory or nation. Christian businesses realize that they are not building an altar of prayer at their workplace just so God can bless them, but because they want to see the presence of God move all across their land.

As prayer altars are established, they even start to break the attitude of praying solely for our own well-being or blessing. There is a sense of joining something bigger, of becoming part of the army of God that is rising up across the entire nation, of joining together to seek the Lord with one purpose: to create an atmosphere into which God is being drawn so He can triumph in the land.

We are seeing this unity of heart rising up all over the world. As people catch the vision, they are not only beginning to have faith for God to move in their families, they are also becoming part of a movement that is impacting their entire nation.

—— JOHN MULINDE AND MARK DANIEL ——

How This Strategy Can Change a Nation

One couple we know of absolutely did not want to do this when they first heard of prayer altars. They avoided praying with one another. They had tried praying as a couple before, but found themselves preaching at each other rather than praying; it was a colossal failure. As the concept of prayer altars was shared with them, they had a completely new vision of how to approach praying together. They started to read Scriptures together for 30 to 45 minutes each morning, then spent time praising, glorifying, and worshiping the God who had been revealed in the Scriptures they had just read. The presence of God grew stronger every day they did this, and they began to experience God, which softened their hearts. This changed the way they prayed.

Instead of praying about how to change each other's lives, they started connecting with God's heart and His desires and ways. They saw that the atmosphere in their home was filled with sarcasm, criticism, and jabs. The woundedness that was in the home began to dissipate. They started to see their children drawn to the things of God, where before they had always seemed uninterested. Before long, their marriage altar turned into a family altar, and they testified that the altar affected their family more than anything they had ever done during their entire married life.

This is a simple story of how the prayer altar changed just one family. And yet, stories like this one are causing families all over the nations to say, "Let's build our prayer altar." As families are establishing altars all across the land, you can see God healing mental illness, putting together broken lives, restoring fathers' hearts to their children, and bringing change to the whole dynamic of the family.

Business people are beginning to build prayer altars and are seeing their workers being saved. There are testimonies from business owners that as they started building prayer altars, employees who had worked with them for over a decade and who had never asked about Christ were now asking questions

and experiencing salvation. Many business owners and managers testify of changing their business practices; as they are
seeking to draw His presence, some are finding they need to
have greater integrity while others find they need to treat their
employees better. The changes then impact other businesses
they are involved with in their industry.

A TV producer was hearing testimonies from around his nation
of people experiencing the presence of God as they were establishing altars of prayer in their workplaces. He heard stories
about how God was changing their industries to be more ethical, blessing the businesses and their workers, and how God's
presence was making a marked impact. This man began to draw
together his crew to read the Bible for 30 or 40 minutes, and
then to spend time praising the God they had read about in the
Scriptures. As they did this, nothing happened; they were not
seeing the presence of God. So he humbled himself and asked,
"God, why are these other workplaces experiencing Your presence and we are not?"

After a time of seeking the Lord, God showed him that the TV
shows they were producing were not glorifying to Him. The
man told the actors, scriptwriters, and others in the studio they
needed to start producing materials that were more glorifying
to God. They started again to read Scriptures and praise the
Lord together at their altar. People were converted, and their
hearts were changed and unified with this man's changed vision.
This marketplace altar even started to have an impact in their
industry.

This is just one story of a business seeking to draw God's presence. The Lord started to move in the business, changing
everything. When thousands of other Christian business leaders
begin to do that, it not only changes the marketplace, but also the
educational, media, entertainment, government, and other areas
of society as well.

In the Far East, there has even been an impact in the medical field, where doctors who have built prayer altars in their work-places have recorded dramatic increases of healing and recovery. This is especially true with psychiatrists.

As individual, family, church, and marketplace prayer altars are built throughout a nation, changes in families, marriages, and business practices become evident. There will also be changes in the Body of Christ. Denominational walls will break down, com-petition between churches will diminish, and strife and selfish ambition will begin to decrease. Everyone's concept of what God can do in a city will increase.

As the church begins to build prayer altars together, darkness will be pushed back and everyone will come to realize they are on the same team. They will begin to work together and come to have the same goals and vision. And as they see the atmosphere change in their city, they will also see souls being saved, families being changed, and their ministries beginning to expand.

A church in Taiwan with approximately 1,500 members began to teach on personal prayer altars and how our heart is the first altar that must be built. The church began to equip and instruct the people about how to minister to the Lord, how to make the Word of God the centerpiece of their lives, and how to draw the presence of God so the fire in their hearts would not go out. God had placed it on their hearts to see at least 60% of the people in their congregation building family prayer altars in their homes. They prayed for this goal and the leadership of the church began to establish family prayer altars themselves. This church fought through the obstacles, challenges, and time constraints that made building a family altar difficult, and they experienced breakthroughs.

Taiwan has a very busy lifestyle and long work hours. Children spend long hours in school, as well as many hours in tutoring after school. These and various other reasons make the people in Taiwan feel as though a family altar is impossible. However, as the leadership of this large church experienced breakthroughs, they started seeing their congregants overcoming their struggles and determining to establish altars in their families. Altars spread to more and more families as the church members shared their testimonies during the Sunday service.

At first, the church members shared their testimonies during one service each month. There were testimonies of marriages that were changed, extended family members coming to Christ because of the presence of God in their homes, neighbors who were won to Christ, and children who began to catch on fire for God again. Over a few months, there were more and more testimonies each week. The congregation began to take that step of faith to build altars in their families, drawing the presence of God into their homes. After a time, every single Sunday there would be at least one or two powerful testimonies of families that were being transformed, healed, and delivered; neighbors who were being saved; and extended family members who were brought to Christ out of Buddhism or ancestral worship.

The witness of the change taking place in this church became so noticeable that other churches around them began to request that they please help them to understand how to establish prayer altars, too. This church has become a lead church in their whole city because of the establishment of prayer altars.

This is just one church's story, but there are hundreds and hundreds of churches experiencing this in Taiwan.

National Breakthrough
In more than 3 years of working with the National Prayer Network of Taiwan to establish personal, family, church, marketplace, and even citywide prayer altars in all 17 provinces of the nation, we witnessed the atmosphere in churches, families, and cities— all across the whole nation—begin to change and become more conducive for the kingdom of God to advance. The atmosphere

became more favorable for unity among spiritual leaders throughout the nation as well as for drawing the presence of God. The change was so evident that nations around Taiwan, including South Korea, Hong Kong, Malaysia, and Mainland China, also began to take note.

The change was so evident that nations around Taiwan, including South Korea, Hong Kong, Malaysia, and Mainland China, also began to take note.

We were able to witness a truly amazing thing as this atmospheric change came to Taiwan: we were able to sit down with the leaders representing the church in the nation of Taiwan and ask them, "What do you sense is the way forward for the advancement of the kingdom in the nation?" We then shared that we believed it was time for a massive soul harvest through bringing together the 4,000 churches of Taiwan to reach half a million souls for Jesus Christ. Many of the leaders in the room said this could not have happened 3 or 4 years ago. Since building the prayer altars across the nation, however, the church has become healthier and stronger. The leaders believe that the nation is ready and that they can go forward and plan a massive soul harvest in the nation.

As the hundreds and even thousands of testimonies from the marketplace, churches, families, and individuals started to be shared, and as the churches in the nation began to come together in unity of heart and purpose and to strategize and pray for a mass harvest, spiritual leaders from countries surrounding Taiwan are asking, "How do we build prayer altars? Will you come teach us how to do this, too?"

Can you see how hundreds, even thousands, of churches coming together to do this could change the atmosphere in the nation? Can you see how building prayer altars across individual lives, families, the marketplace, and communities would raise a much deeper level of prayer? Can you see how building prayer altars across the very fabric of society would strengthen people to stand against the backlash of spiritual warfare as we attempt to push back the darkness over nations? Can you see how this unified effort of prayer can push back and break these forces of darkness that are flooding into the nations? Can you see how this would change the atmosphere in the nation to make it possible for the kingdom of God to advance for massive soul harvests, for churches to grow, and for families to be healed and made whole?

Can you see that we all have a role to play as we follow the strategy God has given is about building prayer altars and spreading them across all areas of society? We all have a role and can be a part of this great work, which is bigger than one denomination, one ministry, or one organization. This is something that only God can do, and He is inviting us to join Him in this great work by building prayer altars across the nations.

But is this strategy biblical? In the next several chapters, we will lay out the principles of this strategy of prayer altars and show that this is the way God worked through Abraham, Moses, David, and many other great men and women in the Bible.

CHAPTER 2.
"BUILD ME AN ALTAR"

*And I sought for a man among them who should build up
the wall and stand in the breach before me for the land,
that I should not destroy it, but found none.*

Ezekiel 22:30

There are unprecedented events happening in our world
today. Every year for the past few years there has been record
damage from natural disasters, such as droughts, floods, torna-
does, earthquakes, and tsunamis. Countries are on the brink of
economic failure, and violence, corruption, and moral and spiritual decay are increasing and spreading across all the nations of
the world.

Around the world, the traditional family unit and the concept of
marriage are changing rapidly, bringing emotional health problems to individuals and families and a distortion of sexuality.
These negative consequences are effecting the very foundation
of society.

The number of marriages worldwide is decreasing, while the
number of divorces is increasing. Single parenting is becoming
the norm in most nations. Due to this, we are seeing high rates of
emotional problems, including:

- Rebellion,
- High suicide rates among teenagers, and
- Increased emotional illnesses (anxiety, depression,
  insecurity, and addictions).

The breakdown of the family unit is causing sexuality to become distorted, bringing about unwanted pregnancies. This is resulting in amazingly high numbers of abortions, promiscuity, experimentation, and confusion of sexuality and sexual orientation. The use of technology is also causing sexual distortion.

The pornography industry is a $97 billion business worldwide. One in eight of all Internet searches are for erotic content. One in five searches on mobile devices are for pornography. The American Academy of Matrimonial Lawyers estimates that in approximately 55% of divorce cases, at least one of the spouses has an obsession with online pornography. Child pornography is a $3 billion industry, and is one of the fastest growing businesses online. The largest consumer of Internet pornography is the 12- to 17-year-old age group. The Christian Post has reported that 90% of 8- to 16-year olds have seen pornography on the Internet at least once.

In addition to this widespread attack on the family, in recent years there have been increases in uprisings, rebellions, protests, revolutions, civil wars, and terrorist activities. The news is filled daily with the number of deaths from suicide bombers, drone attacks, and armed conflicts. Added to this is the increased nuclear threat from Iran, North Korea, and other nations. A great sense of fear and destabilization can be felt all around the world. The increased security we have to deal with just to feel safe is taking a toll on us all.

The recent global financial crisis, the worst seen since the Great Depression in the 1930s, has caused severe worldwide unemployment. Several nations are in desperate financial trouble, including the Eurozone nations of Cyprus, Spain, Slovenia, Greece, Turkey, Italy, and Luxembourg.

Secularism, humanism, and Islam have increased worldwide, and the growth of Christianity has stalled. The small increase in Christianity is mostly attributed to people from the former Communist

Bloc returning to their faith and the growth of the church in China. While Islam and atheism are growing, Christianity is basically at a standstill or even in decline, especially in Europe.

In the UK, once known for revival and as being a hub of Christianity, many church buildings throughout the nation are being sold because of the rapid decrease of people attending church. Once sanctuaries for the believer, today dozens of churches each year are becoming private homes, bars, offices, storefronts, and even mosques! It has been said about "post-Christian" Europe that the two fastest-growing religions are secularism and Islam.

Worldliness and compromise in the church are also evident and on the rise. Christian beliefs held for centuries are eroding (eg, attitudes toward sexuality, sanctity of life, Christ as the only source of salvation, God as the Creator and sustainer of life, the existence of heaven and hell, and life eternal), creating a compromised church. In addition, the church is frequently ridiculed as being hypocritical in its lifestyle. Nonbelievers see a church that is tolerating sin so as to avoid offense or hurt feelings, churchgoers treating church attendance as a social function rather than as a time to worship and encounter God, and churches measuring their success by numbers of attendees and income rather than salvations and discipleship. Rather than being the light of the world and the salt of the earth—discipling their nation—the church has become ineffective and has lost its spiritual and moral authority in many nations around the world as we face increasing darkness flooding the nations.

Natural disasters, economic failures, violence, moral and spiritual decay, increasing perversion, and laboring in vain are all signs mentioned in the Bible which indicate that judgment is beginning to come

> God is provoking us not only to see the darkness that is coming in, but also to see the need to create an atmosphere that will allow Him to come in, cleanse and heal the land, and to stay the judgment that is coming into the land.

into a land (Matt 24:6-7, Luke 21:9-11, 2 Tim 3:1-5). When you look at the nations today, do you see the signs that judgment is coming? In almost any part of the world, the people are seeing that darkness is on the increase. You can see the forces of darkness that are rising up in the nations.

God is provoking us not only to see the darkness that is coming in, but also to see the need to create an atmosphere that will allow Him to come in, cleanse and heal the land, and to stay the judgment that is coming into the land. He is stirring a desire in His people to seek after Him, cry out and come to Him in prayer, and draw His presence so He can begin to move, not only in transforming power, but also by pushing back the darkness that is flooding into the nations.

"Build Me an Altar"

Then Satan stood against Israel and incited David to number Israel. So David said to Joab and the commanders of the army, "Go, number Israel, from Beersheba to Dan, and bring me a report, that I may know their number." But God was displeased with this thing, and he struck Israel. And David said to God, "I have sinned greatly in that I have done this thing. But now, please take away the iniquity of your servant, for I have acted very foolishly."

1 Chronicles 21:1-2,7-8

In 2 Samuel 24 and 1 Chronicles 21, we find an account of how David decided to conduct a census of his armies. Basically, David was trying to gauge how big and strong his army was. This did not please God at all. It was not the vastness or skill of David's armies that had brought him great victories; it had been God all along.

When the prophet came to David with God's message, he instructed David to choose one of three judgments: (1) to face famine for 3 years, (2) to face defeat from his enemies for 3 months, or (3) for pestilence to strike the nation for

3 days. David chose the third option, preferring to fall into the hands of God rather than men. When the plague began, it killed 70,000 people. David's heart was thoroughly smitten and he began to cry out to God for mercy (1 Chr 21:9-14). God does not enjoy destroying people, yet it does not mean He will not do it when sin reaches its fullness. When the plague was sweeping through the land, it grieved God's heart. As the cry for mercy came up to Him, He said to the destroying angel, "Enough! Withdraw your hand" (1 Chr 21:15a).

Many times, when people hear the message of judgment they hate it. They do not want anyone to tell them judgment is looming over their nation. And yet, unless God has mercy upon you, you will never realize that judgment is looming over your nation.

> *And the angel of the Lord was standing by the threshing floor of Ornan the Jebusite. And David lifted his eyes and saw the angel of the Lord standing between earth and heaven, and in his hand a drawn sword stretched out over Jerusalem. Then David and the elders, clothed in sackcloth, fell upon their faces. And David said to God, "Was it not I who gave command to number the people? It is I who have sinned and done great evil. But these sheep, what have they done? Please let your hand, O Lord my God, be against me and against my father's house. But do not let the plague be on your people."*
>
> 1 Chronicles 21:15b-17

David did not see the destroying angel looming over Jerusalem until God commanded him to stop the plague. That was the first time David saw the angel. Like David, if God does not open our eyes, we too will not see the judgment. That is actually His first act of mercy: allowing us to see the darkness of our sinful situation and its effect, as well as our desperate need to change course.

It is only by God's mercy that we see the looming judgment, break down in repentance, and cry for deliverance and grace. That is why, when we see it but do not pray, the angel does not go away. The angel stays in his position with his sword stretched over the land.

What does that imply? God was saying, "Let Me see if the people will do the right thing and create an environment for Me, and invite Me in their midst so that I can have mercy on them. I am looking for a man among them who will see the destruction, and be stirred to stand in the gap on behalf of the land that I may not destroy them" (Ezek 22:30).

When people see God's hand of judgment stretched out over the land and become burdened to create an environment for Him to move on behalf of that land, they are not doing that because they are trying to convince God. It is God who drew them to do that. And only God can put that on our hearts. We are not trying to tell Him, "Please have mercy." He is the One who is saying, "I am holding Myself back. I have withheld judgment for a period. Will you create an atmosphere that allows Me to forgive you and stay the judgment?"

When we create that atmosphere, it begins the journey of reconciliation with God. The problem with most of us is that when we pray and God begins to answer, we stop praying. We need to realize that God is not saying, "I have taken away the plague." Rather, He is saying, "I have heard the prayer. Now I will lead you into what you need to do to restore fellowship between us."

> We must create an atmosphere for Him to come and abide with us so that the real work of restoration and redemption can begin in our land.

That is what it means to "build up the wall" (Ezek 22:30). It has been broken down and we need to mend it. There is a reason why so much darkness is coming into our land. The wall is broken down in many ways. We need God to show us how to build up the wall again. It is not enough to get God to hear us and see some encouragements in society. We must create an atmosphere for Him to come and abide with us so that the real work of restoration and redemption can begin in our land.

What conditions did God give David? He said, "David, go build Me an altar, and I will not just stop the destroying angel, but will remove the plague completely" (2 Sam 24:18-25).

How do we build an altar to hold back the floods of judgment coming into the nations? To answer that, in the next few chapters we will look at how God taught Abraham to take possession of the land by building a network of altars. We will also see how God used that Abrahamic strategy in Uganda to move powerfully across the whole nation.

CHAPTER 3.
TESTIMONY OF UGANDA

Uganda has a very volatile and violent past, but since 1995, we have experienced many positive changes. We have seen God accomplish many things in our nation. However, around 1998, we started to see darkness growing and getting stronger once again. Many were looking and wondering, "What is going on?" We started to lose our spiritual momentum and the darkness began to creep into society again.

There was a call for change throughout the nation. Many were saying we needed change in our government and or in our judicial system. Others said we needed change in our families or in our churches. Some said we needed change in our educational system. There was national agreement that we needed change and that it was needed everywhere; however, many confessed that they did not know where to find the solution.

> We knew we would continue to backslide and that judgments would continue to increase unless the nation woke up and realized that judgment was over our nation.

We (the church), though, realized where the answer lies. We knew we would continue to backslide and that judgments would continue to increase unless the nation woke up and realized that the angel of judgment was stretching his sword over our nation. Like David, we were being called to stand in the gap and cry out for the Lord's mercy so that we could stay the Lord's judgment and create an atmosphere through which He could come down and continue to work in our nation.

The History of Uganda

In the mid-1990s, people around the world heard about the national revival that was going on in Uganda, a nation notorious for its difficult and violent past. In the 24 years between 1962 and 1986, Uganda had 10 presidents, several military coups, bloody war after bloody war, and finally the AIDS outbreak that almost devastated our society. As we were praying and raising up prayer altars all across the nation, we didn't even realize that we were beginning to experience revival; we had been busy seeking God and crying out for His solutions to the manifold challenges we were facing.

In the many years before 1990, whenever upheaval happened in the nation, the church went to prayer to fight against the bad governance in the land. Then, as the government was ousted and relative peace came with the new regime, the church would sit back and stop praying. We did not realize that each time, because of crying out for God's mercy, He had stayed His hand of judgment. He was waiting for an altar to be built, for an atmosphere to be created for Him to come and work in the nation. Yet each time change and relief came, the church slid back into slumber and stopped praying.

Finally, a new situation arose that had nothing to do with bad governance or evil leaders destroying the nation. The AIDS pandemic wasn't like anything we had ever encountered before. In the late 1980s, the World Health Organization reported that Uganda was the nation worst hit by the AIDS virus. The report was extremely depressing. HIV and AIDS prevalence levels were at 36%. The report said that by the year 2000, 30% of the entire population would be dead from AIDS, 30% would be infected by the virus, and the rest would be very old people and very young children, among whom there would be numerous AIDS babies. The sword of judgment hung over the nation.

The church went into a time of seeking God in fasting and prayer, mainly asking God, "What is wrong with our country? Why is it that bad things always happen to Uganda?" When Idi Amin ruled us, we had bloodshed; then Milton Obote came and killed people. The guerrilla soldiers ousted him and killings followed. There was heinous murder, bloodshed, and death in the north of Uganda with Joseph Kony and the Lord's Resistance Army. Now we had AIDS; it wasn't war or bad leadership, but a disease that was killing us.

There was no human leader who could be blamed for this particular disaster. We had to search beyond human enemies and to press further into God.

During that time, God revealed to us that it was the same devil using different tactics to steal, kill, and destroy God's purposes for Uganda. God told us, "You are a weak church because you do not know your enemy."

"You think Idi Amin, Milton Obote, or the rebel soldiers are your enemy, but it is the devil who is your enemy at all times, and he is using different weapons to destroy the nation. He is the one who came through the region killing people, using leaders; now he has changed tactics and is using AIDS to kill your nation. He has only three agendas: to steal, kill, and destroy. People are not your target; the devil and his works against you are your target."

> In His mercy, God allowed us to see the threatening hand of judgment that continued to hang over our nation and invited us to do something to bring His intervention.

In His mercy, God allowed us to see the threatening hand of judgment that continued to hang over our nation and invited us to do something to bring His intervention. The atmosphere that He desired to work in had to be created, so we began to ask Him how to create that atmosphere. What were we to do?

— JOHN MULINDE AND MARK DANIEL —

The Vision

Together with a group of other Christian leaders, we had been crying out to God: "What is the way forward for Uganda? Why do such challenging things happen to Uganda so often? Even the outside world thinks that Ugandans are self-destructive! They think we are killing ourselves." Neighboring countries like Tanzania and Kenya had closed their borders to us. We were stigmatized by the whole world for having trouble and trauma as our perpetual bedfellows.

During this long season of seeking the Lord, I (John Mulinde) received a vision. I saw myself with other colleagues in the ministry going to Lake Victoria for a fishing expedition. We reached the lake and cast out our net. After some time there seemed to be a catch and we began pulling up the net, but it was too heavy and the team members were very few. I said to them, "Go back to the ministry center and call the rest of our colleagues to help us pull this net out of the water. This is a very big catch."

As the workers started to leave, I heard a voice telling me, "John, the work is too big for you. You cannot do it as any one ministry, denomination, or church. Call everyone you can, those who are near and those who are far away, as many as are willing to help." I called back my colleagues and told them, "Go to everyone from every ministry who is willing to come. Go to those who are near and those who are far to ask them to come and help us pull this net out of the water."

After some time, many people started coming to the lake. Some were in small groups and others were in big groups. Each group came with two things: a name and a rope.

The people were from different ministries and churches, and each group came under its own name or identity. Some were from the Full Gospel Church; others were from the Lutheran Church. There were Catholics, Anglicans, Baptists, Methodists, and many others. There were many, many churches and ministries, and their names were written on their placards and banners. Some came in groups of hundreds; others came in groups of tens or fives.

When each group reached the lake, they tied their rope to the net and started to help pull it out. It was heavy work, but everyone worked together, and the whole group managed to get the net out of the water.

To our amazement, when the net came out of the water there were no fish. However, there was a big rock in the shape of the map of Uganda! I wondered, "It is not a catch of fish, but what does it mean?" I heard a voice telling me, "John, give me a net and I will fish your nation out of troubled waters."

I came out of the vision, went into prayer, and asked God, "What do You mean by a 'net'? What about the other people who came with their ministries and their own names?" God said, "If you will institute a network of united prayer all over the nation of Uganda, you will be able to conquer the evil principality ruling over your nation. If you grasp this vision, which goes beyond your ministry and denominational boundaries, so that you can see the bigger picture of My purposes for Uganda, you will be able to overcome the evil principality and establish My kingdom in Uganda."

> If you will institute a network of united prayer across your nation, you will be able to conquer the evil principality ruling over your nation.

God told me "I have many people in many denominations, even in places you cannot imagine. They are in the Lutheran, Pentecostal, Anglican, Baptist, Protestant, and Catholic churches and in numerous other ministries. Every single ministry, denomination, and church has a particular anointing. I have posted people there so that as you come together in unity of purpose, they will come with their unique ministry anointing and covering mantles on their lives. In coming together like that, there will be a greater corporate anointing on the people because of the unity between the different churches, denominations, and ministries. Under that covering, you will have greater legal ground to come against the principality ruling over your nation."

"That is why I told you to call those who are near and those who are far away to join together. No ministry, church, or denomination, no matter how big, could ever single-handedly do the work of bringing My kingdom into any nation; it must be the whole Body of Christ."

I asked, "God how can we do this?" and He said, "I already have people in different parts of your nation. You will work with them. If you go out and share this vision with them, many will come out and work together with you. It does not mean they will turn away from their denominations, churches, or ministries, but I will use them right where they are to build the net of prayer."

"Build Me an Altar"

We started going out on missions, mobilizing people in various ministries, churches, and denominations to pray together, but we did not know how to institute this "net" of prayer. As the time of seeking God continued, I began asking, "God, how shall we make a 'net' of prayer all over the land of Uganda?" The Lord answered, "I am calling for every individual Christian to start praying. Let every Christian family start praying together and let there be prayer going on in every church. Let Christians start prayer in their workplaces. By doing that, you will be giving Me legal ground to work in your land."

I had never heard the terms "legal ground" or "legal authority." As I pondered these new terms and the Biblical basis for what God was telling us, He said, "I am not showing you a new thing. It has

> Imagine a net over your entire nation and then imagine every knot as a prayer altar in your nation."

happened in the Bible. Just as you saw the fishing net woven together, where two threads meet there is a knot. Imagine a net over your entire nation and then imagine every knot as a prayer altar in your nation."

God then brought to memory the strategy He had led Abraham to use to take the land of Canaan, what we call the "Abrahamic Strategy." He told Abraham, "Go, walk through the length and breadth of the land, for I am giving it to you" (Gen 13:17, NIV). He then said to me, "Go to the north, south, east, and west. Wherever you go throughout your nation, set up altars of prayer and call on the name of the Lord."

God was saying, "Build Me an altar and I will rescue your nation."

God spoke to us about this new and strange strategy He would use to save our nation: a net of prayer that would be formed by people praying individually and within groups in various parts of the nation. This would create a spiritual atmosphere that would give God legal authority and legal ground to intervene in the affairs of Uganda and save our nation from total devastation caused by poor leadership and its attendant complications, as well as from the more destructive AIDS pandemic.

This Abrahamic Strategy of taking the land through building up prayer altars is very powerful. It creates an atmosphere in which God can work, and is effective for years and years. Today, even if nations fight against Israel, no matter how many come against her, they cannot take the land. This is because there was a man who went through the land setting up prayer altars, taking the land for the kingdom of the Living God.

At the time I received this vision, I had never stepped outside of Uganda, not even to the neighboring East African nations. It had never entered my imagination that I would ever go anywhere beyond the boundaries of Uganda. And yet, God told me, "As you build prayer altars throughout the land and continue to come to

Me as individuals, families, and churches—as the people of God standing in the gap for this nation—you will begin to see the tide of darkness broken and My presence drawn into this land. This is the strategy you will use, not only in Uganda, but also in every nation to which I send you. These nations, too, will need to use this strategy to purge the land, prepare the spiritual ground, and call upon My presence. You will only find success in what you are doing in the physical realm after you have won the battle in the spiritual realm."

> As you build prayer altars throughout the land, you will begin to see the tide of darkness broken and My presence drawn into the land. You will only find success in what you are doing in the physical realm after you have won the battle in the spiritual realm.

Taking the Land

When we obediently began to walk through the land of Uganda, teaching, preaching, and raising prayer altars in the various households, communities, churches, and villages, and ultimately raised up a national prayer altar, we did not realize what was happening in the spiritual atmosphere over our nation.

As individuals came to recognize that they were priests unto God and that they were called to minister to the Lord at His altar, they began to pray with renewed energy and fire, and prayer increased in the nation. They began to build prayer altars in their homes, offices, institutions of learning, church buildings, and community centers; they were creating openings in the spiritual realm. A fire of prayer was touching every aspect of our society, creating an environment where the presence of God was drawn into those places. It also began to push back the darkness: the corruption, worldly mindsets, sin, and other forms of darkness that were eroding our society.

The covering of destruction that had been thrown over the nation by Satan and his agents to hinder communion between heaven and earth was being punctured as each group of people raised up intercession, spiritual warfare, and supplications for Uganda. These numerous punctures soon perforated the covering of darkness over the nation and it was broken open, meaning that the Holy Spirit could flow through the nation and touch every area of society at unprecedented levels.

The prayer altars are still going strong 20 years later. The heavens over Uganda have remained open largely to the influence of the kingdom of God because of the prayer altars that have been built. We see evidence of this manifested in many ways. There is prayer in the lives of the people of God, in the marketplace, and in the families. Young people have started prayer altars on college campuses, and business people have established prayer altars in their workplaces. Godly laws are much more likely to be discussed and passed by members of Parliament and in government offices. There is a greater unity in the Body of Christ to deal with the important issues and circumstances in our nation.

The spiritual atmosphere of the land has changed and the hand of judgment that was looming against Uganda has been turning away. The rate of incidence of AIDS went from the highest in the world (36%) to the lowest in Africa (6%). Uganda has been blessed by a stable and godly government for a few decades. Corruption has dramatically declined in all sectors of society, especially in the banking system and the political arena. Prayer altars have been established in every form of industry and throughout government. Prayer has become a lifestyle for the people of Uganda, and although there is still a lot of work to do and changes that need to be made, the potential remains to totally transform the nation of Uganda if the church will continue with the level of intercession they started all those years ago.

> The spiritual atmosphere of the land has changed and the hand of judgment that was looming against Uganda has been turning away.

—— JOHN MULINDE AND MARK DANIEL ——

Prayer altars are powerful. They can push back darkness, change the spiritual atmosphere of cities and nations, and bring redemption to elements of society that were eroding. They can bring about the purposes of God and produce tangible fruits of the kingdom of God flowing into the lives of the people of that land. Prayer altars are vital to not only stay the hand of the judgments that are coming against our land, but also to see a great move of God's Spirit upon the land, bringing about a harvest of righteousness and peace.

Altars can open the heavens. It takes a continuously active altar to keep the fire of prayer going up to the Lord. My prayer is to see the heavens in my nation and other nations around the world open as the righteous continue to offer effective fervent prayers (Deut 11:13-17).

Chapter 4.
The Abrahamic Strategy

Where do you find altars in the Bible? Where do you find this strategy that God gave to take possession of the land? Below we discuss what we call the "Abrahamic Strategy," which is the strategy God gave Abraham to build altars throughout the land, pushing back the darkness and claiming the land for the Lord.

> Now the Lord said to Abram, "Go from your country and your kindred and your father's house to the land that I will show you. And I will make of you a great nation, and I will bless you and make your name great, so that you will be a blessing. I will bless those who bless you, and him who dishonors you I will curse, and in you all the families of the earth shall be blessed." So Abram went, as the Lord had told him, and Lot went with him. Abram was seventy-five years old when he departed from Haran. And Abram took Sarai his wife, and Lot his brother's son, and all their possessions that they had gathered, and the people that they had acquired in Haran, and they set out to go to the land of Canaan. When they came to the land of Canaan, Abram passed through the land to the place at Shechem, to the oak of Moreh. At that time the Canaanites were in the land. Then the Lord appeared to Abram and said, "To your offspring I will give this land." So he built there an altar to the Lord, who had appeared to him.
>
> Genesis 12:1-7

God asked Abraham to leave his homeland in Ur of the Chaldeans, and all he was used to, to go to a strange new land. Abraham obeyed and set off for Canaan. When Abraham reached the place the Lord showed him, the Bible says, "he built an altar there to the Lord, who appeared to him" (v 7). Abraham moved from there toward Bethel and pitched his tent with Bethel on the west and Ai on the east. Here, too, he built an altar to the Lord and called on the name of the Lord (v 8). Wherever Abraham went throughout Canaan, he erected an altar to the Lord to create an open gateway for God to interact with His people.

> *The Lord said to Abram, after Lot had separated from him, "Lift up your eyes and look from the place where you are, northward and southward and eastward and westward, for all the land that you see I will give to you and to your offspring forever. I will make your offspring as the dust of the earth, so that if one can count the dust of the earth, your offspring also can be counted. Arise, walk through the length and the breadth of the land, for I will give it to you." So Abram moved his tent and came and settled by the oaks of Mamre, which are at Hebron, and there he built an altar to the Lord.*
>
> Genesis 13:14-18

Why did God tell Abraham to walk through the length and breadth of the land? Abraham could have settled in one place, built an altar, and called on the Living God, but God didn't want that. Why? Because God wanted Abraham to take possession of the whole land, not just one piece of the land.

Abraham knew that the one who oversees the active altar has control of the land. He welcomed the God of heaven to come in and inhabit the land, and have free access in and out of the territory. Everywhere that Abraham went

> Everywhere that Abraham went in that land, he raised an altar, offered a sacrifice, ministered to the Lord, and covenanted the place to God.

in that land, he raised an altar, offered a sacrifice, ministered to the Lord, and covenanted the place to God. This was the strategy God used to lay the spiritual groundwork for this nation to be set apart to Him all those years later when Joshua and the Israelites came to take possession of the land.

The Condition of the Land

The Bible points out that when Abraham arrived in the place where the Lord had sent him, "the Canaanites were in the land" (Gen 12:6). Abraham was not moving into a vacuum. God was careful to mention the spiritual health of the people in the land because the darkness that was in the land was covering and influencing the people of the land.

The Canaanites practiced witchcraft, brought bloodshed on the land, and worshiped pagan gods, all of which attracted spirits of darkness and gave them legal spiritual authority to control the land. The spiritual atmosphere in which they lived was influencing the nature of the people in the territories into which Abraham entered. All the people of the land were under the influence of the ruling principality in that land, which affected the spiritual atmosphere and their behavior, making them live in ways contrary to the ways of God.

> All the people of the land were under the influence of the ruling principality in that land, which affected the spiritual atmosphere and their behavior, making them live in ways contrary to the ways of God. This spiritual atmosphere had an effect on everyone living in the land.

This spiritual atmosphere had an effect on everyone living in the land. For example, when quarreling erupted between Abraham and Lot's herdsmen, the Scripture says that, "the Canaanites and Perizzites were also living in the land at that time" (Gen 13:7), indicating the spiritual atmosphere that was in the land. The strife that erupted shows us that Abraham's household was being affected by the presence of these people, who were connected with a spiritual atmosphere that was different from the spiritual atmosphere in Abraham's home. The Canaanites and Perizzites, living in their pagan ways, were opening a spiritual gateway that was allowing spiritual forces of darkness to flow into the land, affecting all of the people who lived there.

Abraham's situation is not unique to ours today. We are living in nations where spiritual forces of darkness have found gateways through which to come and influence the people in the areas in which we live. These dark forces then influence the people to live in such a way that they are servicing the dark altars, which give the spiritual forces of darkness authority to reign and have control over their territories.

Many times we in the church do not recognize the effect the darkness has over the spiritual atmosphere in our land because we have lived in our land under these dark influences our whole lives. Whenever we travel to a new country or city, we are aware of the darkness there because it is new and not normal to us. In our own land, however, this is more difficult because we have become accustomed to it.

We live in lands where our faith, our prayer lives, and our depth of revelation are at certain levels, which we accept because everybody around us is comfortable with them. We don't realize that the darkness in the land is affecting us. It is not only affecting us, but also elements of our society—the things we see on television, what is allowed at school, and even the mindsets of the people—and it is also affecting the church. A church in a land where darkness is flooding in is being affected by that darkness. It is being drawn into a place of slumber, blindness, and powerlessness. In such a land, churches may see ungodly things going on in their schools, media, and government, but they have no faith or power to see them changed, so they accept the darkness and allow it to continue in the land.

Reclaiming the Land

Wherever Abraham went he set up an altar and called on the name of the Lord. This means that he contended with the spiritual forces of darkness in that area. Then he would go to another place and contend with another spiritual force. Why? Because one of the effects of raising a prayer altar is that it draws the presence of God and breaks the powers of darkness.

When Abraham was raising altars throughout Canaan, he was taking territory that was dedicated to pagan gods by the people of the land and reclaiming it for the kingdom of the Living God. By building altars to the Living God, Abraham was undoing the work of the enemy; he was demolishing strongholds over the land by pushing back the darkness and drawing the presence of God into the territory.

> Just as our holy altars claim the land for God, the unholy altars are trying to draw the presence of evil and claim the land for darkness.

An important point to mention here is that just as the purpose of the holy altar is to draw the presence of God and break the powers of darkness, the purpose of the unholy altar is to draw the presence of demonic powers, counter the influence of the church, and, break the influence of our God from the land. We are truly in a spiritual battle. Just as our holy altars claim the land for God, the unholy altars are trying to draw the presence of evil and claim the land for darkness.

Today, there are agendas and movements all around the world that are trying to come against the purposes, wisdom, and commands of God. Some of these agendas or movements are trying to eradicate the expression of faith and the walking out of Christianity into public life and the public forum. They are taking the Christian lifestyle and belief system to court, and trying to make it illegal for Christians to share their faith, to pray, or to do other kinds of Christian activities in public settings. The main purpose of these efforts is to break the grip of the power of the kingdom of God over society.

There are other movements and agendas trying to force the church to accept lifestyles and ideas that are against the commands and ways of God. These movements and agendas use the courts, the media, and all kinds of other influences to intimidate and force the church to go against the principles and truths of God. They try to play on the sympathies of people and their sense of right and wrong, fairness and justice, drawing us into our human wisdom and away from the divine wisdom of the Lord.

Some people say, "Don't worry about it," and others say, "To each his own." "We will do what we do in the church and they can do what they do in the world." But we have to understand that dark spiritual forces are trying to diminish the influence of the church over the land and to hinder the church from its calling and mission to disciple the nation.

We need to be aware that we do not exist in a spiritual vacuum. The prosperity of darkness in our land is the downfall of the church. It means the diminishing of the church and the failure to complete our mission. It is crucial that we understand that dark and light cannot dwell together; as one thrives, the other falls. There is no neutral ground.

We need to acknowledge that as we are seeking to draw the presence of God so that darkness is broken over the land, the unholy altars are also seeking to draw the presence of darkness so that the kingdom of God is pushed back. In parts of the world today, the church's voice and influence are being pushed out of all spheres of society. Although some would like to say, "Let them be," the darkness is pushing the church further and

> We do not exist in a spiritual vacuum. Dark and light cannot dwell together; as one thrives, the other falls. There is no neutral ground.

further away, and the church is losing more and more of its influence over the land.

The way God leads us to conquer territory is that He leads us into spiritual battles. This is not a conquest of physical territory, but of spiritual territory. We often lose sight of that; we try to fight the battles in the physical realm. We try to fight unrighteous laws and unrighteous ways with petitions and protests, not understanding that we are fighting a spiritual battle.

To understand the importance of this spiritual battle, we need to ask a few questions. Is the church gaining influence over the land or is the darkness gaining influence? Is the church losing its power or is the darkness losing power? Are the thought processes of society turning toward the Lord or increasingly turning toward the darkness?

Sustaining the Claim on the Land

The strategy of building and maintaining prayer altars throughout the land did not stop with Abraham. When Isaac grew up he went on with the ministry of setting up altars:

> From there he went up to Beersheba. And the Lord appeared to him the same night and said, "I am the God of Abraham your father. Fear not, for I am with you and will bless you and multiply your offspring for my servant Abraham's sake." So he built an altar there and called upon the name of the Lord and pitched his tent there. And there Isaac's servants dug a well.
>
> Genesis 26:23-25

In other words, Isaac was sustaining the claim over the land from the gods of the Canaanites by building and maintaining altars of the King Jehovah God.

After Isaac, Jacob continued to build altars to the Lord:

> *And Jacob came safely to the city of Shechem, which is in
> the land of Canaan, on his way from Paddan-aram, and
> he camped before the city. And from the sons of Hamor,
> Shechem's father, he bought for a hundred pieces of money
> the piece of land on which he had pitched his tent. There he
> erected an altar and called it El-Elohe-Israel.*
>
> Genesis 33:18-20

> *And Jacob came to Luz (that is, Bethel), which is in the
> land of Canaan, he and all the people who were with him,
> and there he built an altar and called the place El-bethel,
> because there God had revealed himself to him when he
> fled from his brother.*
>
> Genesis 35:6-7

When he returned from Paddan Aram, Jacob established altars
around the land until he finally settled in Mamre, following the
pattern of his grandfather Abraham. This gives us the sense that
the way to settle into a land is by building altars to the Lord.

> *And Jacob came to his father Isaac at Mamre, or Kiriath-
> arba (that is, Hebron), where Abraham and Isaac had
> sojourned.*
>
> Genesis 35:27

The practice of building altars went on from generation to generation. Think of the altars erected by Moses, Joshua, Gideon,
Samuel, David, Josiah, and Elijah, to name a few. These men were
purging the land and claiming it for Jehovah God. They were contending with the darkness ruling that land as they called on the
presence of God to come upon it and stay. They were claiming
the land from the kingdom of darkness into the kingdom of God.

Go Through the Length and Breadth of the Land

In Uganda, when God was speaking to us about how to apply the Abrahamic Strategy, the word He gave me (John Mulinde) was from Genesis 13:17: "Go through the length and breadth of the land for I give it to you. Wherever you go, set up an altar and call on the name of the Lord." What would happen if all of us set up prayer altars wherever we went? What if we had praying homes, praying churches, praying students, praying politicians, and praying workers in the marketplace? What if we were raising up altars all throughout our lands and honoring our God everywhere we went?

Like Abraham, we would be forming a network of prayer over the territory we have been assigned to. We would be opening up gateways and drawing the presence of God, breaking the powers of darkness over our land. God would then come down and reclaim the land and its people for Himself.

CHAPTER 5.
WHAT IS AN ALTAR?

If we tried to explain an altar with a single definition, we would feel as though we had limited your understanding of it. We would have boxed it in, causing it to become much less than what God intended it to be. In this chapter we are going to try to define and describe the altar from different angles and perspectives, because if you look at it from one angle - like a prism - you will see a beautiful aspect of it. From another angle, you will see something entirely different from what you saw before. As we lay out the description, both from the Old Testament and how it is applied in the New Testament, we should see the concept of the altar expanding instead of being limited.

> What Is an Altar?
> - A spiritual gateway
> - Our hearts
> - A priority in our lives
> - Intimate communion with God
> - A place to offer sacrifice
> - A place of continuous fire

Having a clear understanding of an altar—what it looks like, how and why it functions, where it takes place, and other aspects of the altar—provides the clarity necessary to build and maintain a strong, healthy altar at which we can draw the presence of the Lord, commune and connect with Him, and see Him push back the darkness in our lives and our surroundings.

To help describe and define an altar, we will look at altars in both the Old and New Testaments. We can see from the Old Testament to the New Testament how the concept of the altar deepens and develops.

An Altar Is a Spiritual Gateway

An Old Testament Picture of a Spiritual Gateway. Jacob was Isaac's son, grandson to Abraham. He had grown up in a godly family. Even before he was born, the Lord spoke prophetically upon Jacob's life and said, "I will use him" (Gen 25:23), but he grew up a sinner without the fear of God.

> *Jacob left Beersheba and went toward Haran. And he came to a certain place and stayed there that night, because the sun had set. Taking one of the stones of the place, he put it under his head and lay down in that place to sleep. And he dreamed, and behold, there was a ladder set up on the earth, and the top of it reached to heaven. And behold, the angels of God were ascending and descending on it! And behold, the Lord stood above it and said, "I am the Lord, the God of Abraham your father and the God of Isaac. The land on which you lie I will give to you and to your offspring. Your offspring shall be like the dust of the earth, and you shall spread abroad to the west and to the east and to the north and to the south, and in you and your offspring shall all the families of the earth be blessed. Behold, I am with you and will keep you wherever you go, and will bring you back to this land. For I will not leave you until I have done what I have promised you." Then Jacob awoke from his sleep and said, "Surely the Lord is in this place, and I did not know it." And he was afraid and said, "How awesome is this place! This is none other than the house of God, and this is the gate of heaven." So early in the morning Jacob took the stone that he had put under his head and set it up for a pillar and poured oil on the top of it. He called the name of that place Bethel, but the name of the city was Luz at the first.*
>
> Genesis 28:10-19

Jacob cheated his brother out of his birthright (Gen 25:29-34) and out of his blessing (Gen 27:1-35). He had no qualms about going to his father pretending to be his brother; he did not fear stealing a blessing from God. He could neither apologize nor make peace, so decided to run away from home rather than humble himself.

As he ran away from home, he stopped to rest for the night. When he was sleeping he had a dream in which God spoke to him and he saw angels moving up and down a stairway connecting heaven to earth, meaning there was no resistance in the spiritual realm. When Jacob woke up he thought, "This is the gate of heaven! Surely I didn't know that God is in this place."

He was not looking for the Lord, but simply for a place to sleep. However, God spoke to this sinner through an open heaven, letting him know that even if he was running away, He had a plan and a future for him. God was telling Jacob that He would make him a great nation. Jacob's generations would spread out to the north, south, east, and west. Even if Jacob ran away, God would bring him back. God promised not to leave Jacob until He had accomplished His purposes in Jacob. He would watch over Jacob even though he had run away.

Why was the heaven open so that Jacob was able to see God, to hear the voice of the Living God and see the activities of angels? Because more than 100 years before Jacob came to Bethel, Abraham had paid the price over that land and had built an altar and cried out to the Lord in that same spot (Gen 12:8).

Why was the heaven open so that Jacob was able to see God? Because more than 100 years before, Abraham had paid the price over that land and had built an altar and cried out to the Lord in that same spot.

By raising an altar to God in that place, Abraham had broken the covering of darkness over the land and the heavens remained open. Jacob was not following the Word or ways of God, but because Abraham had opened the heavens with his habit of praying in that place, God could now speak directly to men who traveled through that area.

Abraham had broken the power of the forces of darkness that had ruled over that territory. This not only created an open heaven, it also established God's rule and authority there. God could even speak to the prideful heart of a man who did not know Him. This is the power of an altar, but what exactly is an altar?

A New Testament Picture of the Spiritual Gateway. After Jacob encountered God in a dream, he said, "Surely the Lord is in this place, and I did not know it. How awesome is this place! This is none other than the house of God...the gate of heaven" (Gen 28:16-17). Later, Jesus took this picture of the gateway of heaven and said to Nathanael, "You will see heaven opened, and the angels of God ascending and descending on the Son of Man" (John 1:51). He was saying to the disciples that they were going to see the reality of what Jacob experienced happening to the Son of Man living among them. Jesus was teaching them that the open heaven is not a one-time encounter; it can be a daily encounter with God. They were going to see and experience what it means for a man to live with the abiding presence of God, where angels and all of heaven are available to serve man in the purposes of God. This is what the New Testament reveals about a spiritual gateway.

Since the Fall of man, people have been caught in the middle of darkness; establishing and maintaining the altar is the process God has ordained to break that yoke and attract His presence, which pushes back the darkness. The spiritual realm is being opened up to come and touch the physical realm. We can create a gateway to heaven through the altar. This gateway can open into our homes, families, workplaces, churches, cities, and territories.

As we build an altar, it opens up the spiritual realm, and the layers and layers of darkness that blind, harden, suffocate, hinder, and oppress begin to give way and the heavens start to open, allowing a stronger connection and a greater flow of God's life and resources. As we experience this, we will realize that the spiritual realm can touch and impact the physical realm, whether it is in our own heart and life, our family, or even the region where we live.

Our Hearts

In the Old Testament, there is an element of geography attached to the altar. The Lord says about the temple, "I...have chosen this place for myself as a house of sacrifice" (2 Chr 7:12) and "Now my eyes will be open and my ears attentive to the prayer that is made in this place" (2 Chr 7:15). The people went to the house of the Lord, giving an offering there and making their petitions.

The altar was a specific place with physical features. It was even to be built in certain ways. During their time in the wilderness, God gave the Israelites specific instructions to build the altars with uncut stones (see Ex 20:25, Deut 27:5-6, and Josh 8:31) and to have no steps leading up to them (Ex 20:26). They talked about the stones because they were building a physical structure.

The Lord uses the Scriptures to paint a picture of a specific location where the people would go to meet with Him. They would offer their prayers and sacrifices, and then go to meet with God. The Lord would even say of the temple, "I...have chosen this place for myself as a house of sacrifice...My eyes will be open and my ears attentive to the prayer that is made in this place" (2 Chr 7:12,15). God chose this place where the people would meet with Him. It was a specific geographical place.

In the New Testament, the altar is not limited to a geographical place. The location of the altar in the New Testament is our hearts, which are completely given over to God.

If you love me, you will keep my commandments. And I will ask the Father, and he will give you another Helper, to be

with you forever, even the Spirit of truth, whom the world
cannot receive, because it neither sees him nor knows him.
You know him, for he dwells with you and will be in you.
In that day you will know that I am in my Father, and you
in me, and I in you. Whoever has my commandments and
keeps them, he it is who loves me. And he who loves me will
be loved by my Father, and I will love him and manifest
myself to him. If anyone loves me, he will keep my word,
and my Father will love him, and we will come to him and
make our home with him. Whoever does not love me does
not keep my words. And the word that you hear is not mine
but the Father's who sent me.

John 14:15-17,20-21,23-24

Jesus is showing us if we really love Him, we will submit and surrender our hearts to Him and His will, giving our lives over to Him.
He even describes this love: "If you love Me, you will obey Me."

If we aren't obeying Jesus, we have a love problem, which means
that our hearts are not yielded and surrendered to Him. It isn't
that we have a problem with our willpower, we have a problem
with our heart because that is where the altar is located. He is
saying, "If you love Me, if your heart—your inner altar—is totally
released to Me and yielded to Me, then you and I will be one as
the Father and I are one. My life will flow to you. As My Father
and I manifested ourselves in the Old Testament at the altar, We
will manifest ourselves to you because that altar is ongoing."
Then He says, "We will come and make Our home with you. We
will not just visit you, but will dwell with you, as We did at the
altar in the Old Testament."

> The primary place of the altar is not a physical location. We are the altar. We are the living stones.

He even goes on in other parts
of Scripture, saying in the Great
Commandment that everything
hangs on loving God with all our
heart (Matt 22:37). That doesn't
mean just a lot of our heart; it

means all of our heart. Our hearts are consumed with Him. He also says that our reasonable act of worship is laying our lives on the altar in surrender (Rom 12:1).

In the New Testament, Paul says, "We are the temple of the living God" (2 Cor 6:16). Peter says that we are "like living stones… being built up as a spiritual house, to be a holy priesthood, to offer spiritual sacrifices acceptable to God through Jesus Christ" (1 Pet 2:5). We do not have physical altars made of stone, like in the Old Testament. In the New Testament, we are the living stones that build the temple of the sanctuary of the Lord.

The primary place of the altar is not a physical location. We are the altar. We are the living stones. There is an internal altar inside of us that we want to keep God-focused, yielded, surrendered, and submitted to Him in such a way that we see it drawing and living in His presence in our inner being.

This does not mean we cannot have a physical location where we like to go to meet with God, either personally or as a family. We may have a location we enjoy that has an atmosphere of peace and security so that we can freely give ourselves to God, but the primary place of the altar remains our inner being, our heart.

An Altar Is a Priority in Our Lives
The Old Testament speaks of specific watches and times at the altar: the evening offering, the night watch, the second or third watch, etc. These are particular times when the people would come to a specific place to commune and meet with God.

The story of Ezra is a good example of this (Ezra 9:1-5). When he was facing the issue of intermarriage among the people of Israel, Ezra tore his clothes and pulled out his hair and beard. The Word says that he "sat appalled until the evening sacrifice" (v 4). He moaned and groaned all day; he couldn't even pray. But when it was time for the evening sacrifice, he forced himself to rise from his mourning and fasting in order to go to the evening sacrifice (v 5).

Ezra did not force himself to attend the sacrifice because he was feeling inspired; he did it because it was a specific, daily time of meeting with God and he wanted to keep that time of prayer.

Daniel kept the three times of prayer every day, even when it was outlawed (Dan 6:10).

In the New Testament, Jesus continued to make meeting with God one of His highest priorities. There were two different times He consistently did this, either early in the morning before anyone rose or late in the evening. There were even a few times when He prayed all night. This wasn't something He did randomly; it was something that was a priority in His life.

Paul, who was facing all kinds of hardship, said that he was being renewed inwardly day by day (2 Cor 4:16); this renewal came through his time at the altar. The disciples, when facing all the pressures and demands of ministry, said they needed other people to help service the work because they could not give up continuously reading the Word and prayer (Acts 6:4, NKJV). This was the altar. They made it a priority in their lives.

> Prioritizing our time and giving our first fruits of time to God are key elements in building the prayer altar.

Today it is also good to follow this practice of setting specific times when our personal, family, or other altars will take place. This does not mean that if something comes along and causes difficulty for a day that we go into condemnation or discouragement. However, it does mean that we see that prioritizing our time and giving our first fruits of time to God in building the altar is a key element of what a prayer altar is to be. We do not give Him leftover time. We make time for ministering at the altar a priority.

An Altar Is Intimate Communion With God

What is the difference between a prayer time and a prayer altar? They are very similar, but one of the most fundamental differences is that we measure the success of a prayer time by how much we are following the disciplines of the prayer time, such as reading, praying, worshiping, and even journaling. We are very happy if we have done each of these, and even happier still if we have found some verse or passage that gave us a "feel-good" moment.

For a prayer altar, though, success means breaking through the forces of darkness, encountering the presence of God, and coming into communion with Him. Then, as we come into communion with God, life is exchanged from deep within God to deep within us. When this happens daily, it becomes an atmosphere that we desire to live in; it is communion with God that we want to maintain and dwell in.

> Success for a prayer altar means breaking through the forces of darkness, encountering the presence of God, and coming into communion with Him.

David understood what it meant to come into communion with God. He frequently set aside time to just go before the Lord. David's desire to meet with God to have an intimate time with Him is shown in many of his songs. In Psalm 42:1 he wrote, "As the deer pants for flowing streams, so pants my soul for you, O God." In the same Psalm, David also asks, "Why are you cast down, O my soul, and why are you in turmoil within me?" (v 5). These verses depict David praying but not connecting with the Lord; he was crying out, "My heart is hungry for that communion."

Even though he was in prayer in the house of the Lord, David was aware that he had not yet touched the heart of God. He had not yet experienced an encounter with the Lord. His soul was downcast for some reason, and he was crying out, and yet he was aware that he would meet the Lord at the altar: "Hope in God; for I shall again praise him" (v 5). Verse 7 says, "Deep calls to deep at the roar of your waterfalls; all your breakers and your waves have gone over me." Finally, David made the connection, and the deep within him was touching the deep within God. He was experiencing the waves and waves of God's presence touching him.

The stories of Jesus going into the wilderness or up on a mountain to pray and be with the Father have a strong sense of communion. The disciples would be sleeping, but Jesus would be having time alone with the Father. When the disciples woke and looked for Him, they would not be able to find Him. These meetings between Jesus and the Father were deep and personal. Jesus described His relationship with the Father as being one: "I and the Father are one" (John 10:30).

Acts 10:9-16 illustrates an intimate time that Peter had with the Lord. He went onto the roof of the house to be alone with God while he was waiting for a meal to be prepared. As he was worshiping and praying, God came down and met with him prophetically, giving Peter the same vision three times and saying, "What God has made clean, do not call common" (v 15). What the Lord showed Peter later translated into ministry that opened the gate for the Gentiles to come into the kingdom of God (Acts 10:17-48).

Having a deeply personal time with the Lord is essential, especially at the personal altar. We can always pull away throughout our day to have private time with the Lord, even if it is just to take a short walk or a lunch break in our car to worship and read the Bible. This special time of meeting isn't so much about the particular time, it is more about the purpose of the moment: to get away and be with God.

An Altar Is a Place to Offer Sacrifice

In the Old Testament, offerings in the form of animal sacrifices were placed on the altar. These offerings were made for various reasons, but always had intentional objectives, including atonement for sin, giving thanks, alleviating guilt, and restoring fellowship with the Father.

> *I appeal to you therefore, brothers, by the mercies of God, to present your bodies as a living sacrifice, holy and acceptable to God, which is your spiritual worship.*
>
> Romans 12:1

Today, we are the living sacrifice (Rom 12:1). Our lives are laid on the altar, surrendered and yielded to the Lord. This is a reasonable act of worship. The offerings we lay at the altar include our soft, yielded, surrendered hearts and wills. We come to the altar to offer our lives and give ourselves in submission to God, creating an opening for the spiritual realm to impact the physical realm.

> Today, we are the living sacrifice (Rom 12:1). We offer our lives on the altar in submission to God, creating an opening for the spiritual realm to impact the physical realm.

Through Christ, the Lamb of God, we have atonement for sin, forgiveness, cleansing, and restored relationship with the Father. However, we must remember that we cannot be a worthy sacrifice by ourselves. In the Old Testament, not every animal offered to God was acceptable.

> *When you offer blind animals in sacrifice, is that not evil? And when you offer those that are lame or sick, is that not evil? Present that to your governor; will he accept you or show you favor? says the Lord of hosts.*
>
> Malachi 1:8

God asks, "You bring a lame or imperfect animal to Me? Take it to your ruler to see whether he will accept it." We know that we in ourselves have nothing worthy to offer to God. The only way we can become worthy is through the primary offering of the Lamb of God, which replaces all the sacrifices of the Old Testament (Heb 10:12).

The only thing that gives us the right to come before a Holy God is the blood of Jesus Christ that was shed at Calvary. We cannot approach God with boldness or confidence because we have had a good day or because we feel extra spiritual. The reason we have confidence to approach His throne is because Jesus Christ took our sin upon Himself. He paid the penalty for us and reconciled us to the Father. My faith in Him and what He has done allows me to come and commune with God.

> When we place our faith and focus on the sacrifice of Christ, we have confidence to approach the presence of God boldly.

Approaching God can be precarious until we realize that Jesus' sacrifice on the Cross has satisfied the holiness of God, and God deemed it worthy and sufficient. When we place our faith and focus on the sacrifice of Christ, we have confidence to approach the presence of God boldly.

Paul writes in Romans 3:10, "None is righteous, no, not one," meaning that we are not made righteous by doing enough good works to earn favor with God. Therefore, we are all under a sentence of death, separated from God. The only way we are made righteous is through our faith in what Christ has done, which makes it possible to have peace with God.

In Romans 5, Paul says that we were granted access by faith into the grace in which we now stand (v 2), and then goes on to describe what Christ has done for us. Jesus has accomplished something for us that we could never have accomplished ourselves. Paul talks about how Jesus has freed us from the power of sin and has raised us up into new life. We were bound to the law of sin and death, doing things that we did not want to do, but now Jesus has brought a new law, the law of life and of the Spirit, and He now dwells within us through His Holy Spirit to live with us in this new life.

Paul describes this all throughout the book of Romans, then he comes to chapter 12 and says, "Therefore, since God has done all of that for you through Christ Jesus, what response should you have?"

> *I appeal to you therefore, brothers, by the mercies of God, to present your bodies as a living sacrifice, holy and acceptable to God, which is your spiritual worship.*
> Romans 12:1

This is our spiritual act of worship. When we look at the sacrifice of Christ—He left the glory of heaven, humbled Himself to be obedient, even obedient to the point of death on a cross (Phil 2:8), and gave of that sacrifice to us—we see how hopeless we were and what He accomplished for us. We see the rights, identity, name, nature, and new life that we have in Him.

Paul says that our reasonable act now is to lay our lives down as a living sacrifice (Rom 12:1). The altar is the result of our response to prayerful communion with Him, where we yield our lives in surrender, trust, and submission to His rightful place of authority over us, whether it is during our daily altar time with God or throughout our day.

If we try to approach God based on ourselves (our spiritual feelings, good deeds, or accomplishments), we will have no real confidence to enter into the presence of God Almighty. It is only because of our faith and trust in what Jesus has done that we may approach God, assured of His glad welcome (Eph 3:12). We know that Jesus' sacrifice has satisfied the holiness of God. Our faith is in what He has accomplished and that God accepted His sacrifice. We therefore yield our lives in total abandonment to Him. If I hold onto my life, I will lose it. If I give up my life, I will have life eternal (Mark 8:35)

A sacrifice on the altar is continually ongoing. We are laying ourselves on the altar, saying, "God, my life is not mine, it belongs to You. It was bought at a price with the precious blood of Jesus Christ" (1 Cor 6:19-20). There is a continual yielding and surrendering to His will, not my own will, that takes place at the altar.

A sacrifice on the altar is ongoing. We continually lay ourselves on the altar, yielding and surrendering to God's will.

Although the Israelites could have a time with God in their homes, they were also required to go to a designated place to put a sacrifice on the altar. For example, Moses instructed the Israelites to bring an offering of their first fruits to the altar (Lev 2:12, 2:14, 23:30). Each day as they worked, they set aside the first fruits of their labors, which they brought to the altar on the Sabbath as an offering to the Lord.

We bring offerings of our daily first fruits as well. Although an animal sacrifice is no longer needed, an element of desiring to bring an offering to the altar remains. Every day I come to the altar, bringing my life as a living sacrifice. As I approach Him in worship and humility, my life is yielded and soft to His leadings and Word.

An Altar Is a Place of Continuous Fire

God instructed the priests to not allow the fire on the altar to go out.

> The fire on the altar shall be kept burning on it; it shall not go out. The priest shall burn wood on it every morning, and he shall arrange the burnt offering on it and shall burn on it the fat of the peace offerings. Fire shall be kept burning on the altar continually; it shall not go out.
> Leviticus 6:12-13

In addition to ensuring that the fire of the altar never went out, the priests' duties also included removing the ashes and renewing the firewood. Specific times were set aside to service and tend to the altar in these ways.

Just as the priests in the Old Testament would clear the ash, rekindle the fire, and put new wood on the altar throughout the day, we do the same thing today. We tend to the fire in our heart throughout the day. Pressures and attacks come in that try to extinguish the fire, so we immediately deal with them before the Lord. There are times when we sense our hearts growing cold to the point where they are shutting down, so we go before the Lord, worshiping Him and surrendering to Him, whatever needs to be done to keep that fire going.

Understanding that it was important to keep the fire in my inner being going throughout the day helped me have a more significant time with God and a deeper relationship with Him. It used to be that I (Mark Daniel) would have powerful times with God in the morning, but as the day progressed I would begin to lose that fire. Usually, the fire was extinguished by midday. Now, when I realize that my thoughts are growing negative or fear is coming into my heart, I take these things to the Lord, tending the altar throughout the day. In doing this, I now see that the altar can stay strong all day long.

Because we carry the presence of God with us, we carry the altar with us throughout the day. This means that even though we prioritize the time we have set aside to be with God each day, we also must tend to our altar all day long. We keep the fire burning in our hearts, even during meetings, conferences, or a conflict. We continually tend the altar throughout the day.

The element of tending the fire and not allowing it to go out is very important. It is not so much about saying prayers all day long. It is about having your heart connected, yielded to God, and seeking for the connection to continue throughout the day. You will find things throughout your day that try to shut your heart down, pull you into your flesh, or grieve the Spirit of God. If you tend the altar, then you turn to God through the day, allowing Him to lead you, strengthen you, refocus you, or guide you.

Abiding with God is an entrusting of yourself to Him to be kept inflamed. It is not a work, but a consenting of His work through you. It is the fruit and power of God's redeeming love expressed through a life of intimate communion with the Living God. Abiding is an undivided allegiance of the whole heart to be and do only what He wills. It is a place of entire surrender of our lives no matter what the circumstances. It is in this place of obedience and trust that we will learn the secret of perfect rest in Him as we stand in the promises of who God is, what He has done, and what He promises to do in a life that is completely His.

Testimony From the United States. When Pastor John Mulinde first came to America and started sharing about prayer altars, we had no idea how much impact they would have in the spiritual realm over our lives. One of the greatest influences I (Mark Daniel) have noticed has been in our families.

I remember when the Ugandans first came to the United States and began telling us that we needed to have family altars. To our embarrassment, every one of us confessed that we did not have one. We either prayed together at dinner or did sporadic things together, but none of us had a definite time where we came together as a family and saturated in the Word of God, sought to draw the presence of God, and came into His presence as a family through worship and prayer. The Ugandans looked at us in shock; they knew that we were leaving our families unprotected, allowing the forces of darkness to dominate the mindsets, attitudes, and atmosphere of our homes. This had never occurred to us. We had just been fooled into going along with the customs of our day and time, thinking that we were too busy, that it wouldn't work, or that this was something we didn't really want, but as we began to establish prayer altars, I was amazed at how much they began to change things in our homes.

As we came before the Lord as families, to worship, hallow His name, and read His Word together, the spiritual environment in our homes began to change. A hunger for God grew in all the members of the family, and we saw a huge impact on relationships within the family. There were positive changes in the love between husbands and wives, fathers and children, mothers and children, and between siblings. The fire of God began to spread from heart to heart in our homes.

There were so many things in our homes that we had been unaware of: unloving attitudes, harsh words, sarcasm, manipulative and threatening behavior, and selfishness, but as we established the prayer altars, the atmosphere began to be more honoring, respectful, and godly. The sarcasm, woundedness, negativity, and unloving attitudes began to fade, and our homes became quieter, more peaceful, and more loving.

The spiritual atmosphere began to affect our children's attitudes. It wasn't always instant, but we could see that the prayer altars were affecting the lives of our young people. They became closer to their parents, and began to honor the things of God, treating Him and His ways with greater regard and reverence. In fact, the Ugandans had told us that as we drew God's presence, the need to discipline our children would diminish. They said that the Holy Spirit would begin to convict them and that God would deal with our children Himself. After we started the prayer altars, our children began to come and confess things instead of hiding them and we saw changes in our children that could only have been provoked by the Lord.

As we built our family altars and noticed these changes coming into our homes, we realized that we were building a platform from which we could fight battles. Without the altars, so many times in the past we had no platform from which to fight the battles that would come against our families. Then, as we fought for our children, we started seeing their spiritual appetites changing; they began to pursue the things of God.

It has now been almost a decade since we started to build family altars. In that time, the majority of our children have surrendered their lives to God, given their lives to His service, and desire to fulfill the destiny He has for their lives. Many of our children are now young adults who first started to be part of those altars when they were 10, 12, or 14 years old. They now have altars of prayer in their own homes where they come into the presence of God. They do this because their lives were marked as we went as families before the Lord and encountered Him and met with Him. They saw their parents crying out to God, humbling them-selves before the Lord and ministering to Him.

The tangible changes that have taken place over the past 10 years have been remarkable. It is like a bomb exploded in the spiritual realm and then began to destroy the works of the devil in our hearts and homes.

Summary

What is an altar? People like to have one simple definition of an altar because they believe they can take hold of it that way, but in doing that, they are limiting themselves. It is very possible that their altar would then become routine or lack some essential element.

In this chapter, we have tried to portray a picture of the altar from different angles so that the fullness of it can grow and build in our hearts. Even as you build an altar in your life, you may be initially strong in seeing the intimacy of the altar, the sacrifice, or the importance of making it a priority in your life, but you may not see how to keep the fire going throughout the day. You may still struggle to see how it is a spiritual gateway and how it can push back the darkness, but as you continually walk in the lifestyle of the altar, these other elements will come to you as you go forward.

No one starts with all of the elements of the altar operating at the highest levels; we just want to present the full aspect so that as

God grows you in the other elements of the altar, you will cooperate with Him and see the altar continually growing and building in your life and in your family, and even having an impact on the spiritual realm in greater and greater ways.

CHAPTER 6.
WHICH KINGDOM WILL PREVAIL?

As we look at the altar and why it is important, we need to remind ourselves that there are two kingdoms: a kingdom of light and a kingdom of darkness. At the altar, we build an atmosphere to draw the kingdom of light and receive instructions for how to carry out the mission of the kingdom of light. When we fail to build and service the altar, the kingdom of darkness begins to triumph and prevail.

To discuss altars we need to understand darkness to a degree. However, since we have discussed darkness in great detail in many conferences and meetings around the nations, in this chapter, we are going to describe and discuss darkness very briefly.

The altar is a place where the spiritual realm can intervene in the physical realm. Because darkness is a reality that is part of all of our lives, comprehending darkness is key to grasping the importance of the altar and how it is a gateway.

> Darkness is the spiritual force that comes when people reject the will of God. It gives legal authority to the devil to influence our lives negatively.

Darkness is the spiritual force that comes when people reject the will of God. It gives legal authority to the devil to influence our lives negatively. All men are fallen from the will of God. Therefore, we have all allowed darkness into our lives, so we are all caught up in the different forms of darkness: personal, societal, and territorial. Because of this darkness, men then turn away, and find it more and more difficult to live in the ways of the Lord. The more layers of darkness in a society, the more difficult it will be to know God's will and to live in His ways, to advance His kingdom.

Spiritual forces were not given dominion over the earth; man was (Gen 1:28). Therefore, they do not have the legal authority to control the direction a society goes. But man chooses what spiritual forces he is going to yield to. When man chooses darkness, he is not only inviting darkness to come into the spiritual atmosphere, but also to affect his way of life. He therefore suffers the consequences. Darkness brings blindness; it suffocates the flow of spiritual life. It hardens hearts. It closes up the atmosphere from the things of God. This is a brief explanation of what it means to have closed heavens.

The Scriptures speak about closed heavens, meaning that you labor in vain and there is a famine of the Word of God. Jeremiah lists ways the people weren't seeing the Lord work (Jer 2:6-8). They were not experiencing His presence compared with other times in their history, but no one was asking, "Where is the Lord?" Jeremiah was describing an environment where the heavens were not open; life was not flowing fully from God's throne.

In 2 Chronicles 7:13, God says that He is the one who shuts the heavens: "I shut up the heavens so that there is no rain, or command the locust to devour the land, or send pestilence among my people." He does this because the people "turn aside and forsake my statutes and my commandments that I have set before you, and go and serve other gods and worship them" (2 Chr 7:19).

Haggai also talks about heavens being shut. The Lord said, "You have sown much, and harvested little. You eat, but you never have enough; you drink, but you never have your fill. You clothe yourselves, but no one is warm. And he who earns wages does so to put them into a bag with holes. You looked for much, and behold, it came to little. And when you brought it home, I blew it away" (Hag 1:6,9). They labored, but were not satisfied. This is because the heavens over them were shut.

God has promised that, "If my people who are called by my name humble themselves, and pray and seek my face and turn from their wicked ways, then I will hear from heaven and will forgive their sin and heal their land" (2 Chr 7:14). This is like opening or piercing the darkness, creating an atmosphere where God can come down and move in the land. He has promised that if we fulfill certain conditions, He will hear. Not only will He hear, He will forgive us for anything we have done, and He will come down and heal the land.

God gave the promise that if we turn to the Lord and follow His requirements, we will not only get His attention, He will also hear our prayers and forgive us, removing the legal ground for what the enemy has been doing to us. This draws His presence, which then starts to push back the darkness. Our turning to the Lord and returning to His ways creates the gateway through which He comes to break the power of darkness in our lives and land.

God's Original Intent

God's original intent was that man would live in His presence and with His covenantal connection; that man would live with an inner oneness of the Spirit of God and an outer atmosphere of the presence of God (Gen 1-2).

God's original intent was that man would live in His presence and with His covenantal connection, with an inner oneness of the Spirit of God and an outer atmosphere of the presence of God (Gen 1-2).

Because of the Fall, oneness with God was lost and man developed what the Bible calls the "sinful nature," which is at enmity with God. Man is no longer able to please God and is at war with the Spirit of God. This means that even a person who considers himself "good" can never fulfill God's will because the human/sinful nature cannot do that. The only way to return to being in God's will is to repent of our ways and accept Jesus Christ as our personal Savior.

People who are born again have received the new life of Christ. They can now experience the exchanged life, which is the life that has come into their heart. A connection with God and the ability to receive the life flow of God have been established. However, if a believer chooses to live according to the flesh, he fails to experience this life with God.

The Bible says friendship with the world and carnality are death and enmity with God (Rom 8:5-9, James 4:4). If we choose this, we are forsaking friendship with the Lord and giving the enemy the legal ground to war against us. We then end up living below the fullness and blessedness of what God planned to give us.

> *And you were dead in the trespasses and sin in which you once walked, following the course of this world, following the prince of the power of the air, the spirit that is now at work in the sons of disobedience.*
>
> Ephesians 2:1-2

God intended that we live in the atmospheric presence of His Holy Spirit, just as fish live in water. But because of sin, we lost the blessed presence, the blessed covering of God, and became exposed to the enemy and the presence of powers of darkness, which are roaming over the world and seeking who to influence wherever possible (1 Pet 5:8). We may have the life of Christ, but when we live according to our fallen nature/the flesh, we are giving legal ground to the spiritual forces of darkness to hinder and negatively affect us.

God's Perfect Plan and Desires
When we lost this deep communion with the Lord, we also lost our ability to hear God clearly. We no longer have the life flow of God, which gives us the Christ nature and the ability to understand

and know the will of God as well as the power to do His will. We are no longer able to execute God's will because we no longer have the ability to know His will, desires, etc. We then become limited and even in bondage to darkness.

When I (Mark Daniel) first began building a prayer altar, I had no concept of how much darkness was limiting me, blinding my eyes from revelation and from the truths of God. I did not understand how much it was weakening my strength, my faith, and even my appetite for the things of God. I was living a Christian life the best I knew how, and I was doing as well as anyone else I could see around me. But I was still under the dictates of so much darkness in my culture as well as in my own life. It was deeply limiting and hindering me.

As I began to build the prayer altar and to seek the presence of God, I found that when light comes in, darkness is exposed. As you draw deeper into Him, you see how much the ways of the world are in your thinking and your actions. You have never recognized this before because everybody else is doing the same thing. I didn't realize how much darkness was stealing my spiritual strength, my fidelity, and my oneness of heart with God.

> "As I began to build the prayer altar and to seek the presence of God, I found that when light comes in, darkness is exposed. I didn't realize how much darkness was stealing my spiritual strength, my fidelity, and my oneness of heart with God."

As we come deeper into the light, we start to see that darkness is holding us in bondage. It is blinding us, suffocating the fullness of life that Christ intended for us so that it cannot freely flow.

Even Christians, when they choose to live outside of God's will, lose the power to live according to His will. They then become driven by the lies and deceptions of darkness, the pressures and demands of the people around them, and end up living according to the world's ways, denying the ways of God.

—— JOHN MULINDE AND MARK DANIEL ——

What Is Darkness?

Choosing not to follow God's will results in darkness. Darkness originated when Lucifer rejected God's will, ways, and wisdom, and ended up out of God's will (Ezek 28:1-19). He was therefore in rebellion against God. Whenever we choose our will over God's will, or our ways over God's ways, darkness comes into our thinking and our heart. Layers of darkness can be put on us and begin to hinder us. We even experience a hindrance in communing and drawing near to God or remembering things He has said. Darkness coming in is the reason that often God can speak very powerful revelations to us, but we quickly forget what He said.

The spiritual force of darkness will blind, hinder, weaken, harden, and exert forces against us to continue to push us further and further away from God and His will. The longer we stay in darkness, the more lost we become, the more we see old patterns of sin and flesh coming in, and the more we see godly desires and ways eroding. The Bible tells us repeatedly to not fall into the traps of the enemy, but to be aware that he is seeking to devour us like a lion. Even when we feel him pushing to move us out of the will of God and the wisdom of God, if we immediately submit to God it will cause him to flee (James 4:7). The Bible tells us not to be fooled and for us to be prepared for those times so we can tell when Satan is targeting us. It tells us to be ready for that day of evil, being alert and prepared for those times of attack.

This battle of overcoming darkness is fought by overseeing what we allow into our thoughts and what we come into agreement with in our minds. The Bible tells us to guard our hearts and our minds (Phil 4:7). Paul says to renew our minds to truth (Rom 12:2), and Jesus tells us that if we know the truth, the truth will set us free (John 8:32). Our minds are a gateway that allows darkness in or keeps it out.

We choose whether we are going to follow God's will in our mind. This means that the biggest gate to overcome darkness in the individual is the mind. The Bible encourages us to guard (Phil 4:7), renew (Rom 12:2), and protect (Eph 6:17) our minds. The mind is the main gate that either allows darkness in or protects us against it because we have filled our mind with the truth from the Word of God.

Different Types and Layers of Darkness

There are three different forms of darkness: personal, societal, and territorial. Each form comes through gates that were opened in that specific arena.

Personal Darkness. Darkness comes against individuals. The battle being fought against individuals involves what they submit to and what they trust, as well as whether they will follow the ways of the world or the ways of God. Is it their will or is it God's will?

When individuals turn away from God, they will be more and more surrounded by darkness, which will affect and hinder them. Someone may have received the new life of Christ, but has allowed darkness into his soul (Luke 11:34-35). As darkness comes in, it blinds, deceives, hardens, weakens, torments, draws more darkness, and suffocates the flow of life.

Societal Darkness. Darkness can also affect the way a society functions. There are five recognized "pillars" of society, and each can be affected by darkness: family, economy, government, worship, and belief system.

> Darkness affects the pillars of society:
> - Family
> - Economy
> - Government
> - Worship
> - Belief system

The family is an institution that God formed, and it is the foundation or bedrock of society. When righteousness reigns in society, then the family functions according to the ways of God and there is security, health, and well-being, but when darkness reigns, the family becomes distorted, dysfunctional, and broken. Sexual immorality and other immoral behaviors rise up, affecting the whole family. Children's hearts start to turn away from their parents and rebellion forms in the family. Darkness brings destruction into the family unity.

Another pillar affected by darkness is the economy, the ability of a society to make wealth. Darkness brings greed and selfishness into society, but if the kingdom of God is ruling, there will be generosity, equity, and care for the downtrodden.

When righteousness reigns in society, the government is good to its people; it takes care of them and gives them good leadership. However, when darkness comes into society, the government becomes corrupted and oppressive, and begins to lead the people away from righteousness. The society begins to call good evil and evil good (Is 5:20). This can affect what people worship and give their allegiance to, as well as the concept and direction of the family.

Humans were created to worship; therefore, when the kingdom of light is ruling, society worships the One True God and there is righteousness among the people. However, when darkness comes in, the people start to worship all kinds of other things (wealth, fame, success, superstition, the occult) and their hearts are drawn into the darkness. Worshiping the light or the dark draws either the Lord or spiritual darkness into the society, affecting each of the pillars of society even more.

The belief system is what a society embraces, accepts, and submits to as the way of life in the land. When darkness comes in, it changes the belief system, causing it to become corrupted. If the kingdom of light is reigning, there are words, thoughts, behaviors, and images that are considered unacceptable. Vulgar language, sexual images or behavior, or the portrayal of violence on television or another public forum would cause the society to rise up and declare it unacceptable. When darkness reigns, however, there are very few objections. The people easily accept the unholy or unrighteous thing. For example, words, behaviors, and images portrayed on television, in printed media, or on the Internet that would never have been allowed 10 years ago now come easily into society, with very little notice or comment. There are no protests because the mindsets and behavior of the people have been conformed by the darkness.

When darkness comes into society, it contaminates and corrupts every sphere of that society. This means that instead of helping to build and create a society that welcomes the kingdom of God, it builds and creates one that is in rebellion to God and that draws darkness into the land. The longer a society dwells in darkness, the more each aspect of society gets further and further from the will of God. We can try to fight the unrighteousness that is coming into the land by electing politicians or by protesting the decisions that are unrighteous, but as you see in this chapter, the battle over the land will only be won in the spiritual realm.

As we build prayer altars to the Lord that break through the darkness covering our hearts, homes, churches, and communities and we see the presence of God coming and moving in society, we will also see that nothing is too hard for Him. No nation is too far gone. Our God is able to break through the darkness covering our lands, but we need to rebuild the altar of the Lord.

Territorial Darkness. A third area of darkness is territorial darkness. Territorial darkness is about the spiritual realm: the rulers of darkness, the principalities and powers that rule over territories. You can tell which powers and territorial spirits reign over a land by the character of the people of that land.

Las Vegas is different from Boise, Idaho, or Nairobi, Kenya, and

Tokyo is very different from Frankfurt, Germany. This is because the spiritual forces over the land affect the character and mindset of the people of the land. When we desire to determine which kingdom—the kingdom of light or the kingdom of darkness—is going to rule in a land, we have to deal with personal darkness, societal darkness, and territorial darkness.

We do this by building the altar and drawing the presence of God. The light of God will come and He will reveal personal darkness. He will also reveal the darkness that is in the land. He wants us to break away from those dictates, as well as from the customs and patterns of society that are being ruled by darkness so we can break the powers of darkness in our society. He will show us and help us understand the principalities and powers that are ruling in our territory so that we can start to take authority as the Body of Christ to deal with those powers and principalities in our cities and nations.

Why is the altar important? When we live without the altar, darkness rules society. Without the establishment and maintenance of altars of prayer to the Holy One, darkness would invade, corrupt, and rule society. If the darkness has nothing to combat against it, it will come in faster than it is being pushed back, effecting and hindering us in every way of life.

> When we live without the altar, darkness rules society.

Now that we have a greater understanding of the two kingdoms—the kingdom of light and the kingdom of darkness—we want to discuss why the altar is so important and why nations being overrun with darkness can be largely attributed to the disrepair of the altar in the family, church, and society as a whole.

Holy Versus Unholy Altars

One aspect of the altar is that it is a gateway between the spiritual and physical realms. It is a place where people can engage spiritual forces. Altars are dedicated to some kind of spiritual force, whether it is the One True Living God Jehovah, the pagan god Baal, a New Age god, or the occult.

Activities at the altar draw the attention of spiritual beings. Those who build the altar present offerings, sacrifices, prayer, and worship at that altar, trusting that the spiritual being it is dedicated to will hear and answer. The activities at the altar open the spiritual realm and draw the attention of the spirit that is being ministered to. When the physical realm comes in contact with the spiritual realm at the altar, an atmosphere is created for the spiritual realm to work in and among a people.

> The altar is a gateway between the spiritual and physical realms.

Altars connect with powers of darkness as well as with light; therefore, there are unholy altars as well as holy altars. And just as there is a holy priesthood, there is an unholy priesthood that services the unholy altars. Altars that have been raised to minister to anything other than the Lord God are unholy altars that are drawing the power of the kingdom of darkness into the land. Therefore, an altar erected to anything other than God, the Father of our Lord Jesus Christ, is a cause for concern to the Body of Christ.

Unholy altars are built to minister to spiritual forces of darkness. These altars open a gateway to the dark forces in the spiritual realm, drawing them into a territory. In any city, there are areas where you can feel tangible darkness because altars have been established there that are drawing the presence of darkness. For example, there are places in parts of many cities that have been dedicated to sexual spirits and activities. This affects the people who are in that area by drawing spiritual forces of sexual sin and perversion. People from other parts of the city who go to that area are affected by the darkness that is drawn by these activities. These dark altars affect the hearts and minds of the people in the entire city.

—— JOHN MULINDE AND MARK DANIEL ——

Unholy altars can be focused on sexual perversion, greed, violence and harm, woundedness, New Age, the occult, etc. All over the world, dark altars are connected with blood sacrifice of some sort, whether human blood or another kind of blood. This makes abortion one of the strongest altars, attracting forces of darkness to a territory.

There is no such thing as neutral spiritual ground. Either there will be a predominance of holy altars drawing the presence of God or unholy altars drawing the powers of darkness. Therefore, when we are not building altars to the Lord, dark altars are being built that will take their place. This is why it is very important that Christians work together to build prayer altars to the Lord God all across our cities and territories.

The Prevailing Altar Controls the Land

For when there is a change in the priesthood, there is necessarily a change in the law as well.

Hebrews 7:12

The altar that is most active will control the territory and will influence everything in that territory. Even the lifestyle and character of the people will take on the character of the spiritual being they are serving. This principle can be seen throughout Scripture.

When Lot and Abraham separated, Lot chose to move to the plain of the Jordan, a land that was seemingly beautiful and prosperous (Gen 13:10), but as soon as he settled there, the Word of God tells us that "the men of Sodom were wicked, great sinners against the Lord" (Gen 13:13). This is a statement of the spiritual atmosphere of the land. Later the Scriptures show us the exact nature and character of the people

> The altar that is most active—holy or unholy—will control the territory.

(Gen 19:4-9). Although the principality of darkness is not mentioned, it is obvious that dark forces influence the character of the city. The men of the city were rude and imposing. Their sexual perversion and wickedness are clear. The very idea that all of the men in the city—both young and old, from every part of the city—desired to engage in the sex act with these two people is not human thinking; it is darkness and wickedness. There were no prayer altars to the Lord in the city, so it was covered in darkness.

King Solomon started out as a humble man, submissive to God. He stood at the altar ministering to the Lord in such a way that God honored him by coming down, giving him wisdom and promises of wealth and prosperity. The land experienced the full blessing of God. The boundaries of Israel were expanding and the kingdom was the most prosperous it had ever been or would ever be throughout all of history. In the Song of Songs, you can see Solomon beginning to neglect the altar; the Lord would come to him, but he wasn't willing to respond (Song 5:1-3). Solomon began to allow his wives to raise altars to other gods, causing the hearts of the people in the land to turn away from God. Solomon himself eventually became completely corrupted (1 Kin 11:3-8).

When the altar of the Lord is not being maintained or is in disrepair—not functioning properly or even not functioning at all—altars of darkness start to come into the land to fill the void. This causes the hearts and lives of the people, as well as the direction of the nation, to turn away from God. The only way to turn things back around is for someone in the land to rebuild the altar to the Lord and draw the people back to the altar so they are once more focused on God, communing with Him, ministering to Him, and experiencing His presence carrying their lives forward. The whole spiritual atmosphere will change in greater and greater ways. Examples of this can be found throughout Scripture, but one of the greatest was in the days of Elijah.

In the times of Elijah, the altar of the Lord was in disrepair. The priests of God were in hiding. They were so hidden away that Elijah thought he was the only prophet left who had not compromised himself by bowing his knee to Baal (1 Kin 18:22). The people of the Lord had become so covered with darkness and hindered in their awareness of God that even when they were asked who God was, Baal or the Lord, they didn't have an answer.

When Ahab married Jezebel and took to worshiping her false god Baal (1 Kin 16:31-33), he influenced all of Israel to go in the way of idolatry. The people of the land were soon behaving in the ways of Baal. Ahab and Jezebel had raised altars to Baal that had opened a spiritual gateway for darkness to come in and begin to rule the land and its people.

Darkness prevailed. The priests of Baal controlled the spiritual direction and had the strongest voice of influence over the land. This was the spiritual climate when Elijah came to confront the altars of darkness in Israel. One of the first things he did was rebuild the altar of the Lord. He did this because he realized this was the pivotal place that would determine the direction the nation would go.

And Elijah came near to all the people and said, "How long will you go limping between two different opinions? If the Lord is God, follow him; but if Baal, then follow him." And the people did not answer him a word. Then Elijah said to the people, "I, even I only, am left a prophet of the Lord, but Baal's prophets are 450 men. Let two bulls be given to us, and let them choose one bull for themselves and cut it in pieces and lay it on the wood, but put no fire to it. And I will prepare the other bull and lay it on the wood and put no fire to it. And you call upon the name of your god, and I will call upon the name of the Lord, and the God who answers by fire, he is God." And all the people answered, "It is well spoken." Then Elijah said to the prophets of Baal, "Choose for yourselves one bull and prepare it first, for you are many, and call upon the name of your god, but put no fire to it." And they took the bull that was given them, and they prepared it and called upon the name of Baal from morning until noon, saying, "O Baal, answer us!" But there was no voice, and no one answered. And they limped around the altar that they had made. And at noon Elijah mocked them, saying, "Cry aloud, for he is a god. Either he is musing, or he is relieving himself, or he is on a journey, or perhaps he is asleep and must be awakened." And they cried aloud and cut themselves after their custom with swords and lances, until the blood gushed out upon them. And as midday passed, they raved on until the time of the offering of the oblation, but there was no voice. No one answered; no one paid attention.

Then Elijah said to all the people, "Come near to me." And all the people came near to him. And he repaired the altar of the Lord that had been thrown down. Elijah took twelve stones, according to the number of the tribes of the sons of Jacob, to whom the word of the Lord came, saying, "Israel shall be your name," and with the stones he built an altar in the name of the Lord. And he made a trench about the altar, as great as would contain two seahs of seed. And he put the wood in order and cut the bull in pieces and laid it on the wood. And he said, "Fill four jars with water and pour it on the burnt offering and on the wood." And he said, "Do it a second time." And they did it a second time. And he said, "Do it a third time." And they did it a third time. And the water ran around the altar and filled the trench also with water.

And at the time of the offering of the oblation, Elijah the prophet came near and said, "O Lord, God of Abraham, Isaac, and Israel, let it be known this day that you are God in Israel, and that I am your servant, and that I have done all these things at your word. Answer me, O Lord, answer me, that this people may know that you, O Lord, are God, and that you have turned their hearts back." Then the fire of the Lord fell and consumed the burnt offering and the *wood and the stones and the dust, and licked up the water that was in the trench. And when all the people saw it, they fell on their faces and said, "The Lord, he is God; the Lord, he is God." And Elijah said to them, "Seize the prophets of Baal; let not one of them escape." And they seized them. And Elijah brought them down to the brook Kishon and slaughtered them there.*

1 Kings 18:21-40

When Elijah called for the showdown between the God of heaven and Baal the god of the Sidonians, the Bible says that he had to first repair the altar of the Lord (1 Kin 18:30). Why was the altar of the Lord in disrepair? Because the Lord's altar was not being serviced and maintained as it ought to be. It had fallen into disuse. The people of the land had turned to worship Baal, and the small priesthood of the Lord that remained was in hiding and unable to maintain and service the altar of God. Jezebel was ruling through the strength of the false god Baal and the unholy priesthood that serviced the unholy altars of Baal.

> Whichever priesthood is strongest in the land will rule the land.

Whichever priesthood is strongest in the land will rule the land. This priesthood ensures that their altars are being serviced by offering prayers and sacrifices to their god. The laws of the land will then begin to reflect the wishes of this priesthood, whether holy or unholy, and those spiritual forces will shape the mindsets and appetites of the people.

As Elijah came and repaired the altar of the Lord, he began to operate as a priest of the altar, worshiping God, turning his faith to God. He was opening up that gateway again, making an opportunity for the spiritual forces of God Almighty to touch the physical realm of earth. As the altar of the Lord was restored, the powers of the dark altar were broken and the people were again able to recognize that the Lord is God, not Baal, and their hearts were back to the Lord.

Throughout Scripture, whether it was King Josiah, King Hezekiah, or the Lord Jesus Christ, we see that as they rebuilt the altar of the Lord, then established and lived a lifestyle of the altar, the people of the land began to be drawn to the Lord. Like Elijah, we too can rebuild the altar of the Lord. When we do, not only are we drawing the presence of God Almighty, we are also extinguishing the ability of the false priesthood to draw the presence of their own god and their darkness. The ability of the false god to come down is eliminated. And when the light shines, the darkness cannot prevail.

Holy and Unholy Altars in the Nations

In Uganda, up until the time God revealed to us how to pray for His purposes rather than our problems, the unholy priesthood had thrived in the nation. Witchcraft, ancestral worship, and the occult were widespread. Even though there were few Muslims in the nation, they serviced their altars and were very strong in the land. In the 1970s, with a population that was less than 5% Muslim, President Idi Amin dedicated Uganda to Allah and declared it an Islamic nation. This shouldn't have been a surprise considering the spiritual truth that the prevailing altar and strongest priesthood rules the land.

Idi Amin's declaration was followed by years of turmoil upon turmoil as the Lord endeavored to get the attention of His agents on earth, the Body of Christ. Finally, when He got our attention through the AIDS pandemic, the church went about repairing the altar of the Lord.

After that time came the call to raise altars throughout the nation following the strategy of Abraham that the Lord had revealed to us. As we raised an altar of the Lord over Uganda, the influence of the church and God's purposes soon began to be seen in different areas of the nation.

—— JOHN MULINDE AND MARK DANIEL ——

Corrupt departments like the Uganda Revenue Authority began to change. God raised up godly leaders in the department, and the Uganda Revenue Authority is presently one of the most successful stories of transformation. The banking sector, which had failed so miserably over the years, made a turn-around as prayer altars were raised in the workplace.

President Museveni allowed prayer in the State House, and a prayer altar was raised there. He also handed over the flag of the nation of Uganda to the intercessors at a national prayer rally and said, "If Uganda ever gets into any crisis, it shall not be the fault of me or the government. I put the nation into your hands." These actions came from a man who was a soldier and a socialist, and who did not put much belief in God. They are powerful evidence of the power of an altar and the impact it can have on a nation and its people. President Museveni was effectively putting the control of the happenings in the nation into the hands of the Body of Christ.

Up to this day, whenever anything happens in the nation of Uganda, when the church rises up to pray, God has always intervened in our nation, but when the church loses focus on God and the life of the altar and goes into her own agendas, we see the nation being swayed away from God's purposes, and calamities quickly fall upon the nation.

In the past, in nations where Christianity at one time had a very strong influence, such as in the West, the people saw God moving mightily as they upheld a lifestyle of prayer altars in their families, churches, communities, seats of government, and the marketplace. People in these nations even had a vision and desire to take the gospel all across the known world, such as to the continents of Africa and Asia. Sadly, over time, the focus on prayer began to decrease and the people began to lose their sense of the altar lifestyle. This allowed altars of darkness to begin to be established and even flourish.

Secularism began to grow in the Western world. It has increased to such an extent that many people are even saying that the church doesn't have a place in discussions of the direction of our nations. Humanism has increased and spread throughout the world, its voice getting louder and louder. Those with a humanistic world-view have no sense of a Creator or a God to whom they are obligated; they believe that humans make their own decisions and are the center of the universe. The humanistic voice is being heard by the multitudes in more and more ways, and laws being passed in the nations are drawn from these thought processes.

The United States was founded on a lifestyle of prayer altars. Most of the early settler families had prayer at the beginning and end of each day. However, today, most families in the United States have no time of prayer at all. The altar has fallen into disrepair in our family life. Prayer is declining to such a degree in the West that there are very few praying churches. In most churches today, only a small remnant of people gathers for prayer. As the altars have fallen into disrepair because of the decline in prayer and the altar lifestyle, other unholy altars have been established throughout the nation.

The voices from the priesthood that maintains these unholy altars are being heard in greater and greater ways, and the masses are lining up to follow after them. The voice of immorality and sexual confusion is also getting louder and spreading across the world. It has spread throughout nations where the altar to the Lord has decreased, so other spiritual voices have begun to have the louder voice.

How much more unholiness and darkness do we need to see before we recognize the importance of renewing our efforts, like Elijah did, to restore the altar of the Lord in our lives, families, churches, workplaces, and communities?

Summary

Altars are spiritual gateways that provide an opening for the spiritual realm to intervene in the physical realm. They create open heavens through which the light or the darkness is given authority to interact with the physical realm. Altars are maintained by a priesthood that may be holy or unholy. The priesthood that is strongest raises the strongest altar, and the altar that prevails has control over the territory.

Wherever altars to the Lord prevail, we see the purposes of God prevailing in the land. In contrast, when altars of darkness prevail, we see darkness having control over a city or nation. This is why we must raise up altars of prayer to the Lord: to push the darkness out of our lands.

We have written this book to help re-establish a holy priesthood who will and are able to raise holy altars. Our desire is that altars of prayer will be raised up to God throughout the nations so we can see the darkness pushed back and the kingdom of God advancing in our lives, families, churches, workplaces, cities, and territories.

How can we join together to see this done? One way is through the strategy that God gave Abraham through which he claimed and restored the land back to God. The way God has His people possess territories is not so much by military conquest as by spiritual conquest, and this spiritual conquest is done by establishing altars.

Chapter 7.
The Priesthood

Now when all this was finished, all Israel who were present went out to the cities of Judah and broke in pieces the pillars and cut down the Asherim and broke down the high places and the altars throughout all Judah and Benjamin, and in Ephraim and Manasseh, until they had destroyed them all. Then all the people of Israel returned to their cities, every man to his possession. And Hezekiah appointed the divisions of the priests and of the Levites, division by division, each according to his service, the priests and the Levites, for burnt offerings and peace offerings, to minister in the gates of the camp of the Lord and to give thanks and praise. The contribution of the king from his own possessions was for the burnt offerings: the burnt offerings of morning and evening, and the burnt offerings for the Sabbaths, the new moons, and the appointed feasts, as it is written in the Law of the Lord. And he commanded the people who lived in Jerusalem to give the portion due to the priests and the Levites, that they might give themselves to the Law of the Lord. As soon as the command was spread abroad, the people of Israel gave in abundance the firstfruits of grain, wine, oil, honey, and of all the produce of the field. And they brought in abundantly the tithe of everything. And the people of Israel and Judah who lived in the cities of Judah also brought in the tithe of cattle and sheep, and the tithe of the dedicated things that had been dedicated to the Lord their God, and laid them in heaps. In the third month they began to pile up the heaps, and finished them in the seventh month. When Hezekiah and the princes came and saw the heaps, they blessed the Lord and his people Israel. And Hezekiah questioned the priests and the Levites about the heaps. Azariah the chief priest, who was of the house of Zadok, answered him, "Since they began to bring the contributions into the house of the Lord, we have eaten and had enough and have plenty left, for the Lord has blessed his people, so that we have this large amount left." Thus Hezekiah did throughout all Judah, and he did what was good and right and faithful before the Lord his God. And every work that he undertook in the service of the house of God and in accordance with the law and the commandments, seeking his God, he did with all his heart, and prospered.

2 Chronicles 31:1-10,20-21

Now that we have discussed and understand what prayer altars are and how key they are to a victorious life, the next issue we need to discuss is the priest who serves at the altar.

As we discussed in a previous chapter, the altar opens a gateway between the spiritual realm and the physical realm. Authority is released at the altar to bring the physical and spiritual worlds together to flow in alignment. This makes the altar a vital aspect of life. The priest who services the altar is even more vital.

A priest is a person who will oversee and control the gateway between the spiritual realm and the physical realm that is created by the altar. Only a priest can build and then maintain an altar. There are holy priests, whose purpose is to stand before God to minister at the altar, and unholy priests, who serve the powers of darkness.

In every land there are two priesthoods: an unholy priesthood and a holy priesthood. An effective and holy priesthood draws the presence of God into the land. When the priesthood in the land is righteous, the whole nation will be affected by the presence of God rather than the powers of darkness (Deut 28:1-14, Zech

3:6-9, 2 Chr 31:2-21). The kingdom of darkness has an unholy priesthood that is involved in idolatry, spiritism, and worship of all kinds of false gods and teachings; follows after the ways of the world and the ways of man; and engages in other activities that draw the presence of dark spiritual powers.

The priesthood that prevails—that services the altar most actively and effectively—will have the authority to influence the direction in which the land will go (Heb 7:12).

The Holy Priesthood

> *But you are a chosen people, a royal priesthood, a holy nation, God's special possession, that you may declare the praises of him who called you out of darkness into his wonderful light.*
>
> 1 Peter 2:9, NIV

The priesthood that prevails—that services the altar most actively and effectively—will have the authority to influence the direction in which the land will go (Heb 7:12).

A holy priest is anyone called by the name of the Lord, regardless of age, denomination, theology, or doctrine. Every child of God, whether adult or child, man or woman, is called to be a priest. Together we constitute a royal priesthood (1 Pet 2:9). Anyone who believes that Jesus Christ is the Messiah is considered part of the holy priesthood and is able to minister to God at the altar.

The Word says that Jesus "made us to be a kingdom and priests to serve his God and Father" (Rev 1:6, NIV) and that we "will be called priests of the Lord" and "will be named ministers of our God" (Is 61:6, NIV). Members of this priesthood all have the same desire: to see God's kingdom come and His will being done here on earth as it is in heaven.

We are called to declare the praises of the One who brought us into the light. Each of us is called to take our position as a priest of the Lord, standing in the gap for our various nations. We need to teach our families and fellow believers that we are all priests—in our homes, schools, workplaces, and cities; wherever He has given us a platform—and to seek to carry ourselves as priests in our mindsets, our way of life, and our commitment to one another and to God.

The responsibility of the priest is not just about praying and making petition to God. It incorporates the whole concept of instituting an altar, including being the priest at that altar; offering our lives as living sacrifices at that altar; living as a holy, consecrated people; ministering to the Lord and drawing the presence of God; and bringing our home, community, or nation into covenant with the Lord so the kingdom of God may come and His will be done on earth as it is in heaven.

As the priesthood is renewed in our nations and we establish our hearts as living altars, our homes as places where we gather as a family altar to the Lord, our churches gathering to pray and come before the Lord as a congregation, and prayer altars erected in our marketplaces and throughout our communities, we will see the darkness broken over our nations and the lifestyle of the people in those territories beginning to change. As we do this, we are repairing the altar of the Lord, becoming active and effective priests in the land, and we will see—as in every time in history— that as the priesthood of God becomes active at the altar of the Lord, they will prevail over the territory and affect the direction of their cities and nations.

The Unholy Priesthood

The unholy priesthood does not rejoice in the success, values, or principles of the kingdom of God, but rather in values and principles opposed to the kingdom of God. It thrives in the presence of dark forces, connects with false gods, and prospers with unfair and ungodly practices. It draws its power from a source other than the Holy Spirit, and promotes an agenda that is destructive, ungodly, and damaging, and that leads to death.

I (Mark Daniel) was in Uganda the first time I heard Pastor John speaking about the unholy priesthood. When I returned home I was looking around and wondering, "Where are the unholy priests in America? Who are they?" I was expecting them to be wearing some sort of priestly robes or clothes, but I did not find them. I wasn't home a week before I started to notice that there were many people who were carrying messages and agendas that were clearly against the Word, counsel, and wisdom of God, and they were out trying to win converts. They were trying to sway the mindset of the people of the land. I realized that these were part of the unholy priesthood.

Once I realized that these people are unholy priests, I also realized that they have pulpits. Whenever something of the kingdom of God tries to come into society, they rise up to stand and speak against it and to lead other people against it. They might be speaking out on a news or television show or in a newspaper or classroom; they could simply just be sharing on a blog, Twitter, or Facebook page. Regardless, these unholy priests are standing at their pulpits, espousing views that are shaping people's mindsets, hearts, and attitudes. They are servicing their unholy altars.

There are many types of unholy altars, which include not only physical altars such as mosques, temples, and shrines, but also less obvious altars such as secularism, greed, and hedonism. These altars create an atmosphere that invites dark spiritual forces to interact with the physical world. These forces have spiritual power to control the territory, influence mindsets, and affect the direction of life.

One of the most predominant unholy altars is humanism, which is idealized in societies all around the world. Humanism is defined as an outlook or system of thought attaching prime importance to human rather than divine or supernatural matters. It makes man the center of the world, giving human thought the highest authority. Humanism is held in high esteem in universities and seats of power all over the world, and is a strong spiritual force today.

Throughout our societies there are altars built to greed, pleasure seeking, secularism, false religion, and deception. And when these altars grow in their influence in the land, they draw wickedness and lifestyles devoid of righteousness and purity. Families fall victim, becoming broken and dismantled. We see harmful economic practices, corruption, deception, and a blindness that permeates all the different aspects of society. This blindness rules the mindset and appetites of the people.

In the Old Testament, there were many times when the priests in Israel were servicing unholy altars and going to the altar of the Lord at the same time (1 Kin 11:4-10, 1 Kin 18:21, 2 Chr 36:14, Jer 7:9-10, Jer 32:34, Ezek 5:11, Ezek 8:10-12, Ezek 44:12-13). This was an abomination to God. Today, if we are not building an effective altar and understanding what really needs to take place at an altar, there is room in our heart to service the altars our world is offering us and still go to the house of the Lord. This is very common in the church today, and we must therefore guard our hearts from the possibility of falling into this easy trap.

> If we are not building an effective altar, there is room in our heart to service the altars our world is offering us and still go to the house of the Lord.

The land becomes open to unholy altars and the unholy priesthood when the altar of the Lord is in disrepair. When we see that the voice of the unholy priesthood is louder, more readily heard, and better received by the nation than the voice of the holy priesthood, then we need to look at the altar of the Lord in our respective lands to determine whether it is being serviced properly.

The Effect of the Priesthood on Society

The question of priesthood is not something for the church alone; it encompasses and influences every aspect of society. It not only determines the religious atmosphere of the nation, it also determines
- the foundations of family and marriage,
- economic activities and fairness,
- the way government is conducted in the land,
- the types of laws that will be enacted in the land,
- what is considered valuable in society, and
- the corporate mindset of the land.

This last item is very important. What is the corporate mindset of a nation? It is the automatic way a society thinks, the way it looks at the world and at life, the values of that society, the principles of life that society accepts and honors, what that society considers acceptable or unacceptable, and the way of life of the people in that society. It is the acceptable lifestyle and the way the people submit to the ways of that nation. It is the unwritten code of the society, the "law of the land."

The culture, media, education, and entertainment of the land reflect that unwritten code. It is visible in the ways we educate our people, in what is considered politically correct or incorrect. It is what makes us who we are, what gives us our character. It is the way that outsiders describe us; they will talk about us according to that inner law that governs our society.

We don't recognize, though, that this inner law is actually governed from the spiritual realm. It may be propagated and promoted through education, entertainment, culture, media, and other means, but those agencies are not what create that inner law. They are simply reflections of what is in the spiritual atmosphere of the land.

For example, if the media produces music, a television program, or an advertising campaign that is not in conformity with the spiritual atmosphere, people will say, "That's wrong! You cannot write such a thing. You cannot share such a thing openly on television." Everyone will scream, "No!" Why? Because of the code of society that has been established in the spiritual atmosphere.

Just 10 years ago there were certain idea, images, or language that the media knew was unacceptable to bring into the public. There are things on television today that would never have been able to be shown. If anyone attempted to, society would have cried out against it. Yet today, much of what was once unacceptable is flaunted in the media and no one is making any objections. People are sitting with their families in the living room watching activities on television that yesterday were confined to the privacy of the bedroom.

What has changed? It is not the media that has changed. The media is simply reflecting what has happened in the spiritual atmosphere.

There was a time when godliness was viewed as good and admirable. Businesses would purposely hire a Christian because they knew the person would be honest and have integrity. Today, Christians are portrayed by some as puritanical, small-minded, and intolerant; people to avoid. This thought process has made godliness undesirable and shows the darkness that is ruling in the land.

The spiritual atmosphere has a law, a code of life, and this is what governs the land. It is this spiritual code of life that dictates what will happen in the society and that is reflected in every sphere of life. The spiritual code of life is what dictates the world system in the land.

The Authority of the Priesthood
It is important to note that the spiritual atmosphere of any society is influenced and serviced by the priesthood of that society, whether holy or unholy. Why? Because God did not give the

spiritual powers authority to rule the earth; He gave that authority to man (Gen 1:28). The spiritual powers—whether darkness
or light—do not have God-given authority to rule the earth.

God created man so he may rule over the earth (Gen 1:26). For any spiritual power to exercise authority in the land, man must be involved. This is why "priesthood" is so important.

God did not give this earth to spirit beings to rule; He created man so he may rule over the earth (Gen 1:26). This means that no demons or angels can rule anything or anywhere on this earth without the authority of man. Therefore, for any spiritual power to exercise authority in the land, man must be involved. That is why "priesthood" is so important.

The altar that is being serviced most actively and effectively—
whether holy or unholy—will affect the direction a society goes.
In every aspect of life in that society, whether it is government,
economy, sports, entertainment, education, or home life, the
priesthood has the authority to influence the spiritual realm, so
it will also affect the mindset and direction of the land.

The priesthood will affect what is acceptable or unacceptable
in the attitudes of the people in the land. Therefore, if the holy
priesthood is effectively servicing the altar of the Lord, then the
desires, appetites, and mindsets of the people will be drawn to
the ways of God and the kingdom of God. In this case, if the government passes a law that is outside of the ways of God or the
kingdom of God, the people will rise up and say "that is unacceptable here," but if the unholy priesthood is most effectively
servicing the altar, then even if the government passes a law that
is holy or righteous, the people will reject it and turn against the
government, calling it narrow-minded, controlling, etc.

It isn't the penal code that has the authority; the priesthood that
prevails and influences the spiritual realm has the authority to

truly affect which direction the city or nation is going in. Which-ever priesthood that services its altar most affectively is helping to set what is acceptable and unacceptable, which becomes an unspoken code that society eventually accepts.

The Prevailing Priesthood Controls the Land

For when there is a change in the priesthood, there is nec-essarily a change in the law as well.

Hebrews 7:12

The one who ministers at the altar has the key to what will happen in the physical world as well as in the spiritual world. Therefore, the priest who stands at the altar is not only serving himself, he is opening a spiritual gate. He is aligning the physical world with the code of life that is in the spiritual realm.

Jesus taught us to pray, "Our Father in heaven, hallowed be your name" (Matt 6:9), showing us that the holy priest causes glory, praise, honor, and submission to go forth from the earth up into the heavens in the spiritual realm. He then continues, "Your kingdom come, your will be done, on earth as it is in heaven" (Matt 6:10). Let Your authority, Your rule, and Your insti-tutions of life come down from the spiritual world upon the earth. The priest causes the will of God to be established on earth as it is already established in heaven.

> If the priesthood in the land is godly and holy, a holy influence will come into society.

What is the will of God? It is God's law of life, the code of life in the kingdom of God. It is what God says should happen in worship, marriage, family, the economy, government, education, and in all spheres of life. The will of God is the spiritual code of life in the heavens and the heavenly kingdom.

Remember that whatever happens on earth is governed by the

code of life in the spiritual atmosphere, so if the priesthood in the land is godly and holy, a holy influence will come into society. Glory, honor, submission, and majesty will go forth from the earth unto the Lord of Hosts. Society will honor, glorify, and seek to please God.

How Are We to Be the Prevailing Priesthood?

The people who know their God shall be strong, and carry out great exploits.
Daniel 11:32, NKJV

Daniel was a priest of the Lord; he stood in the gap for his people. He said in his heart, "Israel is my nation. The destiny of Israel and its people is mine, and I'm going to pray and fight for Israel." He searched the Scriptures for Israel, fasted and prayed, and stood as a priest on behalf of his people before the altar of the Lord.

The authority of the priesthood that Daniel represented was not vested in the Levitical order; it was vested in the covenant that God made with His people when He said, "You shall be to me a kingdom of priests and a holy nation" (Ex 19:6).

In the New Testament, we have become priests unto the Lord, not because of the Levitical order, but because of the priesthood of Jesus Christ. We have received this priesthood because we are in covenant with Jesus, and we have also therefore received authority to rule.

But you are a chosen people, a royal priesthood, a holy nation, God's special possession, that you may declare the praises of him who called you out of darkness into his wonderful light. Once you were not a people, but now you are the people of God; once you had not received mercy, but now you have received mercy.
1 Peter 2:9-10, NIV

The Bible says that we are now a chosen generation, a royal priesthood. And not just a priesthood; a royal priesthood. Royal means kingship; it means we have authority to rule. He has called us to be a royal priesthood.

When God calls us to priesthood, He is calling us to kingship. Our Lord Jesus is the Great High Priest, the King of Kings. When you and I choose to be priests of the Lord, we are also given the power and authority to rule and have influence over the land. This is a great privilege, but what does it mean? It means that we have authority over the unwritten spiritual code of the land in which we live. We can influence the "law of the land" that affects the worship, morality, marriage, parenting, economy, justice, government, health, education, media, entertainment, and every other aspect of the society in which we live. And how do we do that? By standing as priests at the altar of the Lord, ministering to Him, drawing His presence, and crying out that His will would be done on earth as it is in heaven.

Over the years in Uganda, there were so many things we thought were impossible to change or resolve, and yet we saw God turn them around, not by the law of the land or the government, but by the spiritual authority we found when we accepted the calling of priesthood.

One of these impossibilities was the woundedness in Uganda. Our nation had experienced a lot of trauma, violence, and bloodshed over the past several decades; therefore, there was a lot of tribal, political, and social hatred. There were strong feelings of injustice, vengeance, and rage that affected the people. But as we prayed and drew the presence of God all over the nation, we saw Him bring healing to the land.

When the Lord began to deal with our nation, the first direction He gave was to awaken and raise up the priesthood. He said, "Go to the north, south, east, and west, and tell My people that I'm calling them to seek My face." He instructed us to go everywhere and to everyone, and to bring them to the altar of the Lord. He said that the altar is not only in the church; the altar should be everywhere. He did not tell us to wage warfare; He did not tell us to change this or that. He simply said, "Teach My people how to raise an altar and call on My name. Teach them how to set up altars in their homes, workplaces, and communities." God wanted us to raise the level of prayer so that all over the nation there would be people calling on His name day and night, morning and evening, midnight and midday.

The unholy priesthood was servicing their altars through idolatry, witchcraft, immorality, sexual promiscuity, greed, and all kinds of other dark activities. But God was telling us, "Raise up an altar for Me. Call on My name and begin to examine your hearts. Call people to go back into My Word. My Spirit will open your eyes and I will show you My way, and as you see My way, bring repentance for your lives, your families, and your nation."

Do you know what He was doing? He was showing us how to raise a priesthood that had more power in the land than the unholy priesthood.

We started small, but the movement grew, spread, and went deeper. The lifestyle of priesthood and standing at the altar of the Lord began to consume people's lives, and after some time the testimonies began to come. There were testimonies from individuals, from families, and from villages all across the nation about the ways that God was touching and changing the land and its people.

The closer we move toward God, the more we are broken free from the darkness. Our prayers gain authority and become more and more effective. As we continue to draw near to God, He continues to draw near to us (James 4:8). Our lives gain a higher authority, our faith grows, our joy in the Lord intensifies, and our ability to resist the pulls of the world increases.

—— JOHN MULINDE AND MARK DANIEL ——

Priesthood is not just saying prayers to God. Priesthood has an element of being set apart from the world, coming to the Word of God, submitting to God, and yielding ourselves to His will. As we pray that His will would be done, our lives are touched, bringing our hearts and desires into submission to Him.

As we continue praying, the prayers begin to flow over the land. As we hallow the name of the Lord, praising Him and glorifying Him, He comes to abide in our praises (Ps 22:3). Every time we praise the Lord, we attract the presence of God, and the Bible says that if He is with us, who can be against us (Rom 8:31)? It also says that one has chased 1,000, and two have put 10,000 to flight (Deut 32:30). In number, then, we may be fighting a greater army, but in power, as we pray amidst the presence of Almighty God, we are even greater. We stand as a holy priesthood that prevails over the land.

Testimony From Uganda. When we first started establishing altars of prayer throughout Uganda, the nation was in a great struggle. The Body of Christ was not working together, and there were divisions and factions in the church. Darkness was holding the church captive and hindering it from impacting society. In fact, society was impacting the church more than the church was impacting society.

As we went out to establish prayer altars throughout Uganda, the first city we went to was Mbale. When we first arrived, there was no effective altar in the city. We were servants of God and the spiritual leaders in the city were servants of God, but we could find no common ground on which to meet and come together. In fact, the local pastors stood against the idea of trying to build up prayer in the city, going so far as to say, "We don't need that."

We couldn't disobey the Lord, so we still went to the city and went into a season of actively seeking the Lord, ministering to Him and drawing His presence, and calling on Him to intervene in the land. The pastors stood against us, so we started with just a few people. But as we continued over a period of 1 or 2 months, God began to open the door. The pastors started coming in and joining us. We started building altars in the city, in the churches, and in our own lives.

Through that, God began to break the principalities of darkness that were ruling over Mbale. In fact, newspapers in Uganda and Kenya started reporting on how witchcraft and the occult were being broken and that the spirits that had formerly been called down by the people could no longer come because the kingdom of God was reigning in the city now.

Through this experience in Mbale, we saw that establishing the altar of the Lord in the people of God changes the spiritual atmosphere in a city. That was the first city where we saw this breakthrough, and even today the strongest prayer network in the nation of Uganda is located in Mbale.

Summary

Not only have prayer altars transformed the nation of Uganda from being a land devastated by war, dictators, and AIDS to a nation that is now known for revival, unity, and miracles, and for churches affecting and changing the whole of the nation, but we are also seeing the establishment of altars beginning to change other nations around the world.

> As the presence of God is being drawn, darkness is revealed. The people see the darkness that has seeped into their lives, families, and mindsets, then repent and turn away, forsaking it.

As we have traveled to many different cities and nations across the world to teach, equip, and train people how to establish prayer altars, we have seen the altars change the spiritual atmosphere and draw the presence of God into homes and churches—even denominations—as well as into cities and territories. As the presence of God is being drawn, darkness is revealed. The people see the darkness that has seeped into their lives, families, and mindsets. They repent and turn away from the darkness, forsaking it. The Holy Spirit gains more and more control in their relationships, their lifestyles, their view of life, and the way they pursue the purposes of God. As the Holy Spirit gains more control, the power of God begins to break through, bringing forth revelation, opening gates that were shut, and establishing and making a way for the advancement of the kingdom of God.

As this is taking place, there is a greater manifestation of the kingdom of God. Testimonies rise up—one after another after another—starting in individual lives, then in families. The numbers of testimonies grow and begin to involve churches, workplaces, and even cities and nations.

One of the nations where we have shared about establishing prayer altars is Taiwan. If you travel throughout the nation of Taiwan, you will see that unholy altars cover the land. Taiwan is mostly Buddhist and is also deep into ancestral worship. There are also unholy altars that you cannot see with your eye that were brought in by the influence of Western culture. Greed, materialism, humanism, and many other kinds of Western thought and activities have seeped into the culture, even into the church. When we first came, the altar of the Lord was in disrepair. Many families did not have prayer altars and in many churches, prayer was in decline. Most people would have to admit that the fire of the altar had grown cold in their own hearts.

As we taught and shared about establishing and rebuilding prayer altars, the National Prayer Network and other ministries in Taiwan spread this message around the nation. The spiritual leaders of the nation would come together, sometimes by the hundreds, and we would teach the principles of how to build a prayer altar, beginning by teaching them how to push back the darkness and draw the presence of God. As we did this, a fire ignited in their hearts, an awakening in their own spirits. It was as if the fire on the altar was catching aflame again. Their hearts began to blaze with a hunger for God and a desire to seek Him with renewed zeal and passion.

We then spoke about establishing prayer altars in the families. Husbands, wives, and children started to come together, saturating in the Word of God, worshiping and praising God together, and seeking to draw His presence into their homes. As families started doing this, they saw breakthroughs taking place in their homes. Their Buddhist neighbors began to come to Christ. Extended family members who had rejected Christ openly—sometimes for decades—would receive Christ as the family drew the presence of God into their home. Testimonies came forth of healings taking place in the family, such as mental illnesses or the restoration of a relationship between father and son or husband and wife. There were also many testimonies of young people beginning to catch fire for God and to hunger for the things of God.

As the prayer altars started to light fires in families, they also began to ignite churches. Teachings about building the prayer altar began to be shared in the churches. People stood up on Sundays to share testimonies about their family prayer altars, provoking more and more families to begin an altar.

Before long, people started taking prayer altars to their workplaces. No matter whether they were psychiatrists, surgeons, lawyers, educators, university professors, manufacturers, or retail shop owners, they began to take the prayer altar into their place of business committing to seek to draw the presence of God into their workplace a few times a week. As the presence of God drew near, He would show them practices in their workplace that were unethical, dishonoring, or a grievance to His presence. They began to repent and change their practices, and God moved in more and more extraordinary ways. Many people were being won to Christ.

Churches began to come together to build city prayer altars. Unity among pastors, churches, and ministries formed where previously relationships had been very fragile, would easily fall apart, or were very shallow and hindered the accomplishment of God's work. As prayer altars were changing the spiritual environment, people began to see the purpose of God for their city and the destiny of their nation, and they joined their lives together to do the work of expanding God's kingdom.

The testimony of the prayer altar has become so profound that the nations around Taiwan, even South Korea, have started to call and ask the Taiwanese to come teach about prayer altars. Why? Because the living testimonies began shaking the nations in that part of the world.

Today, the spiritual atmosphere in Taiwan has changed. The fire is lit in the Body of Christ. We believe that as prayer has been raised up across this nation of 22 million people, it has begun to push back the darkness, and as the prayer altar has been restored and the holy priests are taking their place in this nation, it is now time to seek a soul harvest of half a million or more souls for the kingdom of God.

The prayer altar is powerful. As we open up the spiritual gates and draw the presence of God, there is no limit to what He can do in our lives, families, churches, and nations.

Section 2
What Happens at the Altar?

Section 2
Introduction

I(Mark Daniel) never realized how different my concept of prayer was from that of other Christians from other parts of the world until I started traveling to the nations with John Mulinde, who is from Africa. As I traveled with him, I started to see how radically different our concepts of prayer were. I would have never known that just from speaking with him because we were using the same words and talking about the same things, but after observing him interacting with the Spirit of God, I saw the depths of his entering the presence of God and the results of his time with the Lord. I soon realized that his approach to prayer was very different from mine.

For example, Pastor John tells a story about when he first came to America. He was in Chicago, Illinois, speaking at a conference. Once he got settled in the place where he was staying he went to pray, but he says, "I failed." When I heard that, I didn't know what he meant. I thought maybe he fell asleep because of jet lag or there was some other reason that he said that. I had never even thought of going into prayer and failing.

Pastor John goes on with his story and says, "I went and spoke at the conference session I was supposed to lead. When I came back, I went to pray again and I failed. I stayed there for over an hour worshiping and praying, but I failed again. My heart began to panic because I was used to coming into the presence of God every time I went into prayer." He says, "I began to fall on my face, call out to God, and ask Him what was wrong. Had I done something to grieve Him? Had I done something to hinder the sensitivity to His Spirit in my own heart?"

Pastor John shared later why he was having such difficulty in prayer, but my point here is that as I was listening to him, I realized that many times when I went to pray I did not encounter the presence of God, but I did not consider this a failure. I read, worshiped, and prayed, and many times I got encouragement, truth, or blessings, but the depth of entering His presence was not my common experience, and I realized that what I was experiencing was much more shallow and superficial, and I was content with that, whereas Pastor John was going for something much more substantial and weighty, and that was his norm.

My goal was to spend a certain amount of time worshiping, praying, and reading the Bible, and my success was based on spending that length of time on a regular basis doing those things. But for Pastor John, that was not at all what he considered success. To him, because he knew that all of life and wisdom comes from living in that presence, success in prayer was to be able to break through the hindrances that might be there—the fears, doubts, insecurities, pressures of the day, and all the different obstacles there might be—to come into the presence of God. For Pastor John, coming into God's presence on a regular basis gave him the ability to live the will of God out in his daily life.

The reason I'm sharing this is because when we talk about prayer altars with others, I have found that there are many different concepts of prayer. People often use the same words, but they are not talking about the same thing. So when we discuss prayer altars, talk about the presence of God, or even look at what it means to be in communion with God, we want to lay out these concepts so clearly that our hearts can truly agree on the essence of what a prayer altar truly is.

Some of you may be like me, where you have set up patterns and disciplines for your prayer life, such as journaling, a daily devotional, or a specific time of worship and prayer. You complete these activities each day and then say to yourself and others, "I have a discipline of doing that daily. I have daily prayer or devotions in my life." But that is not what we are aiming for here.

The essence of a prayer altar is to come into the presence of God. We are meant to commune with Him, to allow His life to draw near and touch our lives. It is out of His presence that we have light for our path, we receive wisdom and understanding, and we have power to face the challenges in our lives.

There are dark forces that seek to come between God and us, whether it is sin, our flesh, or things the enemy sends to attack us (fear, discouragement, doubt, physical oppression, diversionary battles, etc). These cause us to pull back our heart or turn our focus, and divert us from our communion with God. When we don't regularly live in the presence of God, we don't notice that we have gotten off track. However, when we do live regularly in His presence and walk in communion with God, we can tell when the slightest thing has come in to hinder that flow of life between our Maker and ourselves.

> The essence of a prayer altar is to come into the presence of God.

Therefore, when we talk about the altar, the first place to start is with that most personal of altars: the one that is in your heart. As you build a personal altar, you will begin to be able to live with a continual sense of the presence of God. Abiding before Him, your heart will be soft, open, vulnerable, yielded, and surrendered to His Holy Spirit. You will be able to be led by Him, trust Him, and allow His life to flow through you. As we learn to create an atmosphere that draws the presence of God, we will see how to build the personal prayer altar in our hearts so we can live in the abiding sense of His presence.

One thing I learned from being with the Ugandans was that I was not spending enough quality time in prayer. My habit was to spend about 30 minutes a day in prayer in my quiet time, but being around the Ugandans made me realize that I needed to spend more time in prayer if I was going to draw deep into God's presence. They spoke about saturating in the Word of God every day, and the need to saturate my soul with God's wisdom, counsel, truth, and commands. They spoke about allowing the Word of God to fill me up every day.

I wasn't doing that. I was reading a few chapters of the Bible a day with about 30 minutes of prayer. They were challenging me to read 45 minutes to an hour a day, and then to come into God's presence for the same length of time to interact with Him in worship and prayer. Because I could see the effect this had on their lives, I started getting up every morning and doing that, spending much more significant time before the Lord.

Slowly but surely, as I spent this time saturating in the Word and interacting with God in prayer and worship, He was cleansing and preparing my inner being and my outer life to dwell more deeply in Him. My lifestyle and thought processes, my appetites and the things that I desired started changing, making me into a vessel that was able to abide in God's presence in a greater reality and weightiness. The depth of communion with God was more than I had known. The greatest change was remaining deeply connected to the Lord throughout the day. As he was working on me inside and out, I realized that He was quieting my soul and softening my heart, and that my will was yielding to the Lord. All this was making it possible for me to walk in communion with Him at levels I had never known before.

As these changes took place, I began to see from further off when things that wanted to encroach upon the work God was doing in me were drawing near. The enemy sends these things against us to shut us down, harden our hearts, or close us off, but I could now see them coming because as God was creating this vessel that was so open to Him, I could perceive anything coming that was trying to close it down. I realized that as we give ourselves to the Lord in a significant way, He positions us to walk in a conscious awareness of His indwelling and abiding presence.

One of the keys to the altar is coming into the presence of God and being in communion with Him, so one of the first discussions we will have in this section is communion and what God meant when He said He wants us to live in His presence. Communion is ministering to the Lord, praising and worshiping Him, saturating in His Word, and offering up our lives as a living sacrifice. Out of that place of communion, God will come and manifest Himself to us, share His heart desires and divine revelation with us, and break the powers of darkness that are opposing His work.

> One of the keys to the altar is coming into the presence of God and being in communion with Him.

CHAPTER 8.
LIVING IN THE PRESENCE OF GOD

O ne of the important things we need to understand if we are going to build a prayer altar is that we were meant to live in the presence of God. We were separated from God's presence, were spiritually dead, were enemies of God, and were under His wrath, but Jesus Christ came to rescue us, restore our fellowship, and reconcile us to the Father. This means that we can now come boldly before His throne of grace, His presence can dwell within us, and we can again have that divine link and communion with Him that He intended for us to have. If we do not believe this is our inheritance as children of God, who have placed our faith and trust in what Jesus Christ completed at Calvary, then we will not be able to fight the forces of darkness that try to cause us to live without that divine communion.

In this chapter we are going to look at how God intended us to live in His presence so that we may thrive as believers.

In the Likeness of God

Then God said, "Let us make man in our image, after our likeness. And let them have dominion over the fish of the sea and over the birds of the heavens and over the livestock and over all the earth and over all every creeping thing that creeps on the earth." So God created man in his

*own image, in the image of God he created him; male and
female he created them.*

Genesis 1:26-27

According to Genesis 1:26-27, God made man in His own image
and likeness. This means that there is something of God that is in
man that is different from every other created thing. It is something that enables men and women to have a divine connection,
a deep communion between themselves and God. It gives man
the ability to tap into God's divine wisdom, knowledge, authority,
and power to rule, and to be able to receive and enjoy all the love
and blessings of his Creator.

Because of this likeness to God, humans have the ability to
connect with God and discern His heart's desires. We can com-
municate with God and receive His divine flow of wisdom and
revelation so that we are able to fulfill the role and purpose that
He has assigned to us.

Genesis 2:7 says that, "The Lord God formed the man of dust from
the ground and breathed into his nostrils the breath of life, and
the man became a living creature." Something from deep within
God was breathed deep into man. God blew the breath of life into
Adam, creating a link between the two of them so that the very
heart and mind of God would flow to Adam. By breathing into
man, God made it possible for man to have deep, personal, and
real communion with the Creator, which would enable man to
fulfill the purpose for which he was created.

God placed His Spirit—His likeness—inside of Adam so that
Adam could do His work. When Adam was asked to name a creature he would receive revelation and know the heart of God for
that piece of creation. We didn't create the creation, but we can
commune with the Creator. This communion with God gives
humans the ability to be led by Him, to walk in a deep sense of
His abiding presence, and to allow Him to work through us.

—— JOHN MULINDE AND MARK DANIEL ——

Think of this. Adam was given the task of naming all the animals (Gen 2:19-20). An animal would pass in front of him and he was supposed to give it a name. What do you suppose Adam did? "I'll just call that big one over there 'elephant.' And see that long-necked thing? I think I'll call that one 'giraffe.'" Do you think that God was just going to accept whatever name Adam gave to each one? No. The Scriptures say that no man teaches God (Rom 11:34).

As Adam named the animals, God wasn't receiving counsel from Adam. Adam was tapping into divine communion with God, receiving revelation and understanding from Him, so that when an animal came and stood before him, Adam would call it by the name God had already determined. Because of this divine connection and communion, Adam knew God's heart and the purpose God intended for each animal.

> Abiding in the divine enablement and communion with the One who made him is the secret to man's authority.

God wanted to maintain this abiding relationship with man because abiding in the divine enablement and communion with the One who made him is the secret to man's authority. Without this communion with God, man's ability to fulfill the purposes for which he was created, or to walk in divine protection and provision, would not be possible. This deep, abiding communion between God and humans is the way God intended for us to live life. It was not His intention that we would exist trying to live for Him through our own strength and abilities, but that we would exist by Him living in and through us with His divine power, love, and grace.

The Importance of Communion With God

How do we get revelation of the One True God? By communing with Him. It is in that communion that we begin to see Him for who He is. We begin to know His heart and His character. We come to know Him, put our hope in Him, and give Him our hearts and our love. We extend ourselves, surrender our lives to Him, and give Him our trust and confidence. The deeper the communion, the deeper the revelation. The deeper the revelation, the deeper the surrender and trust. The deeper that surrender and trust, the more truly He is our God and the more we allow ourselves to be His children.

> The deeper the communion, the deeper the revelation of God. The deeper the revelation, the deeper our surrender and trust to Him.

It is in this divine communion that we can fulfill the calling of God on our lives and the destiny for which we were created. God has a purpose for each one of us, but it is only through that communion that we can tap into His heart. He begins to strip away those things that hinder us from fulfilling His call, and He positions us and shapes us to become that vessel through which He can do mighty and great things.

We were not meant to live disconnected from the Lord. Since the beginning of time, God intended for us to live with His deep, abiding communion and in connection to Him. He is the source of all life: all righteousness, truth, wisdom, and love. He knows that only as we live in the abiding and continual flow of His life can we flourish and thrive as people. Therefore, He intended for us to live connected and abiding in His presence, but through the Fall we became separated from Him.

Broken Communion

> *Now the serpent was more crafty than any other beast of the field that the Lord God had made. He said to the woman, "Did God actually say, 'You shall not eat of any tree in the garden'?" And the woman said to the serpent, "We may eat of the fruit of the trees in the garden, but God said, 'You shall not eat of the fruit of the tree that is in the midst of the garden, neither shall you touch it, lest you die.'" But*

the serpent said to the woman, "You will not surely die. For God knows that when you eat of it your eyes will be opened, and you will be like God, knowing good and evil." So when the woman saw that the tree was good for food, and that it was a delight to the eyes, and that the tree was to be desired to make one wise, she took of its fruit and ate, and she also gave some to her husband who was with her, and he ate. Then the eyes of both were opened, and they knew that they were naked. And they sewed fig leaves together and made themselves loincloths.

Genesis 3:1-7

God wanted to protect the communion between Himself and Adam and Eve so He told them not to eat of the tree of the knowledge of good and evil. Why? What was His intention in giving this command?

God was trying to show them that it is out of this deep communion with Him that life flows; that they had the ability to keep their hearts open, unguarded, unashamed; that they were able to maintain this deep abiding connection with His presence. God knew that in this place of obedience, dependency, and communion with Him, they would be able to fulfill everything they were created to do. And God clearly warned them that the day they ate the forbidden fruit, they would spiritually die because the communion would be broken (Gen 2:17).

However, the devil knows the secrets of man's success and power; he knows that man's dependency, complete trust, and communion with God is how God flows the fullness of His life to man. So he came and tricked the woman into looking at the forbidden fruit of the tree in a new way. After believing the lies of the serpent, she "saw that the tree was good for food, and that it was a delight to the eyes" (Gen 3:6); she no longer believed it was poisonous. And she also saw that the fruit was "desired to make one wise" (Gen 3:6). Whose wisdom? The revelation that comes from God? No. Her own human wisdom. And what happened? Communion was broken, and the first man (Adam) and his wife (Eve) found themselves hiding from God (Gen 3:7).

What happened after the communion was broken? Did creation grow and come into the fullness that God intended? No. In fact, as we read further in the Scriptures, we will notice that corruption, wickedness, sin, idolatry, greed, and all forms of darkness grew in society and the lives of people, and humans turned away from worshiping the One True Living God. Since the time of the Fall, humans have lost the communion with God that enables us to know Him, worship Him, and fulfill the calling and purpose for which we were created.

After man lost communion, he lived in darkness. Layers of darkness were laid on mankind, and the people started worshiping other things. Everything began to unravel. Society deteriorated. Instead of becoming paradise, it became more and more wretched and pitiful.

The nations were becoming so filled with darkness that it was as if God was saying, "If they were not a people, if I took ownership of them, I would have to crush them because they are so wicked and so far from Me. So I am going to call out a people and make them a nation unto Myself."

Jesus Christ Came to Restore Our Communion With God

In His mercy, though, God began to work His plan to restore communion with humanity. For thousands of years mankind could not even come into direct communion with God. People had to go through a priest, sacrificing animals to pay for and atone for their sins. But they were not living in the presence of God or having communion with Him. Even the priests were separated from God by a large and thick veil so they were never truly in His presence. Only the High Priest would go before God's presence, and that was only once a year (Lev 16:1-32).

Jesus Christ came for the sole purpose of restoring communion between mankind and the Father. In fact, while Christ was on the Cross, when He cried out, "It is finished" (John 19:30), the veil in the temple ripped from the top to the bottom (Matt 27:50-51). Jesus made the way for us to come back into God's presence and live in communion with Him.

Before Christ came, where were we?
- We were dead, but now we have been made alive (Eph 2:1-5)
- We were far away, but now we have been brought near (Eph 2:13)
- We were separated from God, but now we have been reconciled to God (Col 1:21-22, Rom 5:10-11))
- We were enemies of God, but now we have been made sons and daughters of God (2 Cor 6:18)
- We were orphans, but now we have been adopted (Eph 1:5)
- We were shut out, but now we can come boldly before the throne of grace (Heb 4:16)
- We were under wrath, but now we are forgiven and justified through the blood of Jesus Christ (Rom 5:9)

We need to understand that Christ won this communion back for us. It is our inheritance and our right as children of God.

What Christ did at the Cross had divine significance in both the spiritual and the physical realms. Before He came, we as people had not been able to come boldly before God; we had to go through priests and sacrifices. After the Fall, the presence of God was found in the Holy of Holies, a place where common men, ordinary people were not allowed to go. But now, through what Christ has done, we can come boldly before God's throne, assured of His glad welcome (Eph 3:12).

This holy, almighty, awesome God now invites us to come before Him. He invites us to draw into His presence. And His presence is healing. It enlightens and brings forth revelation. It secures and strengthens. It gives us new and larger perspectives, and reveals to us His heart's desires and purposes as well as our destiny. His presence begins to reorient our lives; it changes everything.

What Jesus came to do was to restore what was lost from the time of Adam. Through Christ, we can now live in communion with God. We need this communion with God, or our hearts are prone to go astray and chase after what the world chases after. In this place of communion, our hearts are given to Him; we find ourselves trusting Him and loving Him. Out of that love He reveals His divine will, wisdom, and counsel to us so that we may carry out His purposes.

This is the inheritance that Christ won for us. We were meant to live in the presence of God! We were meant to live like a branch attached to a vine, drawing all life from Him. Our altar is meant to be a place for us to come expecting to encounter the presence of God, where we are establishing an atmosphere for our hearts and our lives in which we can walk in communion with God. At our altar we spend time in the Word of God, in worship and prayer, realizing that this place—where I can come boldly before God and allow myself to draw near to Him as He draws near to me—is my inheritance. It is what Christ won for me on the Cross. I don't have to beg for it to happen; it has already been won for me and established by Jesus Christ.

> Our altar is meant to be a place where we are establishing an atmosphere for our hearts and our lives in which we can walk in communion with God.

Sadly, over the years, we have lost the understanding that we have inherited this place of communion at the altar with God, so when we struggle to come near to God during our prayer times, we give up easily and explain away our lack of communion as a "bad day." We do not seek to go deeper because we become accustomed to not touching God's heart or entering into His presence. We are easily distracted, treat prayer lightly, and lose heart because we no longer believe that communion with God is our birthright, and the altar falls into disrepair. It becomes something that has form but no power.

As I (Mark Daniel) was working on this material, thinking back to how my concept of spending time with God changed when I learned about altars, I realized that I had experienced a significant mindset shift as my understanding of altars grew. My concept of prayer has matured over the years. When I first began to have time with the Lord, I saw prayer, worship, and Bible reading as disciplines. I was faithful to follow these Christian practices, just as you would do daily chores at home. This was my normal, daily routine, but it was mostly cognitive and was not piercing deep into my heart.

As I matured, however, I began to understand a more relational model. I realized that I was approaching my Father and that He loved me; I could come near to Him and worship Him. My time with Him was more personal and intimate. I would still read the Word and spend time in prayer and worship, but my concept of prayer continued to mature and my mindset shifted even more.

When I came to the altar I realized that God had said in His word to not let the fire of the altar go out. I saw that the altar He is talking about in the New Testament is my heart. My heart is the altar of the Lord, and it is the fire that we are not to allow to be extinguished. I saw that my time with God is not simply a portion of my day when I just spend an hour with God, but that the altar is something I carry with me throughout the entire day. My heart is the altar and the fire on it is to stay blazing as I go through my day.

As time went by and my concept of prayer continued to grow deeper, I realized that when I came before the presence of God, my heart was open, yielded, submissive, sensitive, worshipful, and in awe of Him. I was yielded to His leadership. I was becoming more responsive to what He was saying, obedient to His leadings and promptings, and more focused on Him. My thoughts were not scattered and I was not looking all around as if I was by myself. My focus was set on Him.

As my prayer life has changed, I now go throughout my day being able to recognize the things that come to shut down my heart and pull my focus from Him. There are things that come that are trying to harden my heart or cause me to distrust Him and take back control from Him.

When you have grasped the concept of the altar, you desire to keep your heart in that place of abiding, yielded to His presence. I have felt the opposition of darkness come in the middle of the day, trying to push against my heart. When this happens, I go before the Lord and begin to praise Him and lift Him up so that my trust does not diminish. I exalt who He is, what He has done, and how He has revealed himself to me in Scripture. Other times, after a long hard day, discouragement or frustration try to set in, but I go home and read the Bible for 45 minutes to an hour, allowing my mind to calm and letting my inner being set on Him. This helps renew the fire of the altar that is on my heart.

The altar is something we carry with us throughout the day. It is not just a moment or specific time in the day; it is ongoing. There are things that come to stoke the fire throughout the day that help refresh it and keep it burning. We must continually tend to that altar, fending off the threats that come to attack it.

When you first begin to build an altar, you realize it is very difficult to come into the presence of God because the altar is in disrepair. Your inner being has not been tended to. There have been many things that have been allowed to come in that grieve and hinder the fire from building up inside you. There are discouragements, fears, insecurities, sins of the flesh, and all kinds of other things. As you approach God, you see these things and start to cast them off and lay them aside. God will even show you what you must get rid of if the fire is going to stay ablaze in your heart.

As you keep approaching God day after day, reading the Word, praying, worshiping God, and drawing near to Him, that fire begins to build, and build, and build. That is when you realize that Christians have to live in the presence of God.

Just like a fish was meant to live in water, we as Christians can only thrive when we live in the presence of God. We were meant to dwell in that atmosphere of His love, wisdom, and leadership, trusting Him and resting in Him. The more we abide in His presence, the more we release ourselves into His presence and continue to keep that fire going. The more we begin to thrive and flourish to see Him bring more and more fruit as He intended, the more His life, power, and love begins to shine forth into our lives.

Drawing the Presence of the Lord

A good example of drawing the presence of God appears in chapter 10 of the Book of Acts. Peter recognized that he couldn't just rely on the one encounter with God that he experienced at Pentecost; he had developed a lifestyle of seeking the Lord and coming into His presence. One time when visiting Simon, Peter went up to the roof to pray and saw a vision from the Lord. He had been praying and worshiping, and began to encounter God. On the roof, the Lord revealed to Peter what was about to happen and how He wanted Peter to respond. In obedience, Peter went to do what the Lord directed, and in power brought the whole household of Cornelius the centurion to salvation.

While Peter was still saying these things, the Holy Spirit fell on all who heard the word. And the believers from among the circumcised who had come with Peter were amazed, because the gift of the Holy Spirit was poured out even on the Gentiles. For they were hearing them speaking in tongues and extolling God. Then Peter declared, "Can

*anyone withhold water for baptizing these people, who
have received the Holy Spirit just as we have?" And he commanded them to be baptized in the name of Jesus Christ.
Then they asked him to remain for some days.*

Acts 10:44-48

Going to the Gentiles with the gospel was a huge step that
went against the entire heritage of Judaism. It required a lot of
certainty on Peter's part to do this because it was so counter-cul-
tural. Peter was able to take this step because of the altar of his
heart. He lived a life in the presence of God, and as he was up on
that rooftop praying, God was able to come and bring forth this
revelation and Peter trusted Him.

If we live in a deepening sense of God's presence, we often find
that there is so much more that God has wanted to give us than
we have been aware of, but because our encounters with Him
have been so seldom or superfi-
cial, we do not experience such
life-changing moments. Peter's
encounter with God on the roof
was significant and changed the
course of the world. It sent the
gospel out to the Gentiles. This
powerful encounter with God
revealed the Lord's heart and
desires to the apostles, and opened
up the gospel to the Gentiles.

> The deeper our communion
> is with God, the deeper the
> revelation, the deeper the
> flow of His life, the deeper
> the anointing, and the
> deeper the release of power.

I (Mark Daniel) have been a Christian for 42 years. From my
experience, the deeper our communion is with God, the deeper
the revelation, the deeper the flow of His life, the deeper the
anointing, and the deeper the release of power.

Living in the Presence of the Lord

When we begin to desire to carry the presence of God, we also
begin to want to understand what attracts His presence, what

makes us sensitive to His presence, and what opens us up to His presence. We want to know what we should do and what thought patterns or actions we have that grieve and hinder His presence. When we seek the presence of God in that way, an altar will be established in our hearts. A fire for God will be lit. We are no longer just saying prayers or reading some passages from the Bible; we are actually seeking God.

The Bible tells us throughout the Scriptures that God is looking for hearts that are completely His (Deut 6:5, Josh 22:5, Matt 22:37, Mark 12:30, Luke 10:27), and that if we seek Him with all of our heart we will find Him (Jer 29:13). In fact, we find that it is impossible to seek God and not encounter Him. Therefore, as we build an altar on which we keep the fire burning, we can continually abide in His presence as He called us to do in John 15:4-9.

An altar is established by seeking the presence of God. As you seek God through the Word, prayer, and worship at a designated time each day, you will come regularly into His presence. A natural by-product of daily communion with Him is that you will seek to walk in His presence throughout the day. His presence will not be far from you. You will not be disconnected from it, so even in the middle of your day, when you find yourself in a circumstance where you don't know what to do, you can turn to Him and seek His divine wisdom. As you feel a pull of something trying to take you

> Seeking to continually remain in the presence of God is the key to the prayer altar.

into darkness, you will turn to Him and choose to stay with Him instead of going along that dark path. You will realize that this altar you have created is not just a time of saying prayers; it is a lifestyle of abiding in the very presence of God, in the place of communion with the Living God that Jesus Christ won for you. Seeking to continually remain in the presence of God is the key to the prayer altar.

This ongoing presence of the Lord creates a continuous open heaven surrounding you. It is like walking in a pillar of fire that has come upon your life, and acts as your protection against the spiritual powers of darkness that are at work in the area. It keeps the heavens open above you. If you develop a lifestyle of prayer and allow your heart to become an altar so that no matter where you are or what you are doing, your heart is always praying and conversing with God, you will maintain that fire so that the heavens remain open. Your prayers will not be hindered; they will go straight to the throne of God.

As we move throughout the land in this pillar of fire, we carry the presence of God with us. This is the beginning of understanding what a carrier of revival is. Someone who walks in the presence of God carries revival, and wherever he goes, whether in his home or in his workplace, it brings impact. This brings chaos to the kingdom of darkness and manifests the power of God throughout our lives and the world. It disrupts the work of the enemy, and as we move, the pillar moves with us. The presence of God will impact lives and situations around us as we move in the physical world.

The mind-changer for me (Mark Daniel) was that I had my quiet time and then I went about my day, but at the altar I realized that as I focused my eyes on God, my heart was becoming very soft, open, and sensitive to Him. As I went throughout my day, I could sense my heart leaving that softness and beginning to go back into a more hardened or distracted state.

At the altar, you realize that you want to stay in that place throughout the day. You want to walk in such a way that your heart remains open, dependent, and yielded to the Lord. As you do that, you will find yourself turning to the Lord in the midst of a conversation or when making a decision, and you will desire to stay very sensitive to the Lord and the leading of His Spirit. Your communion will deepen as the day goes on instead of declining, as it once did before you built your altar, when you only had a time of quiet with Him.

—— JOHN MULINDE AND MARK DANIEL ——

As you are open to the Spirit of God throughout your day, His presence will be with you and go before you. Because of the open heaven above you, as you minister to people, God will have a platform to convict them of sin in their lives or their need for Him. People will begin to repent easily. They will be able to hear and see things they were previously deaf and blind to them. This abiding sense of God's presence will intervene and manifest power throughout your life.

Summary

The key difference between a quiet time and an altar before the Lord is the presence of God. When we decide to establish an altar in our heart, our objective in prayer becomes more than just having the disciplines or forms of a quiet time. We begin to have a heart that seeks after God and desires to enter His presence.

When the objective of prayer changes for you from being about the disciplines of reading, praying, and worshiping to seeking God and His presence, prayer becomes an adventure, a completely different pursuit. When you have just these disciplines, prayer can seem lifeless or boring, but when you are seeking the presence of God, you realize the reality of the battle that ensues against that altar, against that fire being lit in your heart. You recognize that there are forces trying to cause your heart to pull back, harden, or shut down, but as you battle against them, the Holy Spirit will draw you into the presence of God. And as the presence of God draws near, it will impact your life. Everything begins to change inside of you.

> The key difference between a quiet time and an altar before the Lord is the presence of God.

The reality of the altar—spending time daily seeking the Lord, building this fire on your heart, not letting the forces of darkness come against or gain ground, contending for the openness where your heart and life will be an altar built to the Lord so

His presence will be drawn near—will become something you cherish and love beyond measure. This altar will change every aspect of you and your life. In fact, we have never met anyone who has built a personal prayer altar who did not have people around them commenting about how much they have changed. They are different people because that is what the presence of God does to us.

Therefore, as we look at altars, we want to hold onto this truth: a key to the prayer altar is that it is not just about discipline; it is about being in communion with our Creator. This is the inheritance that Christ won for us at Calvary.

> The prayer altar is not just about discipline; it is about being in communion with our Creator.

There is no Word from God that lacks power, but it does need the right atmosphere in which to operate. In the following chapters, we are going to look at how to build the atmosphere that draws the presence of God.

Lord, we thank You for Your heart to draw near to Your people. Bless You that You desire communion with us. Please, Lord, we pray that as we continue to read, You will continue to reveal, teach, expose, and lead us into a deeper communion with You. You are our life and we desire to develop that rich relationship that You have made available to us through Jesus. Open our hearts to understand how to commune with You and minister to You at our altar, drawing Your presence into our lives, families, homes, churches, businesses, communities, and nations. Amen.

CHAPTER 9.

WE DRAW HIS PRESENCE BY MINISTERING TO THE LORD

And they brought in the ark of God and set it inside the tent that David had pitched for it, and they offered burnt offerings and peace offerings before God. And when David had finished offering the burnt offerings and the peace offerings, he blessed the people in the name of the Lord and distributed to all Israel, both men and women, to each a loaf of bread, a portion of meat, and a cake of raisins. Then he appointed some of the Levites as ministers before the ark of the Lord, to invoke, to thank, and to praise the Lord, the God of Israel. Asaph was the chief, and second to him were Zechariah, Jeiel, Shemiramoth, Jehiel, Mattithiah, Eliab, Benaiah, Obed-edom, and Jeiel, who were to play harps and lyres; Asaph was to sound the cymbals, and Benaiah and Jahaziel the priests were to blow trumpets regularly before the ark of the covenant of God.

1 Chronicles 16:1-6

As we seek to live and dwell in the presence of God, to live in this place of communion and connection with His life, and to see the fire of that altar beginning to come forth, we will start to hunger for the things that help draw His presence. We will do the things that attract the presence of God and that make us more sensitive to Him.

In this chapter, we want to look at how to minister to the Lord. As priests at the altar of the Lord, we are called to minister to

Him. As we do that, we draw His presence. We also draw our hearts away from all the busyness, distractions, and temptations around us, and we help our hearts and souls give their full attention, affection, and focus to Christ.

Jesus said, "These people honor me with their lips, but their hearts are far from me" (Matt 15:8, NIV). As we minister to the Lord, our hearts draw near to Him, and as they do, we become more consciously aware of His presence. Our hearts then begin to connect with His heart. That is where we experience real communion.

> As we minister to the Lord, our hearts draw near to Him and we become more consciously aware of His presence.

King David, the "man after God's own heart," is a good example of someone who lived a lifestyle of ministering to the Lord. His desire to commune with the Lord and to draw His presence is clear in the esteem, praise, and reverence that he showed toward the Lord. David even took steps to raise up the Lord's altar and restore the priesthood to the position given them through Moses, understanding the need to minister to the Lord at the altar.

In the New Testament, Peter says that we are "a chosen people, a royal priesthood, a holy nation, God's special possession, that you may declare the praises of him who called you out of darkness into his wonderful light" (1 Pet 2:9, NIV). He also says that we are "being built up as a spiritual house, to be a holy priesthood, to offer spiritual sacrifices acceptable to God through Jesus Christ" (1 Pet 2:5). Like David, Peter understood that ministering to the Lord is vital and that it draws God's presence into our lives.

Today, we have forgotten that we were called to be priests, ministering at the altar of the Lord. We tend to come to church looking for God to minister to us through His servants or His Spirit, to give us hope, strength, wisdom, guidance, and encouragement. We don't realize that we are the priesthood, that we are called to minister to the Lord ourselves, and that ministering to God at the altar draws the presence of God into our lives. Out of His presence all of our needs are met. Ministering to the Lord is a lifestyle we need to cultivate and give the utmost value and priority.

Because communion with God and living in His presence are vital to us, we need to recapture the beauty and God-focused approach of coming as royal priests to minister to the Lord at the altar, making nothing about ourselves and everything about Him. To do this, however, it is important to understand what it means to minister to God.

What Does It Mean to Minister to the Lord?

Ministering to the Lord is when we put our entire focus on God, honoring Him, turning our hearts to Him, and continuing to praise Him until we are not just worshiping Him with our lips, but we are touching something of Him with our Spirit. Our hearts become engaged and we begin to esteem Him. We open our inner being to Him, yield ourselves to His Holy Spirit, and become soft in His hands and open to His leadings.

This can take more time on some days than others. Some days we sense greater hindrances or obstacles coming against us that want to shut down our hearts as we are seeking to turn them to the Lord. We go through some seasons during which we feel so much pushing against us that it is very hard to set our focus on the Lord.

There have been seasons in my (Mark Daniel) life when the stress of ministry and the strain of many trials caused worship to be difficult. I realized that I had to get up an hour earlier than normal so I could spend 2 to 3 hours in His Word and worship. I had to do this so my heart could break through all those different obstacles coming against me and I could begin to touch something of the life of God.

Korean Pastor David Yonggi Cho, pastor of the largest Protestant church in the world, has shared that when he first started his church in 1968, he would spend at least five hours every day in prayer. Because of the idols and temples that surrounded his church, he knew that he had to face spiritual warfare daily, so he determined to spend as much time as needed at his altar before the Lord. He also believed that it was crucial to maintain a consistent connection with the Lord throughout the day to maintain fellowship with the Holy Spirit. Today, after years of prayer and a change in the spiritual atmosphere in his nation, Pastor Cho spends at least 3 hours a day in prayer, although he increases this at least another hour or two a day when traveling to nations like Japan or the United States, because the spiritual forces of darkness over those nations are powerful and need breakthrough.

One of the people in the Scriptures who captured this insight so well is King David. No matter whether he was in dire circumstances or experiencing a great victory, he had a heart that desired to constantly minister to the Lord.

> *Then on that day David first appointed that thanksgiving*
> *be sung to the Lord by Asaph and his brothers.*
>> *Oh give thanks to the Lord; call upon his name;*
>>> *make known his deeds among the peoples!*
>> *Sing to him, sing praises to him;*
>>> *tell of all his wondrous works!*
>> *Glory in his holy name;*
>>> *let the hearts of those who seek the Lord rejoice!*
>> *Seek the Lord and his strength;*
>>> *seek his presence continually!*
>> *Remember the wondrous works that he has done,*
>>> *his miracles and the judgments he uttered,*
>> *O offspring of Israel his servant,*
>>> *children of Jacob, his chosen ones!*
>
> 1 Chronicles 16:7-13

After the Israelites had brought the Ark of the Covenant back into the city, David gave clear instructions to the priests for how to minister to the Lord at the altar. He instructed them to offer sacrifices to the Lord; to sing praises to the Lord; to play lyres and harps, cymbals, and trumpets to the Lord; and then he told them to hallow the name of the Lord by giving thanks to Him, singing to Him, speaking of His wonderful acts, glorifying His name, seeking His face and drawing near to Him, and remembering His miracles. He gave them a wide variety of ways to move their hearts toward the Lord.

Ministering to the Lord involves bringing our hearts to an open and tender place before our Lord. It means to honor Him, not with just our words, but with our whole hearts. To allow our hearts to open up and move toward Him, to engage with the words we are speaking as we praise and worship Him. At first, it may seem like we are just speaking words, but as we keep our focus on God rather than on ourselves and continue to move toward Him with our words, worship, and affection, our hearts will soften and move toward God. We cannot fail to draw near to Him without Him also drawing near to us.

As we first go into prayer, we will find that the eyes of our heart are often focused on ourselves, our circumstances, or other people. Putting our eyes, attention, and affections on the Lord is not always easy. Setting our eyes fully on Christ might be easier if we treat all that is trying to get our attention as a distraction, whether they are thoughts or questions in our mind, circumstances in our day or life, or the needs of the people around us.

We do not come into communion with God by looking at ourselves or at anything else; we come into the presence of the Lord by fully setting our affections on Him. That is why the Bible uses so many different words to describe ministering to the Lord: blessing, praising, extolling, exalting, adoring, honoring, revering, and on and on. These describe the multitude of ways that the people were setting their focus and hearts on the Lord, and as they did, they connected again with who God really is and what He has really said. And as we minister to the Lord in this way, with our focus fully on Him, our hearts will connect with His again and we will come into the true spirit of prayer.

Jesus Told Us How to Minister to the Lord

Hallowing the name of the Lord is a vital part of how Jesus taught us to minister to the Lord. When asked to teach them how to pray, Jesus answered the disciples by saying,

> *Pray then like this: "Our Father in heaven, hallowed be your name. Your kingdom come, your will be done, on earth as it is in heaven. Give us this day our daily bread, and forgive us our debts, as we also have forgiven our debtors. And lead us not into temptation, but deliver us from the evil one.*
>
> Matthew 6:9-14

There are two sections in the Lord's Prayer. The first is focused on God; the second is focused on us. Jesus taught that when we come to the Father in prayer, we don't begin by talking about our problems, struggles, or failures; we begin by calling out, "Our Father" and then focusing on the Lord: "Hallowed be Your name. Let Your kingdom come. Let Your heart's desires be fulfilled, Your commands and instructions be followed, Your will be done on earth as it is in heaven."

These are prayers of surrender and submission to God as Lord and King, centered on the Lord and making everything about Him. We are saying, "I want Your name lifted above all else. I want to see Your kingdom advanced, Your will being done above all else."

We don't start by focusing on ourselves; we don't approach the Lord with our needs or our failures. Before we lay out our struggles, battles, or needs, we declare who God is, what He has done in our lives, and how we want to see His will being done and the desires of His heart being fulfilled. We come to minister to Him, to give our affection and attention to Him, and to draw near to Him as He draws near to us. We hallow His name, declaring His character and qualities to the heavenly realm. Our souls and hearts are drawn closer to Him and connect in deeper ways to His heart as we praise and exalt Him.

Hallowing the Name of the Lord

Hallowing the name of the Lord means that we make everything about Him. We praise and exalt Him. We magnify who He is, what He has promised, and what He has done. We lift up His name over our fears and doubts, over our circumstances, over the darkness and desires of the flesh that are trying to beat us down or that seem to squeeze us, frustrate us, stress us, or make us angry. We lift His name above everything, exalt Him, honor His name, and ascribe to it the value His name deserves. We esteem Him, for He is worthy of all our praise.

> Hallowing the name of the Lord means we make everything about Him, praising and exalting Him, and magnifying who He is, what He has promised, and what He has done.

We don't do this for just a few minutes, like an introduction to our prayer time. According to Jesus, when we come to the Father, we need to hallow His name (Matt 6:9). We need to praise Him and spend time esteeming Him. We need to treat God like God.

Before I (Mark Daniel) learned to hallow the name of the Lord, I usually began my prayer with my problems and my requests, my needs and petitions. Even as we were learning to hallow the Lord's name, I would often begin by treating this like an introduction to my prayer time. I hallowed and praised the name of the Lord and then turned to the list of things that I wanted to get to. I would spend a little time being cordial: "I praise You, God. I give glory to Your name and I honor You," then 5 minutes later I would get down to business: "Here are my struggles, Lord; my battles and my needs." I never seemed to connect with God or to go deep into communion with Him. I struggled many times, and I wasn't seeing the power in prayer that I knew was possible.

However, over the years, I have observed the Ugandans praying and ministering to the Lord. Sometimes they spend 30 minutes to an hour—sometimes more—just hallowing the Lord's name. You can sense the prayers rising up. They praise Him and glorify Him, and as they pray they go deeper and deeper into that conscious awareness of God. Everything else is pushed away and they begin to see God for who He is and what He has done. They continue to proclaim these truths as they see them and hold high the name of our Lord. As their prayers continue, I can feel my heart softening, opening up, and moving toward God, and then I sense His presence drawing nearer and nearer.

For the Ugandans, intercessory prayer comes naturally out of that time spent ministering to the Lord. They glorify Him and come into a conscious awareness of His presence, then move into intercession. When I first began praying with them, I would spontaneously begin to declare my faith that God can handle my needs and my burdens. I would give Him any struggles I had been carrying. And as I ministered to the Lord, I could feel the connection with Him building and building and building, so when I finally took my requests, burdens, failures, and needs to Him, it was out of a deep faith and trust in who He is. I knew that I was in a much higher place of prayer and my requests were laid before the Lord with a deeper sense of confidence than I ever had. After praying for their battles or needs, the Ugandans go back into praising God, giving Him glory and honor, hallowing His name and thanking Him for being their God for another 15 minutes or more.

> Ministering to the Lord and hallowing His name is a lifestyle we need to cultivate.

—— JOHN MULINDE AND MARK DANIEL ——

Ministering to the Lord and hallowing His name is a lifestyle we need to cultivate. As we minister to the Lord through worship and singing, hallowing and praising His name, drawing in and giving our affections to Him, our hearts will connect with the Lord's heart and we will find ourselves in a much stronger place of faith and a much deeper place of communion with the Lord. We will also have a much greater perspective from which to address our needs, failures, temptations, and battles.

When we hallow the name of the Lord, we become much more consciously aware of Him; we connect with Him and come into His presence in a much deeper way than we are used to.

Drawing Near to God

The Scriptures teach us in James 4:8, "Draw near to God, and he will draw near to you." How do we come near to God? Psalm 100:4 says, "Enter his gates with thanksgiving, and his courts with praise!" We draw near to God with thanksgiving and praise. The Scriptures also say that God inhabits the praises of His people (Ps 22:3, KJV). "Inhabits" implies that God comes and dwells with, He moves toward the praises of His people. We can trust that as we draw near to God, He will draw near to us.

As we hallow the name of the Lord, we are declaring that we want to re-establish communion with Him and draw near to Him. The only way we can do that is by praising Him and lifting up His name: "Lord, I praise You. You are my God. There is no other God like You. I give glory and honor to You. You are the One True God, the Savior, the Creator of the world. This very world is sustained by the power of Your Word. You spoke and the sun, moon, stars, sea, mountains, and every created thing came into existence. You are the Mighty One. You are the One who parted the sea, who kept back the superpower of Egypt. You are the One who watched over Your people in the desert, and You are the One who watches over me. I give glory and honor to You. I need not be afraid because You are with me and You guide me. You don't leave me or forsake me. You are not like human beings who break their word. You are a covenant-keeping God. You are the One who is true and faithful. You are not like a man that You can lie. You mean every word that You speak. You watch over everything You say to see that it is fulfilled."

Many of us think we will run out of words after 2 or 3 minutes if we praise God and hallow His name. That is why we need to saturate in His Word. It is the Word that makes us rich with the knowledge of God and who He is. As I (Mark Daniel) began to pore over the Word of God more and more, my esteem for God and my knowledge of Him increased. My capacity to hallow His name multiplied a thousand times over.

> It is the Word that makes us rich with the knowledge of God and who He is.

You cannot praise God just by repeating a preacher's words. You need to personally interact with Him. As God shows you who He is through His Word, it will touch your heart. As you praise Him for what He is showing you, it has the power to connect you with God's heart as He draws near to you. As you do this, the Word becomes more precious to you because you are more aware of how the Holy Spirit uses it to reveal the goodness, love, power, faithfulness, and other characteristics of the Father to you.

The Man After God's Own Heart

As you read through the Bible, especially the Psalms, you see how much David lived a lifestyle of ministering to the Lord. Even in his worst moments, David turned to the Lord to give Him honor, acknowledge His sovereignty, and declare his trust in the Lord's control of the situation. He was a man given over to the ways of God and to pleasing Him. David obviously knew what it meant to minister to the Lord.

What are some of the ways David ministered to the Lord? The Psalms are full of his praise. David didn't have just a few words. His heart overflowed with deep wells of expression of his love, affection, and adoration to the Living God. Even in battles, David turned to the Lord. In one of his worst moments, when everything was taken from him and his army, and his men were ready to stone him, what did David do? The Scriptures say that he strengthened himself in the Lord (1 Sam 30:6).

David's love, devotion, and trust in the Lord saved him time and time again. Think of his victory over Goliath or the time Saul sent men to kill David. David was worshiping and ministering to the Lord with Samuel, and the presence of God was so powerful that everyone fell under the power of the Holy Spirit and began to prophesy. Even Saul, when he went to kill David himself, began to prophesy as he came under the influence of the Holy Spirit (1 Sam 19:23-24).

> Ministering to the Lord is a serious and powerful thing.

David was constantly overwhelmed with gratitude at the promises and covenant God had made with him. One of his greatest burdens was to bring the ark into the city, and when he finally succeeded, what did he do? He danced before the Lord and didn't care how undignified he looked to the people, even though he was the king (2 Sam 6:14,21-22).

How does God view someone who comes to minister to Him? We know that He called David "a man after My own heart" (1 Sam 13:14, Acts 13:22) and covenanted Himself with him (2 Sam 7:8-16). God drew near to David as David's heart drew near to God, and David forever remained the standard by which God measured the kings of Jerusalem and Israel. Every king who followed David was compared to him. God would say, "This one obeyed Me, but not like My servant David," or "This one loved Me, but not like My servant David" (1 Kin 14:8). Ministering to the Lord is a serious and powerful thing.

Living a Lifestyle of Praise

How do we develop hearts that overflow with the kind of esteem and love toward the Lord that David had? How do we live in in such a way that we are constantly hallowing, blessing, and honoring the Lord's name?

Today, most of us have difficulty sustaining prayer for prolonged periods of time. People will lift up praise to the Lord, but run out of words after about 5 minutes. They repeat the same words over and over, and their hearts find it difficult to engage and really be able to minister to God. How do we begin to open up these wells? How do we develop hearts that overflow with ministry to the Lord, like David had?

About 10 years ago, while I (Mark Daniel) was listening to Pastor John preach in St Louis, I remember thinking that Pastor John holds God in much higher esteem than I do. He treated God with such honor and reverence, such respect and tender love. He had an adoration and regard for Him that I didn't have. And even though I had been in ministry for a few decades, I realized that he had greater depths and wells of love in his heart for God than I did. And I asked God, "What can I do to get that kind of love flowing in my heart?" I began to be convicted and broken, and the Lord showed me that the answer was saturating in His Word.

After that, I began to pore over the Word of God more and more, and my esteem for God increased. My knowledge of Him expanded, and my capacity to hallow His name grew and grew. I came into a deeper knowledge of who He is, what He has done, and what He has promised to do as I read the Word, expecting it to reveal God more and more to me (He is bigger than we can know).

We have already mentioned that the altar is different from a quiet time. The altar is something we keep going as we go through our day; we keep that fire going in our hearts. Many of us often have powerful times of connection with God in the Word and in our morning prayer times, and have felt such softness of heart, sensitivity, and yielding to His Holy Spirit. But then, as we go through our day, it is as though those things drain away. We lose that sensitivity, and our hearts harden, our spirit becomes less yielded, and our connection with God seems to grow more and more faint. It's as though in the morning we filled up a bucket full of holes, but as we go about our day the water we had filled it with is now draining away.

This happened to me many times until I learned about the altar and how I must keep watch over it throughout my day. I realized that ministering to the Lord is not achieved in prayer time alone, it is achieved through my lifestyle. I need to live a lifestyle of praise. Many times I lost my connection

> Ministering to the Lord is not achieved in prayer time alone; it is achieved through our lifestyle of the altar.

with God during the day because I would leave a lifestyle of praise for just prayer, and then I would go about a day that did not have much praise in it at all.

I found that as I went about my day, attacks would come to turn my eyes away from the Lord, trying to turn me to fear, doubt, discouragement, self-pity, or a variety of other such things. They would try to create mistrust and a tightening of my heart, getting me to pull my heart back and to hold it in my own hands instead of leaving it yielded before the Lord. As these pressures came, I started to come into agreement with them and to speak out words of negativity, fear, doubt, and pity. The more I spoke out the negative words, the more they affected the spiritual atmosphere of my heart.

After spending weeks and weeks praising God and touching His Presence, it would all drain away because my lifestyle was negative, critical, or fearful. Praise God that the Holy Spirit started to train me so that as I went throughout my day I was able to retrain my inner being. The Lord showed me that as I faced challenges, I was not to speak out discouragement, but to speak out praise. When I began to feel fear tighten around me and wanted to pull my life back, I was to intentionally look to the Lord and declare the greatness and faithfulness of my God, and to hold His name high. During this training time, I learned that going through my day praising, acknowledging, and ministering to the Lord kept the atmosphere of God's presence, and that the spiritual atmosphere that I was experiencing every morning was remaining with me throughout the day.

The fire of the altar can stay strong as we live out a lifestyle of praise.

Fighting the Fight of Faith

Isaiah 7:9 says, "If you do not stand firm in your faith, you will not stand at all." Everything we have described above about ministering to the Lord is a fight of faith. Every day you need to establish the name of the Lord, glorify and praise His name. Begin to bless His name, honor it, and ascribe to it the worth it deserves. As you do that, you will experience darkness being pushed back. What has been burdening you and pushing on you will diminish. You will begin to see life, peace, and promise. Everything of God will begin to flow to you. You will become more sensitive to Him, and as you read the Word, you will comprehend more of it. All of this will happen because you have maintained an attitude of praise and engaged the fight of faith.

The enemy wants to hinder, oppose, and weaken our faith. If we don't protect it, then it can be weakened and vulnerable to attack.

When I (Mark Daniel) started to create a lifestyle of praise and hallowing the Lord's name, I found it wasn't easy. I couldn't just say the words and then it was done. And for a long time I didn't treat this lifestyle of faith as something I needed to fight for. I didn't realize the enemy wants to hinder, oppose, and weaken my faith, and that if I didn't protect it, then it could be weakened and vulnerable to attack.

We have all been living lifestyles that don't actively, aggressively, or powerfully praise the Lord, so when we begin to do this, we often find ourselves struggling and hindered. I remember a time when I was very discouraged. I didn't have a lot of hope, faith, or confidence and didn't know the way forward. Most of the time my prayers were focused on myself. I was telling God, "I need You. I'm weak. I'm weary. I can't do this without You." This was just feeding my low position. But I would hear some of the others I was praying with, and they would be focusing on Him. Some-times I would listen for 15 or 20 minutes. I was praying and getting nowhere, but hearing their prayers helped me to prog-ress and go forward.

One day during this time I decided I was going to praise the Lord while walking around the block in my neighborhood, but intim-idating thoughts were coming that were trying to stop me from praising God, so I started to say, "God, I praise You because You are good. You are faithful. Your faithfulness reaches to the heavens." Then all of a sudden I had these thoughts: "This is just emo-tionalism; this isn't real." It stopped my prayers for a moment. So I was pushed back. I began to praise Him again. "Lord, You are good. You are my God. You know me. You know the number of hairs on my head." Then I heard, "You are just trying to work yourself up. There is no power in this." Again I stepped back. So I started again: "God, I give You the glory because You are the cre-ator of heaven and earth. You know everything about creation. You know everything about my DNA." The thought came again: "This isn't going anywhere. You are wasting your time." Finally, I stopped and asked, "Who is doing all this talking to me?" I'm trying to focus on God and there is some other party here trying to invade my conversation with God. At that moment I realized that the enemy was trying to keep me from praising God and coming into His presence, and I said, "No. I'm not putting up with this!"

If you have ever been to a sporting event where one side begins to cheer and then the other side begins to cheer louder, you will understand what happened next. I said, "If you're going to speak against God to me, I'm going to speak even louder for Him. If you're going to start saying things against God, against His ways or His character, then I'm going to praise Him twice as much. I'm going to raise His name even higher. If you want to try to push me back, I'm going to push you back." I started to praise Him and lift up His name. Then a push would come and say this is going to happen or that is going to happen. I said, "My God is faithful. He did not fail David. He did not fail Daniel. He did not fail Abraham. He did not fail Paul. He will not fail me." I began to praise and then felt a push again. I pushed back and said, "He is able. His grace is sufficient. His love is unfailing. His wisdom is without limit. His power knows no end. He is victorious. He came to destroy every weapon of the enemy." Finally I began to push forward; my faith and confidence grew stronger. As I pushed back, I could sense something breaking in the spiritual realm. Then finally it burst open and the presence of God came down. I just wept and wept, and gave Him glory and praise. I said, "Oh, God. There is nothing like Your presence. There is nothing like Your presence."

We can be sure that as we fight for our faith, as we determine to praise and hallow the name of the Lord, even as we are pushed and intimidated by the enemy, He is faithful and true, and will draw near to us as we minister to Him.

Summary

Saturating in the Word of God helps us hold onto Him and cherish Him. It broadens our revelation and understanding of God, increases our esteem and affection for Him, and builds our faith and trust in Him. Our hearts connect with God as we draw near to Him, and then we have words to use to minister to Him and to hallow His name, words that are not coming from just our lips, but from the depths of our hearts.

As we minister to the Lord, we experience His presence in deeper ways for longer and longer periods of time. Like David, we desire to abide in His presence and to develop a lifestyle of praise and thanksgiving. We desire to esteem and exalt Him however we can, whenever we can. We want to hallow His name and live a lifestyle of ministering to Him. As we do, the importance of saturating in His Word becomes clearer, and we make God's Word the centerpiece of our life.

CHAPTER 10.

WE DRAW HIS PRESENCE BY SATURATING IN THE WORD

Only be strong and very courageous, being careful to do according to all the law that Moses my servant commanded you. Do not turn from it to the right hand or to the left, that you may have good success wherever you go. This Book of the Law shall not depart from your mouth, but you shall meditate on it day and night, so that you may be careful to do according to all that is written in it. For then you will make your way prosperous, and then you will have good success.

Joshua 1:7-8

The Bible says that this world was created by the Word of God (John 1:1-3). Hebrews 1:3 says that all things are sustained by the power of the Word of God. It is the Word of God that is holding the sun, stars, and moon in place (Jer 31:35). The power of the Word of God is what causes the winds, lightning, hail, and all other things going on around the world to take place (Jer 10:13, 51:16).

David asked how a young man should keep the way of the Lord. The answer is by hiding the Word of God in his heart (Ps 119:9). How shall one avoid the pitfalls of life? By holding onto the statutes of the Lord (Ps 119:1-8). Psalm 119 is the longest psalm in the Bible, and every verse states one thing: a cry for the Word of God. It is a continuous cry to be grounded in, instructed in, and built up in the Word of God. David was expressing how precious the Word of God is. He was willing to give up everything else if only God would just instruct him and build him up in the Word of God.

Jesus said that heaven and earth shall pass away, but the Word of God will never pass away (Matt 24:35). He even said to the Jews who were challenging His teachings that He would not be the one to judge them; the Word of God would do that (John 12:47-48). Jesus said that life comes from His Word, and that man does not live by bread alone but by every word that comes from God (Matt 4:4).

The Word of God has the highest importance in the kingdom and government of God. Hebrews 4:12 says that the Word of God is living and active; it is breathed and anointed of God (2 Tim 3:16). The name of God is definitive, descriptive, and representative of Him, and yet the Bible says God has exalted His Word above His own name (Ps 138:2). If we really understood the importance of the Word of God, we would push all other things aside and make it the primary focus of our life.

One of the foundational elements in building an atmosphere in our hearts and in our lives is to make the Word of God the centerpiece of our lives. We will draw the presence of God dramatically—the weightiness of the reality of God—when we saturate our souls, minds, and hearts daily in the wisdom and counsel of the Word of God.

Do Not Let the Book of the Law Depart From Your Mouth

Joshua served the Lord and Moses for decades. He served Moses as the Israelites wandered in the desert for 40 years, so he had experienced and learned how to do a number of things according to the ways of God. However, when Moses died and the Lord called Joshua into leadership, the first thing God told Joshua was to be strong and courageous, and to do all that Moses had commanded the Israelites to do (Josh 1:6-7). And then He gave Joshua the key to how to be strong and courageous. He said, "This Book of the Law shall not depart from your mouth, but you shall meditate in it day and night, so that you may be careful to do according to all that is written in it. For then you will make your way prosperous, and then you will have good success" (Josh 1:8).

What does it mean to meditate on the Law day and night? The Lord was saying to Joshua, "Commit yourself to the Word. You should be so saturated in its contents that its words are always on your lips and stirring in your mind. They should be flowing in your heart, touching your attitudes, and shaping your perspectives."

God is speaking to us about letting His Word be so deeply in us, so deeply in our soul, that we are saturated in it. We soak in it and it fills us through and through. It becomes so much a part of us that even as we speak, counsel, rebuke, or encourage, whatever we are doing, the wisdom, counsel, and thinking of God is flowing through our words and our inner being.

In Malachi He demanded of the priests that wisdom should flow out of their mouths; people should hear only the wisdom of God: "For the lips of a priest should guard knowledge, and people should seek instruction from his mouth, for he is the messenger of the Lord of hosts" (Mal 2:7). Throughout both books of Kings, God instructed the leaders of the land that they must constantly be in the Word of God so they would walk in His ways.

God was saying to these men—and to us—"Saturate yourself so deeply in the Bible that every time you open your mouth, the wisdom of God comes forth. Meditate on it day and night so that it is stirring in your thoughts as you drive your car, cook your dinner, or wash dishes. The words and counsels of God need to be so rich and full inside of you that they are on the forefront of your mind rather than in the background of your mind. In every situation, your words, thoughts, meditations, imaginations, and dreams need to be touched by the Word of God."

—— JOHN MULINDE AND MARK DANIEL ——

What did that mean to Joshua, Malachi, and the priests? It meant they were going to have to change the way they lived their lives. They were going to have to create quality time and a good quantity of time to saturate themselves in the Word of God so that their lives were being shaped by it.

Joshua had been serving the Lord for a long time, yet when God called him into leadership, He emphasized the need for Joshua to meditate on, "eat," and internalize the Word. He is not the first or only one to whom God had said this. God told Ezekiel to "open your mouth and eat what I give you...So I opened my mouth, and he gave me the scroll to eat" (Ezek 2:8, 3:2). God did the same with the Apostle John (Rev 10:9-10). We need to recognize that God wants the Word to sink into us also.

In John 8:31-32, Jesus said to the Jews who had believed in Him, "If you abide in my word, you are truly my disciples, and you will know the truth, and the truth will set you free." John 15:7 says, "If you abide in me, and my words abide in you, ask whatever you wish, and it will be done for you."

If you are going to create an atmosphere that is drawing God's presence, His Word has to be the centerpiece of your life. This doesn't mean that you just give more space to reading the Word; it requires coming to the Word with a new and deeper sense of humility and reverence.

> If you are going to create an atmosphere that is drawing God's presence, His Word has to be the centerpiece of your life.

Testimony From Uganda. When we had the visitation from the Lord in 1988, the first thing He told us was, "Don't even deceive yourselves that you know Me. You think you know Me, but you know Me very little, and you hardly know My ways. There are lots of things you have done in your ignorance, and I have blessed them because I love you. But above all, I love the people you minister to and I want My name to have a testimony among them." We knew that none of us truly knew or understood the Word, and that none of us knew God.

Many of us even found it hard to praise the Lord in those days. We didn't have the words stored in our hearts to exalt God because the Word of God was shallow in us. The more we began to flow in the Word of God, however, the more the praise, gratitude, thankfulness, esteem, and exaltation of who God is was built up in our hearts.

God showed us that He is far beyond our mental capacities, and that when our minds try to grab and shape Him so that we begin to think we know Him, we immediately limit Him. God showed us that the way He chooses to reveal Himself is through His Word, and that as we saturate ourselves in His Word, He begins to reveal greater and greater depths of who He is and the realities of His being and His ways. He was telling us not to let the Word of His Book depart from our mouths.

> Read the Bible as students, seeking to know our God. Who is this God in these pages? What is He like? What does He want? What are His plans? What are His attributes and values? Come with open hearts and minds to learn, discover, and understand who this God.

God began to teach us to approach the Bible with humility and a hunger for revelation to flow forth. We approached the Word like little children who don't assume they have God figured out. We began to read the Bible as students, seeking to know our God. Who is this God in these pages? What is He like? What does He want? What are His plans? What are His attributes and values? We came with open hearts and minds to learn, discover, and understand our God.

We understood that if we approached the Word the way God was leading us that His Holy Spirit would be there to teach us. He would reveal more and more of Himself to us, and allow us to see what we could not see in our own abilities.

During our altar time, we started reading the Bible for one purpose, not to get a teaching or a good feeling for the day. We read the Bible so that the words, wisdom, and truth of God were flowing in our souls. We were no longer reading each day just to get direction to handle a problem or to have a moment of peace; we were reading to have our souls saturated in the Word of God.

Since the altar is the place where we draw God's presence, we wanted to be captivated by His presence, so as we read for an hour, we would be praying with eyes open to see the beauty, greatness, and wonder of who God is, and we were able to respond to that. The daily and prolonged reading of the Word washed over us, and we came with only one purpose: not to get a teaching, but saying, "God, we want You to reveal Yourself to us. We want something of who You are so our souls can grasp the pages of Scriptures, so our souls can delight in and esteem You for who You are."

There is a humility we come into when we realize we need our hearts to be captivated by God. This is how we get life. It is what will sustain us and enable us to maintain reservoirs of faith and a high and exalted view of God.

> Our hearts need to be captivated by God. This is how we get life. It is what will sustain us and enable us to maintain reservoirs of faith and a high and exalted view of God.

As you read the Word each day, take a moment to meditate on this question: "Who is this God who I am coming before?" As you meditate, allow your heart to be impressed by what the Word is revealing of Him. When you then go into worship and praise, you are not just speaking words into the air; you are connecting with the One you have found in the Word. You are drawing the presence of the One who is revealing Himself and having communion with Him.

Saturating in the Word of God

We are living in a day when many, many people do not think highly of the Word of God. And many of those who confess to love the Lord do not have a first-hand experience with God through His Word. There are people who are committed to reading the Bible from cover to cover once a year, but these people are usually pastors; others don't normally see the need to do that.

It is mostly pastors who will commit themselves to a reading plan that will lead them through the entire Bible from cover to cover, but I (John Mulinde) have also been at pastors' conferences where more than 70% of attendees confessed that they had started with a plan but had not been able to finish it. In other words, they are never able to read the Bible all the way through.

Many people believe they read the Bible every day or every now and then, but what they do is "snack" on what they think is good to hear. One day they are in the book of Kings, the next day they are in Corinthians, another day they are in the Psalms, and another day in Matthew. I did that for many years and thought I had a good habit of reading the Bible. Then I realized I never understood the difficult parts of the Bible because I read like that. We tend to go to those passages that are easy, enjoyable, and appealing. We don't read books like Leviticus; we even wonder why it is there, although we know God has a purpose for it.

Many years ago I read a book by Pastor Yonggi Cho from South Korea, who said he had met pastors who pray only 20 minutes a day, and I thought that he couldn't possibly be telling the truth. That would be impossible. While I was in England shortly afterward I mentioned this in a leaders meeting; a pastor came to me later and said, "Pastor John, I pray 20 minutes a week." I said, "What? And you still preach to God's people? What do you preach and where do you get it from? When do you touch the heart of God? Are you ministering in your wisdom or the wisdom of God?"

—— JOHN MULINDE AND MARK DANIEL ——

The Word doesn't just instruct us and help us learn things, it is breathed of God. It has life in it that builds reverence, awe, respect, honor, and esteem for God, and helps us become God-centered and God-focused in our living instead of self-centered and self-focused. It changes our appetites and our perspectives. It is powerful.

There is no way to build an altar without the Word of God saturating our souls. That is why we don't want to read just bits and "snacks" of the Word of God. We want to soak ourselves in it day by day by day.

The Word of God Reveals Who He Is. When we want revelation of who God is, we meditate on the Bible. We obey the Word that says, "Be still and know that I am God" (Ps 46:10). In other words we are quiet before Him and we meditate on who He is.

Listen to some of David's words: "Make me to know your ways, O Lord; teach me your paths" (Ps 25:4). It is not enough to know about Him; now we want to know Him. It is that particular element that opens us up to praise and worship.

We can encounter God every day in different degrees throughout the pages of the Bible. The first chapter of Genesis alone is an amazing chapter. He said, "And let there be this," and it was. "And let there be that," and it was. He speaks to the ocean, "You go here," and it does. He says to the mountains, "You stop there," and they do. Everything obeys His Word (Gen 1:3-27).

What a mighty being! He is not constructing something; He is speaking the Word, and the Word has such power! To this day it is still upholding the oceans and the seas. It is still making the sun rise and set. It is still keeping the seasons. What a powerful Word!

Hebrews says that God upholds and sustains all things by the power of His Word (Heb 1:3). You can stop there, but if you take it further and consider whether that is the power of His Word, then you will want to see how people have handled His Word throughout the Bible. You want to watch the language of the people who listened to Him and those who did not listen to Him. You study a man like Cain; he gave an offering that God rejected, and God comes to him and says, "Why are you so gloomy? If you do right, won't you be accepted? But if you don't do right, sin is crouching at your door, and its desire is for you. But you must resist it" (paraphrase, Gen 4:7).

Remember who is speaking. It is the same One who said, "Let there be light," and there was light. He comes and warns you, "If you do right you will be accepted." Just think about that. The One who said, "There shall be sunrise and sunset" so many years ago—and it is still happening today. He is giving you a key! He is saying that if you do right, you will be accepted.

That is a sure word. God does not speak crooked words. Then He says, "But if you don't do right, sin is crouching by your door. Its desire is to take you. But you must overcome it." That is scary. He just said there is no escape. "If you choose right, I will accept you. You will enter into the inheritance I have for you. If you don't choose it, there is not any other way; you are going to go into captivity, and you are going to be destroyed."

But we read the Word every day and we argue with it. Why? Because we do not remember who is speaking to us. The One who is speaking is the One who said to Moses, "Don't cry to Me. Those Egyptians you are seeing now, you are seeing them for the last time. Stretch forth your rod." Creation obeyed. The sea opened! No one had ever heard of that. A road was cleared, and they walked through. That was the last time they saw those Egyptians.

This is the God we are talking about. It is the same God still talking to you and me. It is the same God who is demanding, "Give Me your life. I will be faithful with it." He who said, "Let there be light" and there was light is the same One who says, "Trust Me," and we struggle with that.

Do you know why we argue with the Word of God? We do not go back into the perspective, the bigger story. Who is this speaking to me? We argue, "Lord, that is too hard. Lord, how do I do that?" Do you know who you are talking to? Do you know who you are arguing with? Do you know the power of His Word?

You say, "Lord, it is too hard." For whom? For the Creator or the creature? Which one is now arguing that it is too hard? It is the heart that does not know who it is talking to that argues with God. That is why worship is the most important thing any human being could ever do because it brings us back to seeing the greatness and wonder of God. And true heart worship can only come from saturating in the Word of God.

> Worship brings us to see the greatness and wonder of God. And true heart worship can only come from saturating in the Word of God.

The Word Builds Esteem and Reverence for the Lord. The only way we can come to the place where we say, "Yes, Lord," is when our hearts and minds are saturated in the awareness of who our God is. In that perspective and sensitivity of God, we don't treat His Word lightly. It has weight and power because we know who it has come from. When we walk with that kind of awareness of the Word of God, our hearts stay in a yielded position before Him. The slightest prompting of His Spirit or the slightest use of His Word toward us raises up an immediate "Yes, Lord" in our inner man because we know with whom we are dealing. We know who is speaking these words. As we are saturating in the Word of God, every page of the Bible helps build esteem and reverence for God.

When they spoke, the people in the Bible had no fear. Why? Because they knew the One who was speaking to them. Whether it was Elijah at Mt Carmel, with the whole nation standing before him, knowing that God would bring fire down because God had spoken that to him (1 Kin 18:21-39), or whether it was Samuel speaking to King Saul, telling him that the throne was being taken from him while the king was begging him not to allow it. Samuel confidently said it would be done because the Lord had spoken and He does not lie or change His mind (1 Sam 15:29).

The New Testament says, "In the beginning was the Word, and the Word was with God, and the Word was God. All things were made through him, and without him was not any thing made that was made. In him was life, and the life was the light of men. He came to his own, and his own people did not receive him. But to all who did receive him, who believed in his name, he gave the right to become children of God" (John 1:1,3,4,11-12).

The Word says that the things we see were made by the invisible Word of God (Heb 11:3), that "without faith it is impossible to please him, for whoever would draw near to God must believe that he exists and that he rewards those who seek him" (Heb 11:6), and that "faith comes from hearing, and hearing through the word of Christ" (Rom 10:17).

The altar is a place from which we draw God's presence and seek to commune with Him. There is no way we are going to go very far or very deep without the Word of God. God is so vast and so beyond our mental concepts and comprehension that it takes His Word to reveal those dimensions and qualities as well as those things that captivate our hearts and make them yielded and open to the Living God. Without the Word of God, our time with Him becomes more human, shallow, and common, and we fail to come fully into His presence and communion with Him.

Therefore, as we build our altar, one of the key foundational pieces is saturating ourselves in the Word of God, allowing it to wash in and through our minds and our inner being every day, building up reservoirs of the whole knowledge of God, the full scope of who He is, until we realize there is an atmosphere in our soul that is beginning to reverence Him, to have a larger view of Him, and to esteem Him.

In Acts 17:22-28, Paul writes about the Greeks, who say, "We live in him. We breathe in him. He is all around us." And yet He was still unknown to them. So unless God brings His Word, we cannot know anything about Him. Jesus said, "No one knows the Father except the Son and anyone to whom the Son chooses to reveal him" (Matt 11:27b). John 1:14 says that, "The Word became flesh and dwelt among us." It is only through Jesus, the Word, that we can know the reality of the Father.

The Word helps us to better know God and His ways, demands, character, plans, and heart. It does something tangible in us, revealing the mystery of God, and teaching and instructing us how to walk with God, obey Him, and do the things He desires. The Word begins to build an atmosphere in our hearts of reverence, esteem, honor, and love for God. Nothing does that like the Word of God. It teaches us how to avoid what God hates and what He says will be harmful to us.

Create the Time to Saturate in the Word. The more we understand how powerful the Word of God is, the more we realize we need to make time and room in our lives for it to be able to saturate our souls. The Lord challenged us, revealing to us how our souls were being saturated in the Internet, television, media, the world, and so much else around us, but our souls were barely soaking in the Word of God. The more we heard and saw how the esteem of God, being captivated by God, and building praise and hearts of worship in our lives unfolded the mysteries of God, the more we desired to humble ourselves and saturate in the Bible day by day.

Start by reading large chunks of the Bible, perhaps five or 10 chapters every day. Don't mix studying and reading. Just read; studying is different. You cannot study the Word of God until you have invested a lot of time planting it inside of you, so at the beginning don't worry about doing any studying, just read.

When you are reading, differentiate between the Word of God and the word of men. You may have a wonderful study Bible with study notes. Don't read the notes as part of the Bible reading; they are not part of the story of the Bible. They are not the Word of God; they are man's interpretations and understandings. When you have leisure time, you can go back into the notes, but when it is your Bible reading time, stay with the Scriptures. Even the subheadings you read in the Bible are not the Word of God; those are created by men trying to categorize and outline what the Word of God is saying. Don't let those define for you what the Word of God says. Stay with the Scriptures.

There will be times when you won't understand or enjoy what you are reading. Don't worry; just read. If you are sleepy, take the Bible and walk back and forth, but keep reading. David said, "Sustain me...then I will meditate continually on your decrees" (Ps 119:117, NLT). David used to talk to his soul (Ps 103:1-2). Tell your soul, "Why are you sad inside of me? (Or weary? Or bored?) Praise the Lord, Oh my soul, for He will yet come through for you."

Take your Bible and say, "My soul, you are not enjoying this, but you are going to have to take it in." Why? Because when you hide the Word of God inside yourself, it will come through for you when you need help. He will come through.

In the beginning it may not make sense, but the time will come when you have hidden enough of it inside of you that it will begin to speak to you with wisdom beyond human understanding. It will give you answers when no person can. It will build your faith. When others are trembling, you will be firm. It will give security and calm to your soul. It will guard your mind, keeping you secure, firm, and stable.

—— JOHN MULINDE AND MARK DANIEL ——

Romans 12:2 warns us to not let the world squeeze us into its mold. The world constantly tries to fill our lives with so much that seems important or essential, but these things begin to crowd our lives so that we don't have time for the things of God. We then give God the leftover time, instead of making Him our priority and giving Him the first portion of our time.

Oftentimes, when we talk about spending time saturating in the Word, so that the esteem, worship, and revelation of who God is can come into our lives, we say, "I don't have time for that," and allow ourselves to be robbed of the wonder of coming to know Him and to walk in deeper communion with Him. Jesus said, 'This is the way to have eternal life—to know you, the only true God, and Jesus Christ, the one you sent to earth" (John 17:3). If we are to know God the way Jesus implied in this verse, we will need to build an altar and give significant time to reading the Word so that our souls will not get just a light shower of the Word of God, but so they can be saturated in the Word of God.

Read the Whole Story of the Bible. The Bible as a whole helps you to know God. After I (John Mulinde) first got saved, this is how I would read the Bible. I would want to read in John, the first ten chapters. I would get as far as chapter two, and I would get stuck because something touched my heart. I would begin to study. I would take a word and try to decide what it meant. I would analyze it and try to relate it to my circumstances, try to get the lesson out of it. I would write it down, saying it was speaking to my heart, teaching me, and then the Lord said to me, "What is your point of reference for studying the Word?" It took me many, many days to understand that, but then I came to understand that the only point of reference I had for studying the Word was my experience of life, my circumstances. I would take what it said and wonder what it meant, for example, in my life and in my experience. Then the Lord would say to me, "Go back to this part of the Bible and just read the whole book."

By reading the whole book I could see the perspective from the Jewish history, from the situation in which it took place, from the background of the events, to why that Word was spoken. Then I would realize the whole situation this Word was referring to was totally different from my present circumstances. I had taken the Word out of context. It said what I wanted it to say. I was taking it, applying it to my life, and telling the Lord, "But You said." And He would say, "No, I never said that." Because I had taken it out of context, I had made it say something He did not intend to say.

What does this mean? It means that if I don't have the bigger picture of how God is revealing Himself to mankind through the ages, the background of what happened to lead to a particular word being spoken or a particular principle being laid out, then I am bound to interpret it in my own human wisdom and live by that in my own way. Many people do this today. We try to study the Word even though we have never internalized the bigger picture.

This happens when someone has just come to the Lord and we give him a Bible and a Bible study guide that tells him to read a little bit of the Old Testament and a little bit of the New Testament and then to take a verse, keep it in his heart, and meditate on it all day. What is his point of reference for his understanding? Why would we even assume we know what God is saying? He is a mystery! And He will remain a mystery until we humble ourselves and say, "Lord, I want to know You."

> "Come to the Word to seek to know Me. Don't try to study Me and understand My deep things. Just try to say one thing, 'Lord, I just want to know You.'"

The Lord says to us, "I want you to read the Bible as though you have never heard of Me. You don't know Me. I have visited you; you acknowledge Me, but you don't know Me. You don't know My ways. You don't know My statutes, My standards. So come to the Word first of all to seek to know Me. Don't try to study Me and understand My deep things. Just try to say one thing, 'Lord, I just want to know You.'"

When we approach it like that, then our approach to the Word is simple: we saturate in it for information, instruction, and revelation. The first emphasis is go to the Bible for information: "I just want to know You. I'm not trying to study You. I'm not trying to analyze You. I'm not trying to argue with You or resist You. I just want to know You. I want to know what You say and what You think. I'm not trying to say, 'How do I apply this?' I just want to know You." So I want the narrative element of the Word of God. Who is this God? What is He like? What does He want? Why did He create me? What is His purpose with man? What are these things happening around?

This is how the Holy Spirit taught me to approach the Word. I'm not saying you have to do it this way, but when I read and realized the Holy Spirit is the real author of the Word of God through man, I said, "Every time I approach the Bible, I am going to take a moment to become aware that the Holy Spirit, the author of this Bible, is here with me."

My reading is not just reading; I'm actually receiving a story from the Author. And this Author knows things that happened before I was born. He knows what He is talking about. I want to listen. I want to receive the Word as I listen to His heart. I don't just want the letter of what it says; I want to catch the heart of the Author. So as I read the Bible, it was as if I was listening to a storyteller tell me, "And then this happened, and then that happened. And then the Lord said this."

At times I would pause and wonder, "Why did He say that? What is the background to that?" Sometimes I would go back in the story several pages, not to analyze or study, but to understand the flow of the story. How did events come to that? How did God come to say such a thing? Sometimes it didn't make sense, but I would just keep going.

What I'm trying to say is, "Just get the story." Approach the Bible simply wanting to get the story from Genesis to Revelation. You are not trying to analyze but just getting the story. Say to yourself, "I would love to do this three or four times a year. I want to be able to go through the Bible with just one intention, to get the story, the God story." Come back to the storyteller, the Holy Spirit. And sometimes you say, "But why? Why did He ask Isaiah to live a life like that? Why did He require this of Ezekiel? I don't even remember why. But when you go back to the story, you are not going back to study, you are just trying to see how it came about, how it ended. Did this man obey, and if he did, what was the result?

Is that the only way we can read the Bible? No. We have to read the Bible in many different ways. Study it. Meditate on it. Memorize it. But this way—reading to get the story of the Bible—helps to bring the bigger perspective. Then when we go to study, we have the reference from the big story. You begin to see, "Ah! This is what God is requiring. Yes! It's here. He required it of this one and of that one." So as the stories unfold, you can see the consistency of God. It's not just here; it's all throughout the Bible.

Every day as we read the Bible, we can encounter this God. We can come to that place where we say, "Wow." If you take what we have just been sharing about the Word, the power of God's Word, take what you saw in the first chapter of Genesis into your reading time as you read the second chapter of Genesis, He will continue to expand the power of His Word.

Drawing the Presence
of God by Saturating in the Word

In Uganda, the Lord had to say to us, "Come to the Bible as if you don't know Me. Read the Bible as if you are reading to get the whole story. Read from cover to cover and then go back from cover to cover, then read it again from cover to cover." For a season, that is all we did. We were not studying; we were just reading large chunks of the Bible, just getting the story. This way we began to see how things connect and the continuity of the story and all that the Word includes.

A time came when God said, "Now, make time to meditate on My Word. Make time to go back to the story and just look for one thing: to see Me. Read the Word and pray for the ability and a heart that desires to see Me in My Word. Ask the Holy Spirit to help you see My character, nature, desires, and values. Ask to see how I deal with challenges, with disobedience, or with pride."

The Lord gave us instructions for how to seek Him in His Word: Discover Him, and then as you sit and behold Him, allow your heart to melt by what you are seeing of God. Allow your heart to meditate and be impressed. Don't be a cold-hearted, detached reader. Allow your heart to be involved. In other words, experience that God. Allow your heart to feel that God, to feel His heart, to feel what He feels when He watches the people He loves going into sin, how He feels about people going into rebellion. Allow your heart to touch that. As your heart allows that to happen and begins to respond, you will come to know who He is. He is the Good and Almighty God. As you respond to Him, be led into praise.

> "Come to the Bible as if you don't know Me. Read it from cover to cover as if you are reading to get the whole story."

As we discover God in the Word, praise is released. It is out of that discovery of who He is that we can praise His holy name. We can pour out praise and say, "You are the Almighty God. You are the One who knows everything. You can do all things. You are capable of destroying the whole world in one day, yet You watch and are patient and longsuffering with this sinful generation. Oh God, who is like You?"

We declare to our soul and to the heavenly realm, "Oh, my God! He is an Almighty God. He is an Awesome God. He reigns forever." The reaction is not just because you read it in the Scriptures, but also because your heart is being impressed by what you are learning about God from His Word. The power of the Word can usher us into the release of praise.

After your heart becomes full, praise begins to be proclaimed. As you continue proclaiming the truth, as it has been coming through your meditation, your heart gets softer and softer toward God. Sometimes you feel your heart is just melting before Him. As you allow that to happen and you express that, it becomes worship.

> The power of the Word can usher us into the release of praise.

Whether your worship is expressed in a song or word doesn't matter. Sometimes it just touches your heart and you have no words; you are in silence, but that silence can still be worship to God. Sometimes you close your eyes and all you can think or say is, "Oh my God. Oh my God. Oh my God!" But that is worship. Sometimes you will just want to lie prostrate or bow down in His presence or you want to lift your hands to Him. Sometimes tears will flow and you find yourself crying.

Treat those moments reverently; don't take them lightly. Treat this time before God as precious and make it quality time. Choose a time when you can say, "Lord, I'm here." Allow no interruptions. When your mind is not distracted and is settled, it can receive more revelation from the Father. Allow your heart and soul to say, "I just want to be here, Lord. I just want to give You everything I have."

The Lord will allow you to rise up to that revelation and respond to Him because you are not squeezing your altar into a time when you will be bothered or interrupted. Therefore, you are able to have a deeper experience of worship than you would otherwise, and through that experience of worship is when you meet the heart of God. You feel as if you have come into an embrace with Him, with His heart.

As you are praising His character and hallowing His name, "Lord, You are sovereign. You are the Name above all Names. There is nothing impossible for You!" a situation in your life—whether it concerns your children, spouse, church, or job—suddenly comes before you and you speak to the Father, saying, "Oh Lord, help me with this. Help my child with that." Instead of praying in your normal vein, take a moment and just proclaim His name in that situation. "You are the God who has control over all things. You are King over everything. Your Word is the law. Your Word sustains all things." Just proclaim His name. Suddenly you will find the mountains, challenges, and battles that seemed so impossible to you fall into perspective before your God. And when God is on your side, who or what can stand against you?

As you proclaim His name, establishing His name in the situation, everything dwindles in size in comparison with Him. Then instead of pleading, "Lord, look what they are doing to me," you begin to say, "Even though the world shall rage, I shall be secure in You, Lord, because You are able to handle this." You are no longer the fearful one, pleading. You are now proclaiming your position in Him, saying, "Lord, You are mighty, and I can stand. I don't even mind if everything I stand upon is taken away. Even if the ground on which I'm standing disappears, I will still be secure because Your promises are true."

We normally come to God conscious of all our problems and circumstances, crying out, "Lord, help us! Help us! Will You do this? Won't You do that?" But what does the Bible teach us? The Word says to enter His courts with praise! Come into His courts with thanksgiving. Make a joyful noise to the Lord (Ps 95:2, 100:4).

As you approach the Lord, remind your heart that He is good. His mercies are new every morning. Remind yourself that He is our Maker and we are His people. He is the Shepherd and we are the sheep of His green pastures. Remind yourself who it is you are approaching. You are not just coming into the presence of some king, desperate and pleading. No! We have been given the right to, "Come boldly to the throne of grace, that we may obtain mercy and find grace to help in time of need" (Heb 4:16, NKJV). In that place of yieldedness and confidence in who God is, you are not approaching God from the understanding of your weakness and your hopelessness; you are approaching Him based on who He is and what He has pledged to you. That makes an enormous difference. That facilitates prayer with faith. Because the whole story of the Bible is a backdrop, you won't just pick a phrase and verse to speak out, such as "I can do all things through him who strengthens me" (Phil 4:13). You will also remember that He is the One who brought down the walls of Jericho. He is the One who parted the Red Sea. So when you read Philippians 4:13, the verse has all that context with it that floods through your soul with a sense of faith, assurance, and certainty of who spoke those words and the power that He has to help you in your time of need.

> In that place of yieldedness and confidence in who God is, you are not approaching God from the understanding of your weakness and your hopelessness; you are approaching Him based on who He is and what He has pledged to you.

Summary

It is out of spending quality time in God's Word and seeking to know Him that you see His heart's burden. You will see His causes and purposes, and pray for the purposes of God because there is nothing else worthy of giving your life to. You can afford to ignore everything, even your own personal discomforts, because what He has in His heart is all that matters.

All the prayers in the world will not change our nations until we come back to these simple truths that we are talking about here. The Word of God is key to knowing God, and we need be feeding ourselves on the Word and then allowing it to turn into praise and prayer. If you invest a few weeks in doing that you will want to go beyond reading five chapters a day; you will start to desire to do more than just read—good! Take the Word into meditation. Determine to see God in the Word, and when you do, praise Him and worship Him and allow Him to take you into that deep prayer which is born from that place of worship.

If you saturate yourself in the Word of God and then allow Him to penetrate your heart, He will prepare you to be a worthy altar that will send up incense acceptable to Him. You will then soon see the results in your personal life, your family, your church, your business, and your community. In other words, if God is being blessed in your heart, you can choose to open a door for God to work, not by power, not by might, but by investing your life in seeking to know God.

Closing Prayer

Let's take a moment for prayer:

Lord, let me yearn after You, that I may have an appetite for Your Word and for worship. Draw me to Yourself, oh God. Let me see You as I read the whole story in Your Word.

Lord, I may be busy, please but give me the grace to make time for Your Word and let it become a priority in my life. Reorder my day so I can make spending time with You a priority in my life.

Lord, give me a hunger for You and for Your Word. Make me hungry for You. Make me yearn for Your Word. And when I read Your Word, please give me the grace to take it in and keep it in.

Thank You, Lord.

Please spend a few minutes praising the Lord.

- Praise and exalt Him for what we have just been discussing.
- Tell Him about His Word: "Oh God, Your Word is wonderful. Your Word created the heavens. The visible was created out of the invisible by Your Word."
- Hallow His name and tell Him how wonderful He is, how much you want to know Him, how much you want to love Him, and how much you want to walk with Him.
- Lift up your voice and speak praises to Him. Lift up His holy name and fill the air with His praises.

SECTION 3
THE LIFESTYLE
OF THE ALTAR

SECTION 3
INTRODUCTION

In the previous chapters, we discussed the things we do at the altar as the chosen, royal priesthood of God that draw His presence. We commune with God and minister to Him, we saturate in His Word to get to know Him in deeper and more intimate ways, and we offer ourselves as a living sacrifice on the altar of our hearts that we have raised to Him. All these actions draw the presence of God closer to us.

As we pursue, love, and esteem God, to give ourselves more fully to Him, we find that His presence is both within us and rests upon us. Not only does His Spirit indwell us, He also surrounds and embraces us.

As we will be discussing in the following chapters, it is out of this deep communion and awareness of God's presence that He enables us to fulfill His purposes. He equips us and strengthens us. He gives us wisdom, power, and authority. He makes covenant with us and exchanges His divine nature for our corrupt nature. We begin to receive divine guidance and prophetic insight, and find ourselves able to push back darkness, break strongholds, and destroy the works of the enemy. All of this results from establishing and maintaining a holy altar unto the Lord, the fruits that come from this deepening communion with Him.

It is through our lifestyle at the altar that we draw the presence of God, and it is through His presence that He gives us what we need to advance His kingdom.

Lord, help us to understand the concept of the altar and then see how to bring it into reality in our hearts and lives. Our desire, Lord, is to fulfill the purposes for which we were created. We desire to see Your kingdom come and Your will being done "on earth as it is in heaven."

Please bless us, Lord, with eyes to see and ears to hear so we can understand what You are calling us to, and please give us willing hearts that we may become part of that pure and spotless Bride You desire to meet on That Day.

Amen.

CHAPTER 11.
THE ALTAR BRINGS FORTH SACRIFICE AND COVENANT EXCHANGE

And fire came out from before the Lord and consumed the
burnt offering and the pieces of fat on the altar, and when
all the people saw it, they shouted and fell on their faces.
Leviticus 9:24

As you develop the lifestyle of an altar where you are drawing the presence of God through ministering to the Lord and hallowing His name, you will find that the affections of your heart, your attention, and your thoughts are focusing more and more on Christ. As you saturate in the Word of God, you will find yourself internally becoming much more God-centered and God-focused, and less self-centered and self-focused. You will find your internal ways of processing and thinking, even your sensitivities and appetites, beginning to change.

In this atmosphere, you are much more sensitive and aware of God's heart. Instead of looking at things from just a human point of view, you will see them from God's perspective. You will see them the way He sees them. And it won't be simply that His will becomes information to you; your heart will burn with what His heart burns for. When you read His Word, you will tremble before it. When you are at the altar, in communion with God, His Word will have greater impact and you will have a greater reverence for it inside your inner being.

With all this going on, you will see things in your life that are not honoring to Him, things in your culture that are against His Word and His counsel, things in your own attitude that don't line up with His Word. Instead of treating these lightly, simply as information or something that you just acknowledge is against His ways, you will want to get rid of them; your inner being won't want to stay in that state. Something within you will want to release and get rid of all those things that are dishonoring to God.

At the altar we offer up sacrifices. We surrender and lay down everything that is not of God, is against His will, and that grieves His heart's desires. As we come deeper into His presence, we see our own thought processes, our actions, and our attitudes, and we begin to surrender them. This isn't something we are told to do; it is the work of the Spirit of God. He is drawing us deeper into His presence, removing those things that hinder us and keep us from lives that are fully given over to Him.

As we go into this chapter, we will be looking at the altar as a place where we offer up sacrifices and experience covenant exchange. Laying down our sacrifices on the altar is a natural response as we yield ourselves to God in surrender and draw His presence in increasingly deeper ways.

The Altar and Sacrifices

There is always sacrifice at the altar. This has been true since the beginning of time. It is the price that is paid to see the divine intervene and cause change in the physical world. God Himself raised the very first altar at Calvary before the foundation of the world (Rev 13:8). He offered His very best: His only begotten Son, Jesus Christ (John 3:16).

> It was now about the sixth hour, and there was darkness over the whole land until the ninth hour, while the sun's light failed. And the curtain of the temple was torn in two. Then Jesus, calling out with a loud voice, said, "Father, into

your hands I commit my spirit!" And having said this he
breathed his last.

Luke 23:44-46

For in him all the fullness of God was pleased to dwell, and
through him to reconcile to himself all things, whether on
earth or in heaven, making peace by the blood of his cross.

Colossians 1:19-20

God also established an altar when He slaughtered an animal to atone for the sin of Adam and Eve in the garden of Eden (Gen 3:21), and then used its skin to cover Adam and Eve's nakedness. God needed to redeem and re-establish fallen man, but could not intervene in the situation of sin and broken covenant with Adam and Eve without an altar and a sacrifice. He therefore created that altar Himself, through which He reclaimed man and re-established relationship and communion with him. An altar was immediately raised as the animal's blood was shed.

Since that time, God has required altars to be raised to Him so He can visit mankind through the gateway created by the altar.

Every Altar Requires a Price

King David took a census of Israel, which made God angry enough to send a plague against the nation. In repentance, David fell face down and pleaded with the Lord: "Was it not I who gave command to number the people? It is I who have sinned and done great evil. But these sheep, what have they done? Please let your hand, O Lord my God, be against me and against my father's house. But do not let the plague be on your people" (1 Chr 21:17). To halt the plague, God told David to go up and build an altar to the Lord on the threshing floor of Ornan the Jebusite (1 Chr 21:18).

So David went up at Gad's word, which he had spoken in
the name of the Lord. Now Ornan was threshing wheat. He
turned and saw the angel, and his four sons who were with

him hid themselves. As David came to Ornan, Ornan looked and saw David and went out from the threshing floor and paid homage to David with his face to the ground. And David said to Ornan, "Give me the site of the threshing floor that I may build on it an altar to the Lord—give it to me at its full price—that the plague may be averted from the people." Then Ornan said to David, "Take it, and let my lord the king do what seems good to him. See, I give the oxen for burnt offerings and the threshing sledges for the wood and the wheat for a grain offering; I give it all." But King David said to Ornan, "No, but I will buy them for the full price. I will not take for the Lord what is yours, nor offer burnt offerings that cost me nothing." So David paid Ornan 600 shekels of gold by weight for the site. And David built there an altar to the Lord and presented burnt offerings and peace offerings and called on the Lord, and the Lord answered him with fire from heaven upon the altar of burnt offering. Then the Lord commanded the angel, and he put his sword back into its sheath. At that time, when David saw that the Lord had answered him at the threshing floor of Ornan the Jebusite, he sacrificed there.

1 Chronicles 21:19-28

To stop the plague, David determined to build the altar that the Lord required. He asked Ornan to sell him the threshing floor so that he could offer a sacrifice to the Lord, as he had been instructed. Ornan graciously offered to give the threshing floor, as well as everything else that David would need for the burnt offering and the grain offering. There is a price to pay to institute an altar, and although he could have easily accepted Ornan's offer, David insisted on paying the full price for the sacrifice needed for the altar.

The New Testament Altar
Like David, we too are asked to raise an altar and provide a sacrifice to see God work and bring change into our lives, family, church, business, or community. Today, the offering we bring has

nothing to do with animals, but everything to do with ourselves. Like Christ, we are asked to surrender our lives on the altars of our hearts.

In the Old Testament the priest approached God on behalf of the people. Today, everyone who believes in Jesus Christ and follows His Word is a priest unto God. God wants you to enter into your own priesthood and erect a prayer altar to Him, and then He asks that you surrender yourself to Him as an act of worship and devotion.

Every altar raised to the Lord requires a price. The greater the impact of your altar in the territory, the higher the price that will be required.

That is why the early church had such a great impact. Throughout the New Testament, there are stories of rejection, persecution, stonings, beatings, hunger, shipwreck, imprisonment, and even death (Acts 4:3; Acts 5:18,40; Acts 7:58-59; Acts 12:2; Acts 16:19-24; 2 Cor 6:4-10; 2 Cor 11:23-27). When you read about the price the apostles paid to see the gospel spread and the great impact it had, you can see the price they so willingly paid at the altar that drew the presence of God and enabled them to be used by Him in great and effective ways.

> The greater the impact of your altar in the territory, the higher the price that will be required.

In 1 Corinthians 4:8-13 and 2 Corinthians 4:7-12, Paul reports the price the apostles paid to serve the Lord. They gave up their lives and chose to be poor, dishonored, hungry, thirsty, homeless, cursed, persecuted, and slandered. What was the impact of their sacrifice? They shook up their entire world. The Bible says that when they entered a new city, the people would say, "these men who have turned the world upside down have come here also" (Acts 17:6).

Time and time again the book of Acts illustrates how the apostles and other believers stirred up the passions of the people, both negatively and positively (Acts 3:2-10, 7:54-58, 8:5-8, 9:32-35,36-42). These men laid a strong foundation for the redemption, revival, and transformation of the world in which they lived.

What Is the Price We Are Asked to Pay Today?

Therefore, I urge you, brothers and sisters, in view of God's mercy, to offer your bodies as a living sacrifice, holy and pleasing to God—this is your true and proper worship.

Romans 12:1, NIV

Living for Christ means that we lay down our own will and desires. We give ourselves as a living sacrifice by laying our lives on the altar. We approach the throne daily, yielding ourselves to God's ways and His will. The old nature is gone—it has been put to death—and we begin to live as new creatures. We nail our passions and desires to the cross (Gal 5:24), crucifying our flesh. We take off the old and put on the new (Eph 4:22-24).

> Anything we have to endure, withstand, or give up to have Him is nothing compared with what our Lord Jesus Christ endured on the cross.

Any time you think the price is too high, read the passion of Jesus Christ in Isaiah 53 and remind yourself that Jesus took up our infirmities, carried our sorrows, and was stricken, smitten, and afflicted by God. He was pierced for our sin and crushed for our iniquities (Is 53:4-5). Let yourself come into the realization that there is no price high enough to repay. Anything we have to endure, withstand, or give up to have Him is nothing compared with what our Lord Jesus Christ endured on the cross. The price He paid to purchase our souls is much higher than anything we could ever repay.

> *Do you not know that your bodies are temples of the Holy*
> *Spirit, who is in you, whom you have received from God?*
> *You are not your own; you were bought at a price. There-*
> *fore honor God with your bodies.*
> 1 Corinthians 6:19-20, NIV

My Life Is Not My Own; It Belongs to Jesus Christ. The Bible makes it clear that our lives are no longer our own; we were bought with a great price. We are to no longer live for ourselves, but to live for Christ. This is our "living sacrifice," our "spiritual act of worship" (Rom 12:1).

> *And he died for all, that those who live might no longer live*
> *for themselves but for him who for their sake died and was*
> *raised.*
> 2 Corinthians 5:15

We no longer plan our future, but submit to walking with God and following His ways and commands. We want to see His purposes accomplished and the desires of His heart fulfilled. We surrender our lives to Him and submit to the calling He has placed on our lives.

I No Longer Live; It Is Christ Who Lives in Me. We must come to the place where we realize that we no longer live for ourselves; we live for Christ. We live for His glory, His honor, and His will. We no longer want to accomplish our will, but His. As we lay our lives on the altar and allow God to bring us to a place of true surrender, abandonment, and total trust in Him, we see who we really are; how truly wretched our flesh is. Then, we no longer want to keep our lives for ourselves, but to give them to Christ so we can take on His life.

> *I have been crucified with Christ. It is no longer I who live,*
> *but Christ who lives in me. And the life I now live in the*

flesh I live by faith in the Son of God, who loved me and gave himself for me.

Galatians 2:20

Our human nature is corrupt and spiritually blind; it cannot please or obey God and is powerless to take hold of spiritual truths. Our will fights against God's will, our desires aren't His desires, and our flesh tries to take control and have its way. The worldliness and woundedness inside of us scream for attention. Lies dominate our thoughts.

The only way to overcome is through Christ who lives within me, the Righteous One, the One who obeys, follows, trusts, and believes God. Why should I give up my life, laying it on the altar as a living sacrifice? So that my old sinful nature will die, allowing Christ to live through me.

Why must I lay down my life? Because it's the only way Christ can live His life through me. Where He rules in me, His righteousness and love flow through me, and His fervency for the Father dwells in me. It is the way through which I can minister to the Lord at the altar.

Why must I lay down my life? Because it's the only way Christ can live His life through me.

Why should I fight my self nature to submit to Christ, subduing my fears and insecurities, daily placing my life on the altar? So that I will no longer live and that Christ will live through me; so that the life I live in the body, I live by faith in the Son of God.

As we spend time saturating in the Word and worshiping God as He is revealed in the Scriptures, we will see Him more and more clearly. He will captivate our hearts and we will yield our lives more to Him. As we do this daily, we then see what it means to be dependent on God. And as we become more dependent on God, we will stop looking to ourselves for wisdom, direction, strength, security, or provision. We will just look to Him. We will see ourselves as new creations.

> *Therefore, if anyone is in Christ, he is a new creation. The old has passed away; behold, the new has come.*
> 2 Corinthians 5:17

This new creation is spoken of throughout the Bible. It includes new attitudes, deeper faith, stronger trust, growing righteousness, and changing thought and behavior patterns. Someone who has struggled with faith in the past will notice he isn't turning to fear or fretting over every problem so easily. We may have been quick to criticize, but now find ourselves full of praise and thanksgiving. We start to realize that the old nature is waning; the new is getting stronger and more evident. And we become thankful because we know this is not a work we can do; only God can bring about a new creation. This is the result of laying ourselves on the altar and abandoning our lives to the Lord.

The Offering Is Taken to the Altar Daily

The Scriptures tell us to crucify the passions and desires of our carnal nature. They use words telling us to "cast off" and "put to death" our fleshly desires. The words used in the Bible are strong and exacting, telling us to eradicate and die to our earthly nature and to lay down the lust of our flesh, once and for all (Rom 6:6-11). In reality, though, our flesh deals with our carnal nature, not by eradicating or casting off, but by suppressing, covering, denying, pretending, and white-washing our fleshly desires.

As you build and establish the lifestyle of an altar, of coming into the presence of God on a regular basis, the distinction between what is of this world and what is of the kingdom of God will become increasingly clear to you. You will see the distinction between the Christ-life that is within you, this beautiful life that Christ has given to you through His sacrifice, and the life of your flesh nature. The more time you spend at the altar, the more you will see the reality of that Christ-life. At the same time, you will begin to recognize the old nature, your old life, and see that it is wretched, blind, pitiful, and rebellious against the things of God.

As you spend time at the altar, you will realize that these things must be put aside. And as you come to worship the Lord, drawing into His presence, seeking Him, and spending time deep before Him, you will also realize that He is calling you to come closer and closer to Him but you are finding it difficult to go. These fleshly things are clinging to you and making your heart shrink back, unable to fully go where God wants you to go. You will realize that you have to let go of the fleshly desires of your carnal nature so you can keep progressing onward with God.

For instance, you may see that you have to trust Him and step out of your fears if you are going to go into the depths He is calling you to. And out of that place of understanding, that divine wisdom you received from being before the Lord, you lay those carnal things down as a living sacrifice on the altar. You cast them off and give them up because you want to keep going further and deeper with God.

At the altar, you will often experience a natural reaction—a response compelled by love—that comes when you are worshiping, hallowing His name, and saturating in the reality of who He is, what He has done, and what He has promised to you. You won't even be trying to make it happen; you will just speak out words of surrender, to lay yourself before the Lord in a position of submission unto His Holy Spirit. You will speak words of abandonment to Him because those are the words of worshipers: you will begin to yield, to surrender. Over time, you will come to realize that your heart remains yielded to the Holy Spirit at the altar. Without the altar, our hearts harden, and we become self-serving. Our human nature rises up and we become stubborn, rebellious, and callous to the things of God.

The more we touch the reality of God, the more we trust Him.

—— JOHN MULINDE AND MARK DANIEL ——

The more we trust Him, the more we yield ourselves to Him. The more we yield ourselves to Him, the more we don't want control of our own lives anymore; we give them fully and completely to God. And the deeper He takes us into surrender, the deeper He takes us into the Christ-life and His anointing.

Sacrifice Leads to Covenant Exchange

As New Testament priests—a chosen people, a royal priesthood (1 Pet 2:9)—God calls us to come to the altar and lay down our lives. Like David, we cannot build an altar that costs us nothing. The Old Testament priests brought cattle, sheep, and goats, but we bring our hearts and lives. We lay ourselves on the altar and become living sacrifices.

At the altar, we consecrate our lives to God, yielding our wills, and submitting our hearts and souls to His commands and purposes. This is not a sacrifice we make just once; we make a continual offering at the altar.

As we lay our lives on the altar and surrender them to the Lord Most High, we no longer look at things or value them the way the world does. We no longer exalt what the world exalts or find our identity in anything that comes from the world system. We are not of this world, although we are still in the world. We have been redeemed and purchased with a great price. We have exchanged our self-nature for the very nature of Christ.

Making and Renewing Covenant With God

> And God said, "This is the sign of the covenant that I make between me and you and every living creature that is with you, for all future generations: I have set my bow in the cloud, and it shall be a sign of the covenant between me and the earth. When I bring clouds over the earth and the bow is seen in the clouds, I will remember my covenant that is between me and you and every living creature of all

flesh. And the waters shall never again become a flood to destroy all flesh. When the bow is in the clouds, I will see it and remember the everlasting covenant between God and every living creature of all flesh that is on the earth."

Genesis 9:12-16

Know therefore that the Lord your God is God, the faith-ful God who keeps covenant and steadfast love with those who love him and keep his commandments, to a thousand generations.

Deuteronomy 7:9

At the altar, we make and renew covenant with God. Covenant is very important to Him. The Scriptures are full of descriptions of the covenants that God made between Himself and man, both in the Old and New Testaments. In fact, the Bible is separated into these two sections by the covenants they each represent, the old covenant God made with the people in Moses' day and the new covenant made between God and man at the altar of Jesus Christ.

Covenant Is the Basis of Man's Relationship With God

God acts by covenant; it is the basis of His relationship with man. It is the way He has always related to man from the beginning of time. Throughout the Scriptures we see Him making covenant with Noah, Abraham, Moses, David, the nation of Israel, the apos-tles, and the church. He covenants Himself to people, nations, and lands. The way He works is by finding people who will not only give themselves to Him in covenant, but who will also commit to serve Him and His purposes in their nation.

Throughout history, from the time of Adam up until today, people have made covenant agreements with God. They have cove-nanted themselves, their marriages, their families, their lands, and their lives to God to see His purposes fulfilled. Stronger than a promise, covenant is the security that He gives to people. They can know that God Almighty had come down to the human level, saying He was binding Himself to them through covenant, guaranteeing to fulfill all the agreements He had made in that covenant.

From the beginning of time God created covenant to bind Himself in relationship with humans. God only relates to men by covenant, and the place where that covenant is made is at an altar. This makes establishing and maintaining altars crucial because they enable covenants to be made, to be renewed, and to be strengthened.

> Establishing and maintaining altars is crucial because they enable covenants to be made, to be renewed, and to be strengthened.

The foundation of Christianity is covenant relationship with God. That key position of covenant is the basis by which we pray, worship, believe, trust, surrender, and obey. It is through covenant that God trusts us with His heart desires. And it is only as we are walking in this covenant relationship that our hearts are able to stay in a place of strength and confidence in Him.

Throughout Scripture God reveals how serious He is about covenant.

> And he said, "Behold, I am making a covenant. Before all your people I will do marvels, such as have not been created in all the earth or in any nation. And all the people among whom you are shall see the work of the Lord, for it is an awesome thing that I will do with you.
>
> Exodus 34:10

This verse is like God declaring to Israel, "I am covenanting Myself to you. I will fight your battles. I will bring you victories. I will be with you. I will not forsake you. I will reveal Myself as your God." And He told them, "Your part is to give yourself to Me.

Worship Me and nothing else. Your love and loyalty will be to Me. I want you to abandon yourself to Me, trust Me, and submit to My ways. I will be your God and you will be My people. Then I will show Myself mighty among you and you will be a blessing to all the nations of the world" (Ex 34:10-24).

You can see throughout the Scriptures that the whole basis of relationship with God is covenant. It is not just a moral code, a belief system, or a religious experience. If it were based on a religious experience, then we would only be "up" when we are having those experiences. But sometimes we are experiencing struggles or feeling beaten down; we are walking through very low, insecure times. In those times, rather than standing firm and strong because of a religious experience, we can stand firm because we are in covenant with Almighty God.

> Rather than standing firm and strong because of a religious experience, we can stand firm because we are in covenant with Almighty God.

We know that no weapon formed against us can prosper (Is 54:17, NKJV). This assurance comes, not because we have a strong faith and feel confident today, but because we are in covenant with the One who is in control of all things. If we base our lives on ourselves and our experiences, we will have a rollercoaster ride. But if our lives are based on covenant, then our walk is firm and solid. Even in the midst of the storms of life, our hearts can stay in communion with God and anchored in covenant.

Covenant Partners Bind Themselves to One Another

Partners entering covenant bind themselves to one another, such as the marriage union between husband and wife. This is the way God operates. He asks us to covenant ourselves, our families, and our lands to Him. And we don't just covenant ourselves to God, we also covenant ourselves to His purposes being accomplished in the land.

Covenant involves deep abandonment and unity. It involves bonding our family and future generations to another party. In ancient times, when people entered covenant, they knew it was a serious matter and that covenants could not be broken. The two parties would seriously discuss their relationship and what entering covenant would mean. It would sometimes take up to 3 years of negotiations to come to the terms of the covenant. Both parties knew they were entering and creating a binding relationship that would affect their descendants for generations.

Each party was fully aware that part of the covenant would involve giving up their personal rights. Whatever one person owned would become available to the other. If one had a need or a debt, the other was taking on the obligation to fill that need or take care of that debt. If one partner was in a battle or someone was chasing him, he would run to his covenant partner, who would stand beside him and join the battle. Why? Because they were in covenant together.

In covenant, two become one. There is a bonding of life. All I have, all my resources, and all my strengths become yours. And all you have, all your resources, and all your strengths become mine. The two parties enter into a shared life, declaring that they will lay down their lives for the other's benefit and good.

After coming to agreement and negotiating the terms, the covenant partners would go through a ceremony then make promises and covenant themselves to each other. Each party understood and agreed to the terms: I bind myself to you. Everything I have is yours. I will be there with you in every battle you face. I will not abandon you. We are family. If something happens to you, I will take care of your children. Your family will be watched over. I am here.

But the Lord was gracious to them and had compassion on them, and he turned toward them, because of his covenant with Abraham, Isaac, and Jacob, and would not destroy them, nor has he cast them from his presence until now.

2 Kings 13:23

The two partners would no longer be separated; they became one. Covenant was—and is—sacred and serious. It is permanent.

God Will Not Break Covenant

God is a covenant-keeping God. He will not break covenant: "Yet the Lord was not willing to destroy the house of David, because of the covenant that he had made with David, and since he had promised to give a lamp to him and to his sons forever" (2 Chr 21:7). He says it would be easier for the mountains to disappear than for Him to break His covenant with Israel: "'For the mountains may depart and the hills be removed, but my steadfast love shall not depart from you, and my covenant of peace shall not be removed,' says the Lord, who has compassion on you" (Is 54:10).

God promised David, "I will establish your offspring forever, and build your throne for all generations" (Ps 89:4). God later promised David that even if his sons turned their backs on Him, He would punish them, but He would never break His covenant with David (Ps 89:30-37).

These Scriptures reveal to us who God is and how steadfast He is. They also tell us that He is faithful, He cannot lie. When He makes covenant, He will keep it. It would be easier for the sun and moon to disappear than for Him to break His covenant (Jer 33:19-21,25-26). As Paul said, even "if we are faithless, he remains faithful" (2 Tim 2:13).

For this is the covenant that I will make with the house of Israel after those days, declares the Lord: I will put my laws

into their minds, and write them on their hearts, and I will
be their God, and they shall be my people.

Hebrews 8:10

Like David, we can trust that God cannot—that He will not—break the covenant He has made with us. Hebrews 6:19 tells us that we have an anchor of hope for our soul, firm and secure, and that we can trust God to uphold this promise. Why? Because He made an oath; He bound Himself in covenant. This is our anchor.

When the wind beats against us, when the enemy intimidates us, when Satan roars at us with all his power, we can say, "I stand upon the covenant of my God!" Even when we go into battle against the darkness and are being buffeted and struck down, we can rise up in strength. Why? Because God has bound Himself to us in covenant.

Uganda Testimony: Covenanting the Land to God to Fulfill His Purposes

I (John Mulinde) would like to share something I learned in my walk with the Lord. In my lifetime, I have seen God move many times and in many ways in my nation. There have been four very distinct waves of the Lord's intervention in Uganda: in the 1970s with Idi Amin, in the 1980s in the times of war with Milton Obote, in the 1990s when we were dealing with HIV and AIDS, and in the early 2000s with the war with the Lord's Resistance Army in Northern Uganda. We saw many different moves of God in Uganda, but new difficulties and challenges kept rising up. We learned many treasured lessons during this time, but the most important was that we were not approaching God as covenant partners; we were just crying out for a crisis to be alleviated. Therefore, every time we prayed, we would see a breakthrough, but we wouldn't see long-lasting change. One problem would be stopped, but another would soon arise because we weren't functioning as covenant partners with God.

The greatest move of the Holy Spirit in Uganda—the East Africa Revival—began in Ruanda-Urundi (the present-day nations of Rwanda and Burundi) in the late 1920s. It swept throughout eastern Africa, including Uganda, in the 1930s and 1940s. This revival led to significant church growth throughout the region, and its influence continues today.

When Idi Amin came to rule over Uganda, he was determined to turn the nation into an Islamic state. He believed that to be able to survive as leader of our nation, he needed to get the petro dollars of the Arabs and the support of the communists, which he did. To convince them he was serious, he tried to prove that he was a devoted Muslim. He banned the churches in the nation, beginning with the ones that were most vocal and visible. Year after year, he added more churches to the list of churches not allowed to operate in the nation.

By 1975, only three churches were allowed to operate in Uganda: the Catholic Church, the Anglican Church, and the Orthodox Church. All others were illegal. Not only was it illegal to practice Christianity openly, it was illegal to practice Christianity in your own home. Praying in any other place except in the three churches sanctioned by Amin was banned. Even those three were only allowed to practice their faith on Sunday mornings. Within those churches, anyone caught praying on any other day was arrested; some were even killed.

In 1977, Idi Amin declared Uganda an Islamic state. In 1979, as he was preparing to declare Sharia law, he was overthrown. The most evident reaction of the deposition of Amin was the joy of having freedom of worship once again.

During his reign, Idi Amin also tried to eradicate sorcery and ancestral worship. Because of this, those who practiced witchcraft, sorcery, and occultism had gone underground. When he was overthrown, there were two spiritual reactions in the nation. One was that there was a great move of the Holy Spirit, which gave birth to many churches. Signs and wonders even followed this move of God, and many young people gave their lives to the Lord and to ministry.

There was also a great revival of witchcraft and ancestral worship. Shrines that had been taken underground came out into the open. People began to advertise their occult clubs, temples, and covens on the radio, in newspapers, and on billboards. Witches and sorcerers began to come to Uganda from other African nations; a great witch from Mombasa was even promoted. This growth and strengthening of the occult was an unexpected by-product of the breakthrough of prayer that came with the overthrow of Idi Amin.

In the 1980s, when Milton Obote was President of Uganda, there was war in the land. Because the government could not pay the soldiers satisfactorily, in order to keep the troops loyal to him, the President decreed that the soldiers could take whatever they wanted from the people without cost. This allowed the soldiers to rob, kill, and destroy openly.

Every night, buses full of soldiers would come from the barracks to different parts of the city. When they heard the buses coming, people would leave their houses wide open so the soldiers did not have to break the door. They would then go hide somewhere until the soldiers left. That was the only way to save your house, even though you would lose whatever the soldiers found and took. Sometimes you would hear people screaming in the middle of the night because they were caught in their house; then you would hear the gunshots. Every morning it was common to ask if anyone was killed, and to hear, "Yes, two or three were killed." This was a daily thing.

When we prayed, God answered our prayers and change came. Peace and security returned to the streets and cities of Uganda. But as these things returned, so did the nightlife. Bars remained open longer; nightclubs and discos opened, and people stayed out late to enjoy the nightlife. Promiscuity and all that goes with the nightlife returned and even increased. Young people who had not known freedom suddenly found they could spend the whole night dancing in a nightclub. This caused sexual promiscuity to become a trend. Because this time was just after the war, the infrastructure of the nation and the medical field, as well as almost everything else, was broken down. It did not take very long before Uganda was declared the nation worst hit by AIDS/HIV. We had the highest levels in the world at that time.

In the early 1990s, a minister from the government invited national pastors to pray over the nation. He read to us a report from the World Health Organization, which declared that Uganda was certain to become a failed state because of the AIDS situation. The World Health Organization said that in the next 10 years—by the year 2000—30% of the population would be dead from AIDS and another 30% would have HIV and be waiting to die. The remaining population would consist of mostly children and older people, who would not be able to sustain the economy. Uganda was going to be a failed state.

This government official was a born-again Christian who worked as Minister of Security in the Office of the President. He said, "I am here in the name of the President. Government has no answer. The medical world has no hope. The international community has no solution. Men of God, will you mobilize the nation to pray?" The government was appealing to the men of God to deal with a situation that was impossible. It had no scientific, economic, political, or diplomatic solution, so the government was turning to the church, saying, "Only God can help us in this. Will you mobilize the nation in prayer?"

"Until you seek to connect with My purposes for the nation, you will never understand how to fight for the nation."

After that meeting, the pastors prayed from morning to evening.

Late in the afternoon, a prophetic word came to the small group of people who were remaining that changed our understanding. I am paraphrasing what the Lord spoke to us: "In spite of all the pain and fire you have been through as a nation, you have still not learned any lessons from it. You still believe that your enemy is flesh and blood. That is why you were holding bitterness and hatred toward Idi Amin and his henchmen, and for Milton Obote and his soldiers. What you are holding onto is preventing Me from doing what I want to do for you as a nation. Right now you don't know how to pray because you don't have a human agent to point to. You need to know that you are dealing with spiritual powers of darkness that are trying to ruin this country because of My destiny for this land. Until you seek to connect with My purposes for the nation, you will never understand how to fight for the nation."

That was the point where we took our eyes off the problems in the land and began to seek the heart of God for the land. This was difficult because the problems were present and challenging. Every one of us was losing loved ones. Every family in Uganda had someone who was dying of AIDS. Every family knew what it meant to watch someone waste away until they were no more.

God was covenanting Himself to us for our land. He was saying to us, "Take your eyes off the problems and begin to seek Me, My heart, and My purposes and plans for Uganda. When you connect with that, you will be able to pray according to My will for your nation." We had seen Idi Amin overthrown, but then witchcraft and the occult rose up. We saw Milton Obote defeated, but then the nightlife was restored and promiscuity increased. Then, as we saw AIDS ravishing our nation, God started telling us to pray for His purposes, not our problems. This was a key lesson and a turning point for our nation.

The Faithfulness of Our Covenant Partner
When you fully lay your life on the altar and give yourself in trusting, humble surrender to God, you will see that He binds

Himself to you. One of the first examples I (Mark Daniel) saw of that is when we first started building the prayer altars in our church. There was a lady in our church whose husband had left her. She found herself trying to raise several children alone, with very little financial support. Everyone around her started to give her all kinds of different advice about what she needed to do.

Up to then, she had stayed home with her children, so she had no job and no income. People were telling her she needed to go back to college to earn a degree because she had no career in front of her. Others were telling her to go to the government to apply for financial aid to help her with food, housing, and other expenses. Some were advising her to start looking for another man to marry so he could help take care of the family. Others told her she needed to ask her parents to take care of her and help support her children.

At the time, I was preaching about the life of surrender, how God is calling us to give ourselves fully to Him. I was sharing this week after week, and this young mom was listening to these sermons and struggling with the message. In her struggles, she started seeking the Lord and asking, "What do I do?" As she sought His guidance, God began speaking to her: "I don't want you to look to anybody to take care of you except for Me. I don't want you to look to the government, to another man, to your parents, or to anyone else. I want you to trust Me to take care of you and your children."

She struggled with this for several weeks. None of us knew this was happening, but as she prayed at the altar she came to that place in her heart where you lay down sacrifices. One day while she was at the altar in prayer, God led her to step across a line and say, "God, I will look to nobody else to take care of me and my girls. I will only look to You."

No one knew that she had that kind of encounter with God at the altar. Two days later, before the Sunday service had started, someone in our church who is fairly well-off financially came up to her and said, "I have never done this in all of my life, but God has led me to give this to you." He gave her a blank check and said, "Write this out for whatever you need."

Now, picture this. If you had just crossed a line and said, "God, I'm not going to look to anybody else to take care of me. Just You." You took this terrifying step to trust God, and then 2 days later a wealthy person comes up to you with a blank check and says to make it out for whatever you need. She later shared that in that moment God was showing her, "I've received your sacrifice. I'm making a covenant with you. I will take care of you."

Over the last several years we have watched God take care of her and her family in dramatic ways. I remember several times when people were moved to bring money into the church office saying, "Give this to her now. God says it must be today." When the secretary called to tell her, she would start crying and saying things like, "I needed that exact amount to pay rent today." We watched this happen over and over. God was faithful and took care of them. It was miraculous, and we were all inspired by His faithfulness to her.

A few years ago, a couple came to her and said, "We are moving, but believe the Lord is telling us not to sell our house, but to rent it to you for whatever you are paying for your apartment." It was an almost new, extremely large house! She struggled with this a few days and came to the place of saying, "Lord, I'll trust You with this. I'm not sure how I'll pay the higher utility bills and other expenses, but I'll trust You." A few weeks before she was supposed to move into the bigger house, the couple came to her and the husband said, "I've never heard God's voice in my whole life, but I know for sure He is telling us to give you this house for free for as long as you need it." Again we saw God and His faithfulness! He had bound Himself in covenant and was intervening in her life because she had laid it down on the altar and had given herself to serving Him and His purposes.

When the economic crash came a few years ago, this man's business was deeply affected. He could no longer afford the payments for his own house and the house he had given to this woman and her family, and made the decision that he was going to have to ask her to move out. It made sense to everyone. He went to bed that night, settled in his heart that he was going to do this. In the middle of the night God woke him up and spoke to him, saying, "You will not touch that house." And he knew for sure he could not take that house from her, that God had told him what to do. As the man was telling me this story, I marveled at how God had defended what He had done for this lady. Like He did for Abraham when Pharaoh had taken his wife, God woke the man up in his sleep, fighting battles for this lady and her children.

Summary

As we come to the altar and lay our lives down as a sacrifice, as we continually respond to the reality of who God is and give ourselves over to Him, He shows us His heart's desires and He gives Himself to us. He binds Himself to us in covenant and He intervenes in our lives. He opens up His work and His purposes to us, so that we can go forth to carry out His purposes.

As you spend time at your altar, hallowing the name of the Lord, saturating in His Word, creating an atmosphere that is increasingly—day by day, week by week—becoming more pregnant with the presence of God, you will experience a deeper and deeper reality of God's presence and His abiding love. As you do that, the presence of God will begin to cause you, in response to His love, to begin to yield to Him wholeheartedly. He is so much greater than us. He is so much greater than us that our natural reaction is to fall down and yield ourselves to Him in every way. In Scripture, anyone who encountered God immediately humbled themselves, acknowledged who He is, and yielded themselves to Him because of His rightful authority over them.

During your time at the altar, as you are worshiping and praising Him, drawing closer to Him day after day, the Holy Spirit begins revealing God to you, and the laying down of your sacrifice becomes a very tangible reality: "Not my will, God. Let Your will be done. Not my ways, Lord. Let me follow Your ways." This grows deeper in your life, and as you lay down that sacrifice of surrender, yieldedness, and submission to Him on the altar, God binds Himself in covenant with you. He begins to show you His heart's desires and His purposes for our generation, and to speak words of covenant: "If you do this and trust Me with that, then I will accomplish this and fulfill those things in your life." He invites you to join His purposes and then binds Himself to you in covenant.

CHAPTER 12.

THE ALTAR BRINGS FORTH PROPHETIC INSIGHT AND A PLATFORM OF BREAKTHROUGH

...that the God of our Lord Jesus Christ, the Father of glory, may give you the Spirit of wisdom and of revelation in the knowledge of him, having the eyes of your hearts enlightened, that you may know what is the hope to which he has called you, what are the riches of his glorious inheritance in the saints.

Ephesians 1:17-18

If any of you lacks wisdom, let him ask God, who gives generously to all without reproach, and it will be given him.

James 1:5

> God wants us to live by prophetic insight and divine revelation, not by human wisdom and human thinking.

God wants us to live by prophetic insight and divine revelation, not by human wisdom and human thinking. Our thoughts aren't His thoughts; our ways aren't His ways (Is 55:8-9). It is only as we live by prophetic insight and divine revelation that we can do the work of God, that we can walk in the ways of God and see the fruit that only He can bring.

As you build a lifestyle of the altar, both personally and in your family, when you or your family faces a crisis, you will go to the altar to seek wisdom and revelation. Even business and marketplace people who have established altars can go to the altar when they face a crisis to seek wisdom and revelation from God.

When an altar is successfully built, people can go into prayer to get direction for how to face their burdens and battles, and they come out in victory. When the altar is not successfully built, the people go into committees to try to solve their problems, and they come out with projects and human solutions, which result in human results.

A lifestyle of the prayer altar develops the ability to live in the presence of the Lord, which we call His abiding presence. In that place, we experience continual communication and connection with God, and sensitivity to His Holy Spirit. This is one of the things Charles Finney did, and is probably what made his ministry so powerful and anointed. Finney, a revivalist in the Second Great Awakening in America, called this a "spirit of prayer." He said, "If I ever felt there would be a hindrance to that spirit of prayer, I would stop everything and then go and seek the Lord." It is in this place that we receive wisdom, insight, guidance, and direction from the Lord.

> A lifestyle of the prayer altar develops the ability to live in the presence of the Lord, which we call His abiding presence.

King David's life was based on the lifestyle of a personal altar. David didn't live by human thinking and wisdom. Because his life was an ongoing altar, he was always ministering to the Lord, drawing the presence of God, and living a life of surrender and abandonment to God. Even in the middle of his battles, decisions, or life issues, David would call on the Lord for divine revelation and insight, and God would answer, giving him the direction he needed to have victory in every situation.

> *And David inquired of the Lord, "Shall I pursue after this band? Shall I overtake them?" He answered him, "Pursue, for you shall surely overtake and shall surely rescue."*
>
> 1 Samuel 30:8

> *And David inquired of the Lord, "Shall I go up against the Philistines? Will you give them into my hand?" And the Lord said to David, "Go up, for I will certainly give the Philistines into your hand." And David came to Baal-perazim, and David defeated them there.*
>
> 2 Samuel 5:19-20a

> *And the Philistines came up yet again and spread out in the Valley of Rephaim. And when David inquired of the Lord, he said, "You shall not go up; go around to their rear, and come against them opposite the balsam trees. And when you hear the sound of marching in the tops of the balsam trees, then rouse yourself, for then the Lord has gone out before you to strike down the army of the Philistines." And David did as the Lord commanded him, and struck down the Philistines from Geba to Gezer.*
>
> 2 Samuel 5:22-25

There are several times when David sought the Lord for direction about whether to counterattack or go after an army. He would ask, "Should I attack or not?" and God would say, "Yes," then give David assurance of victory. He also sometimes gave specific instructions for how to fight the battle: "Go around them, then I will blow through the trees. It will sound like marching and you will know that it is time to attack." God gave David the exact insight and information he needed.

The Altar Is a Place of Revelation and Insight

The Bible is full of people receiving revelation from God. For example, when the Moabites and Ammonites were coming against Judah, King Jehoshaphat sought the Lord and proclaimed a fast in Judah. He caused the whole nation to assemble and seek help from the Lord; as they did, the Lord encouraged them to stay brave, then gave them guidance and direction (2 Chr 20:1-21).

Jehoshaphat had developed a lifestyle of the altar where he went before God and met with him regularly. At this altar, he learned to be led by the Lord and not by his own human wisdom and human thinking. He also lived in a covenantal way with God so when the nation faced a crisis, Jehoshaphat called the nation to join him in prayer.

The altar is not limited to prayer time or devotional time. It is a lifestyle of being before the Lord and living in His presence.

Daniel also developed a lifestyle of the altar. When Nebuchadnezzar had his dream, no one was able to interpret it except Daniel. His time with the Lord offered him the information and revelation needed to interpret the king's dream (Dan 2:16-47).

> The altar is not limited to prayer time or devotional time. It is a lifestyle of being before the Lord and living in His presence.

No one today could say to a ruler, "Give me 3 days." Anyone saying such a thing must have a relationship so deep with the Lord that they are sure God is going to protect them and provide what they are seeking. This certainty and boldness comes from the commitment they have made to live their life at the altar before the Lord.

The three young men, Meshach, Shadrach, and Abednego, were also living in covenant with God, so they would not bow down to idols (Dan 3:14,16-18). They were willing to die rather than bow down to an idol. Their behavior points back to the lifestyle to which they and Daniel had committed themselves (Dan 1:8-20).

When you study the life of Daniel, you discover a man of prayer. He was at his altar praying three times a day, which he wouldn't abandon even when the decree made the practice unlawful and his life was threatened (Dan 6:10). He was a man of the Word; that is how he discovered the prophecy of Jeremiah (Dan 9:1-2). Daniel was also a man who waited upon God. When he didn't have understanding, he sought the Lord. Daniel sought divine revelation repeatedly.

Daniel is a good example of how a lifestyle of an altar before the Lord provides us with all we need. Through communion with God on a deep daily level, we find the instruction, boldness, wisdom, and revelation we need to live the Christian life and fulfill our destiny.

When the kings of Judah who had a functioning altar faced challenges, they would turn to the Lord and seek direction and protection. Because He was their covenant partner, the Lord would always give them revelation and understanding of what He wanted them to do. The kings who did not have that altar lifestyle faltered, and would turn to something or someone else to handle their problems, such as armaments, alliances with other nations, or material goods. They would end up with disaster and ruin because they turned elsewhere rather than to God.

One of the encouraging things about the lifestyle of an altar is that the Lord will reveal things to you before they happen. He prepares you for what is coming. As Paul was being taken to Rome, he sought the Lord for guidance. As the ship he and the Roman soldiers were on started to have difficulty, the Lord told Paul exactly what needed to be done to save their lives along with the lives of the ship's crew. Paul told the soldiers to get rid of the lifeboats so the crew couldn't leave the ship. He told everyone to eat since they had fasted for days. He told them that if they followed the instructions of the Lord, none of them would lose their life. All this revelation came from Paul's time spent in the presence of the Lord at the altar (Acts 27:9-36).

Testimony From Uganda

One morning about 14 years ago, I (John Mulinde) was in prayer in the new place we had acquired. I was seeking the Lord, wanting to get a fresh word from Him. We had just come into the city and bought this new place, so there were a lot of questions in our minds. What are we going to do? What are we going to call the place? How are we going to order the activities? I began to pray.

As I was there, I felt sure the Lord brought this passage to me. It took a long time to grasp the inner meaning in my heart. It says, "In the fifteenth year in the reign of Tiberius Caeser, Pontius Pilate being governor of Judea, and Herod being tetrarch of Galilee, and his brother Philip tetrarch of the region of Ituraea and Trachonitis, and Lysanias tetrarch of Abilene, during the high priesthood of Annas and Caiaphas, the word of God came to John the son of Zechariah in the wilderness" (Luke 3:1-2).

I really struggled with all the details in these Scriptures that the Holy Spirit included just to tell us the Word of the Lord. Why did He have to go into all these rulers in all these different places just to tell us that the Word of the Lord came to John at that time? Then it began to sink into my soul; He is painting a picture for us. He is trying to show us what kind of world it was when the Word of the Lord came to John.

In these Scriptures, the Holy Spirit is showing us an ordinary world going about business in the ordinary way. He is talking about the time of Tiberius Caesar and reminding us that we are looking at the bigger picture of the Roman Empire. It is not just John somewhere in the desert, maybe in a cave, communing with God. There is a picture being painted of the Roman Empire and everything that goes with it, the Roman culture, the Roman law, the political system, the economic system, the resentment between Jews and the Roman rulers, and everything else that is involved. It is saying to us that all of that doesn't just hang in the air; it affects the minds of the people who live under the system. It shows us the atmosphere in place when John received the Word of God.

That's not all. Pontius Pilate was the governor of Judea, and Pontius Pilate was Roman. He wasn't a Jew. Herod was a tetrarch of Galilee, and his brother Philip was a tetrarch of Ituraea and Trachonitis. And Lysanias was the tetrarch of Abilene. These are territories or regions within the land of Canaan or Israel, but they were being ruled by different people. Each ruler has a different personality, and that comes through in his rule. Every ruler affects how the people react to him and how they react to life. He affects what people think about, and how they think about themselves, the life, the system, the things around them, and the way things are done. Everything—the taxation, economic system, political system, and social system—are affected by these people.

This all came to me when I was seeking the Lord wondering what we should call this new place. The Lord was showing me, "Do you realize you're trying to find something to fit into the system? You're trying to find a name that will appeal to the system. You're trying to find a system of work that is going to be acceptable to the people. You are trying to do all these things, but why are you here? I called you. I told you what I want to do with your life. I told you I want to accomplish this in the nations of the world. You don't even know how you can go out of this place."

Those who have been to our old Trumpet Center saw that it looked like a cave. It was a very, very humble place and there was no way we could even imagine that out of that humble place people would go out across the whole world. And the Lord was saying "Why are you bothering to try to do something that the world will understand and relate to? There's no way after being understood you are even going to plan how My Word is going to be fulfilled. So why bother with all those questions? Come before Me and say, "Lord, what do You want me to do with this place?"'

I had to humble myself and repent and say, "Lord I'm sorry. I'll wait upon You."

Then He said to me, "You know how you have a roll of carpet, and then you begin to unroll it? My calendar is similar to that. As everything is being unfolded, it is just the next thing on My calendar that you should be in this place with the work I've given you. It's not something you have prayed through. It's not something you have labored for. It is just the next thing in My plan for you. When the right time comes, I'll get you out of this place, but now that you are coming in, this is what I want you to do. Turn this place into an altar of prayer that goes on twenty-four hours a day. I want you to intercede for My purposes as I will show them to you."

And He said, "Be careful who you put on the platform to speak from that place, because that is My platform. If you allow just anyone to come speak, then you will lose the fire that I'm going to release in that place, but if you are careful to ask Me and wait for My approval of who is going to stand on that platform to speak to My people, then I will keep My fire there."

A fellowship had met for a long time at the place I was taking over, so there were several Christians who felt they belonged to that place. But God said, "You are not going to work with any of these people; the majority are going to go away. I'm going to bring people who are handpicked. I'm going to bring them here; one from a city, one from a village. Respect them. Give everything I've taught you to them, for through these men and women I will start to take nations and cities and begin to turn systems upside down."

At that time I had nothing to stand on to be able to say, "This is what God is going to do." I would have sounded crazy. But because of my altar and the time I spent before the Lord, I was confident of what I had heard and what my God had told me.

God Sees What Is Coming

The Lord knows what is ahead. If He tells you to be careful and not be intimidated, like He said to Jeremiah (Jer 1:7-8), take His warnings seriously. If He tells you four times to be strong and courageous, like He said to Joshua (Josh 1:6-7,9,18), give your whole heart to it because He knows what is in store for you. He knows there are difficult times that are going to come that will make you want to shrink back and quit.

There are times you will feel inept and overwhelmed, but God will say, "Be strong. When such moments come and you want to quit, remember that I told you, 'Be strong.' It is part of the rule of life to which I have called you. Be courageous. When everything in you is trembling and you feel like that is the end and you want to run and hide, remember that I told you, 'Be strong, and be courageous.'" At the altar, He will give you the insight to be in position for what is ahead.

> The altars we build and maintain give us a platform to break strongholds and push back darkness.

Any time the Lord warns you or encourages you, take that into your spirit. Any time the Lord says, "Be careful not to do this. Be careful not to shame or defile My name," know that a moment is coming when you will have to stand on His Word, in His strength. He speaks because He sees what is coming, and He gives you that Word so that when the moment comes it will be there as an anchor. You will be able to successfully pass through.

Drawing God's Presence Helps Us in Warfare

There is a link between prophetic insight and spiritual warfare.

The altars that are built and maintained give us a platform to break strongholds and push back darkness. As we walk in this lifestyle of seeking God to draw His presence, experiencing God drawing nearer and nearer to us, and our hearts yielding more and more to Him, we begin to grow more God-conscious and God-confident. When we do not live at the altar, we become self-conscious and self-focused, and therefore, our battles continue. They will overwhelm, confuse, and provoke us to turn to human resources to fight them. However, the more time we spend in the presence of God, the more we become confident in His ability to lead us, guide us, and provide for us. The more we saturate in His Word, ministering to His Spirit, and experiencing His abiding presence leading us through life, the more we realize that He is who He says He is, that He will do what He said He will do, and that He is a covenant-keeping God. As He was with Daniel in the lion's den (Dan 6:16-23), He will be with me in the valley of the shadow of death. As He was with David as he faced Goliath (1 Sam 17:32-54), He will lead me through to victory.

As you spend quality time at the altar, you become aware that our God is a covenant keeper and that He has bound Himself to you. Your battles are now His battles; your needs are now His needs. You will then also find peace and security in trusting Him and turning to the altar to receive the guidance and wisdom you need, even in the midst of battle or in the midst of increasing pressure and difficulty.

A good example of this is David, who had a life at the altar. David was a man who sought after God. As you read through the Psalms, you see that David was a man who ministered to the Lord continually. He constantly surrendered himself before God. As David would lay out his burdens to the Lord, he would say things like, "I give myself to You. I choose You and Your ways." He would talk about his battles and his difficult circumstances, and then he would declare his choice to trust in the Lord.

After David was called to be king, he rose in fame and success;

everyone was singing his name in the streets (1 Sam 18:6-7). It must have been very encouraging to David to see that he was on track to fulfill the prophetic word that God had given him through Samuel. Then King Saul became jealous of David and turned against him. Saul even started to look for ways to kill David. When Saul tried to hunt David down, David went into hiding. During this whole time, David turned to the Lord and trusted Him to give guidance for how to deal with Saul. And even though the king and his entire army were hunting David, he continued to trust and believe that the Lord would protect him.

A day came, though, when David could no longer find a hiding place in Israel, so he went to live in the Philistine territory (1 Sam 27:1-4). David and his men lived for over a year in the city of Ziklag, which the king of Achish had given them (1 Sam 27:5-7). Although the king of Achish had insisted that David and his men fight on the side of the Philistines as long as they lived in his land (1 Sam 28:1), when the Philistine army one day decided to go up against Israel, the commanders of the Philistine army insisted that David and his men be sent away, for fear that they would turn against the Philistines during the battle (1 Sam 29:1-4).

David now found himself in an even more difficult situation; he had nowhere else to go. To make things worse, when he and his men got back to Ziklag, they found that all their possessions had been captured in a raid by the Amalekites; their children, their wives, and all their goods had been taken (1 Sam 30:1-3). At this point, David not only had nowhere else to go, he had also lost everything and his men began to turn on him and talked of stoning him: "And David was greatly distressed, for the people spoke of stoning him, because all the people were bitter in soul, each for his sons and daughters" (1 Sam 30:6a).

The situation could not have been any worse, but what did David do? The Word says, "But David strengthened himself in the Lord his God" (1 Sam 30:6b).

David encouraged himself in the Lord! He turned to God—he went to the altar—and he began to praise God, focus on God, minister to God, and glorify God. And as he was ministering to the Lord and pouring out his praise, David was not making the time in God's presence about his circumstances, he was talking about the greatness, faithfulness, and unfailing love of his God. He declared how God saw David through several battles and his trust that God would continue to be faithful to him. David encouraged himself in who God is, what God had done in his life, and His character, and then sought direction and asked God, ""Shall I pursue after this band? Shall I overtake them?" (1 Sam 30:8a). He asked for direction and guidance, and God gave him prophetic insight and assurance of victory. He and his men got back all their families and possessions. It was only a few weeks after this challenging time that David was made king over Judah (2 Sam 2:4).

David was a man who lived at the altar, so even when he found himself in the midst of the greatest warfare without any allies on either side of him, and it looked like everything he possessed was lost, he didn't panic or go into human thinking. He didn't run away or try to figure out a way to resolve the situation. He turned to the Lord because the altar was in his lifestyle. It was the way he had walked through battles and difficulties throughout his entire life. And because God is faithful, we see in the Word that He brought great victory into David's life. As we trust in God and depend on Him, He can accomplish things that we could never accomplish. God gave David prophetic insight as well as victory. The altar lifestyle helps us find guidance and direction, and also helps us obtain victory.

> As we trust in God and depend on Him, He can accomplish things that we could never accomplish.

In warfare, there is often so much tension, stress, strain, fear, and anxiety that if we don't go to the altar, we will operate out of our human nature or our human ways. We don't experience victory while we are fearful or anxious because we don't have the Lord's presence to calm us, settle us, or help us focus on the Lord. The altar gives us the ability to fight the battle because at the altar we can see God's way forward and are able to take hold of His authority; this gives us the platform to push back darkness and to gain the victory.

The Power of Darkness Is Broken at the Altar

The story of Hezekiah in 2 Kings 18 and 19 is a good illustration of how the altar is not only a place where revelation is received, but also where darkness is broken and victory is gained.

The Assyrian commanders were standing before the walls of Jerusalem, speaking out so all the people could hear, spreading threats all throughout Israel. The Assyrian kingdom had been winning victory after victory in city after city, and the commander of the army was even boasting of all of their victories, speaking in a way that was causing fear to spread to the people.

Most political leaders at a time like that would panic or try to come up with a strategy to solve the problem. But because he was a man of God, Hezekiah went to the altar. This was where he had found answers before. It was where he had found direction and been given God's wisdom. Hezekiah took Assyria's threats and taunts to the altar, and God spoke and revealed how the victory would come.

> *"Therefore thus says the Lord concerning the king of Assyria: He shall not come into this city or shoot an arrow there, or come before it with a shield or cast up a siege mound against it. By the way that he came, by the same he shall return, and he shall not come into this city, declares the Lord. For I will defend this city to save it, for my own sake and for the sake of my servant David." And that night the angel of the Lord went out and struck down 185,000 in the camp of the Assyrians. And when*

*people arose early in the morning, behold, these were all
dead bodies. Then Sennacherib king of Assyria departed
and went home and lived at Nineveh. And as he was worshiping in the house of Nisroch his god, Adrammelech and
Sharezer, his sons, struck him down with the sword and
escaped into the land of Ararat. And Esarhaddon his son
reigned in his place.*

2 Kings 19:32-37

As King Hezekiah and the nation of Judah depended on the covenant God had with them, and turned to Him at the altar, God
not only protected them from the invasion of Assyria, but also
destroyed the enemy army and its leader.

When you go to the altar, worshiping and ministering to the Lord,
praising Him and acknowledging Him, a calm comes over you.
You are reassured of who is in control. All the panic, discouragement, and fear that can come from the warfare eases, and you
become calm and subdued and quieted before Him. In those
moments, God can speak and give direction, showing you His
path of victory. He can show you the way He is going to accomplish His purposes so you know how to cooperate with Him and
submit to Him.

In those times, however, God will also reveal what is in you that is
giving the enemy legal ground for attack, and will show you what
needs to be done to get rid of those things. King Josiah is a good
example of that.

In 2 Kings 22 and 23, King Josiah finds the Book of the Law and has it read to the people of Israel. He returns to the altar lifestyle and sees the many things in the family life, the national life, and the life of the kingdom that were against the ways of God. He starts a movement

> God begins to cleanse you at the altar so the enemy doesn't have the legal right to attack you.

of national repentance and cleansing of the land. Discovering how far they had strayed from the ways of the Lord, King Josiah renews the covenant of the people with the Lord, and begins to cleanse the nation of idols and unholy altars. At the altar, God begins to cleanse you so the enemy doesn't have the legal right to attack you.

Testimony of Joseph Kony and the Ugandan Army. A contemporary example of the power of darkness being broken at the altar is the war in Uganda with Joseph Kony and the Lord's Resistance Army. Since the mid-1980s, Joseph Kony has led a group of rebels that has abducted and displaced thousands and thousands of children and adults in northern Uganda. The LRA initially stated that their mission was to overthrow the government and make way for a new regime that upheld the Ten Commandments; eventually, however, they became a group of rebel soldiers with no clear mission or ideology.

The rebels have been known to attack villages, schools, churches, and other large gatherings of people, killing the weak and old, maiming some as a warning to others, and kidnapping children to bring into their camps. They forced the boys to become soldiers and the girls to become sex slaves. Those captured were often forced to rape or kill family members so they would have no hope of returning home; those who resisted were tortured and killed. It has been estimated that since the 1980s at least 30,000 children (and possibly many, many more) have been abducted and over 2 million people have been internally displaced. In 2001, the United States declared the LRA a terrorist group, and in 2005, the International Criminal court indicted Joseph Kony for war crimes and crimes against humanity.

The Ugandan government had fought Joseph Kony for over 20 years, but had been unable to stop him. He was holding the nation captive. His army would hide in the bush of northern Uganda, or run away to Sudan, where the government could not enter. If the army set up an ambush, Kony would become aware of it and he and his men were able to escape. Even with technological, military equipment, and other aid from western countries, such as the US, Britain, and Germany, the Ugandan government was not able to stop Kony and his rebels.

During this time, the nation of Uganda was experiencing a move of God across almost all the land. At first, the church was unconcerned about what was going on in the north; that was the government's problem. However, as national pastors and leaders began to gather and share testimonies about answers to prayer and the move of God they were seeing in their regions, the northern people began to cry out and say, "You are describing all these answers to prayer, all of this transformation that is taking place in your part of the country, but we're not experiencing anything. Is God a respecter of persons?" The church leaders were convicted by this question and the obvious fact that the whole nation was being touched by God except for the area targeted by Joseph Kony. It started to become obvious that Kony had a spiritual power of darkness helping him. The national leaders responded by humbling themselves before the Lord.

As the leaders prayed, the Lord showed some of them that because this was a spiritual battle, it could not be won by military means. The pastors shared this insight with some military leaders, one of whom was a general who said the Lord had told him the same thing in a dream. The general helped arrange a meeting for one of the pastors with the President. As this pastor shared the revelation from the Lord with the President, he also shared the location of three or four of the places where Kony had built unholy altars, from which he was receiving power and knowledge. Astonished, the military leaders said that the locations of those altars were the places they had encountered the greatest resistance and defeats.

The President agreed that there were spiritual influences at work, offered to send the Ugandan army into Kony's territory along with the pastors, and asked the pastor for a strategy. After much prayer, the pastors came back with a strategy that was two-fold: to call the people in the north to repentance and to call the nation to a fast.

Over the centuries, there had been alliances made and things done in individual lives, in churches, and in the region that were giving legal ground for the forces of darkness to control the territory. The pastors started to hold campaigns, preaching the Word and drawing the presence of God, and people started bringing witchcraft items to the altar; they brought items they had made that had given the darkness rightful hold in their land, and they began to repent and break the unholy altars of witchcraft they had created. To protect themselves from Joseph Kony and the LRA, the people had also made alliances with them, which they confessed and repented. People in the region started to share about unholy altars and the spiritual powers behind Kony. The people repented of any place, way, or unholy object that had given legal ground for the darkness to have a hold in their lives, families, churches, and communities. Many people gave their lives to the Lord during this time; almost 3,000 at one meeting alone. The darkness was being cleansed from the land.

The second part of the strategy was to call the nation to a 2-week fast to seek God for guidance of how to have a spiritual victory over Joseph Kony and his army. During the fast, the Lord showed the national pastors how to prepare themselves to go to where Joseph Kony's unholy altars were with the intention of breaking the powers of darkness over those places. The military sent gunships and tanks along with the pastors and intercessors. They went in and broke the power of darkness at every one of those unholy places. As they did, there was clear evidence that God had prevailed: soldiers were getting saved and baptized. The presence of God was moving. Joseph Kony never won another victory in Uganda after that time. The power of darkness had been broken. Within a year, Kony was out of Uganda and has never returned.

It is impossible for most of us to picture what the people of Uganda were facing at that point, but they began to come together to seek the Lord at prayer altars in their families, churches, villages, and cities. This drew the presence of God, and the people began to receive His insight and direction, and then a platform from which the powers of darkness could be broken was established over cities, villages, and the nation.

The Power of the Altar in Our Lives

We, too, can experience the power of the altar. Like the people of Uganda, as our hearts yield to God and the altar lifestyle, God's Word will shape us, transform us, and draw us deeper into Himself. Then, as we draw into the presence of God, He will reveal the darkness that is in our lives. We will see the sin and other things in our lives that go against His Word and His ways. He will show us the things of our own flesh that are warring against His Spirit, as well as our spiritual blindness, the woundedness we are carrying around in our lives, and the darkness that is holding us captive. Whether it is the world's ways and thinking or the enemy who has a stronghold on us, God will reveal to us those things that need to be cleansed and broken.

> At the altar, as God strips away the layers of darkness and brings you to places of repentance, you will begin to feel spiritually strengthened, to see more clearly, to have more stability in your spiritual walk, and to have more passion and spiritual energy to go forward.

God will identify the darkness at the altar. He will show you how the darkness is not of Him and how it is affecting you. Once you see it and repent of it, you will realize how blind the darkness has made you. At the altar, as God strips away the layers of darkness and brings you to places of repentance, you will begin to feel spiritually strengthened, to see more clearly, to have more stability in your spiritual walk, and to have more passion and spiritual energy to go forward.

As you allow God to continue to expose and strip away the layers of darkness, which can be from many sources, such as the choices you make, the belief system you follow, or the culture you live in, you will be amazed at how much darkness there was and how it has been affecting you. At the altar, God begins to strip these layers off and to break their legal hold on you.

Many of us have lived with darkness for so long that we can't picture ourselves apart from it. We can't imagine not being afraid, anxious, doubtful, or intimidated. We don't feel safe without the anger and rage we've used to protect ourselves. Many of us find it difficult to acknowledge the haughtiness, self-righteousness, and judgmental spirit that the Lord reveals at the altar. However, as we repent of these things and begin to choose the Lord and His ways, He will strip the darkness away and we will come alive. Spiritual strength and power rise up within us, and God will be able to break the legal grip the darkness had on us. When this happens, we will be able to rise up in spiritual authority.

Rising up in spiritual authority does not mean you just begin to command spiritual forces; it means that you start to clearly see how to take hold of the victory that has been purchased for you by the blood of Jesus Christ. When the legal ground is broken, you become less intimidated and are able to rise up in authority. You become more certain of the victory that has been won for you through Jesus Christ, and more confident that He has destroyed every work of the devil and has gained victory over every weapon of the enemy.

The confidence and rest in the Lord that we find at the altar allows us the ability to face spiritual battles without panic. We will no longer try to fight battles with our human wisdom and power, but will go confidently before the Lord, knowing that He can bring about the victory. This is the platform—the staging area—that is built at the altar from which we can engage in spiritual battle, dependent on the Lord and not on our own flesh or human ways.

CHAPTER 13.
THE LACK OF A
HOLY ALTAR ALLOWS
DARKNESS TO PREVAIL

Every Man Has a Breaking Point

When we base our lives on nothing but human wisdom and ability, we will only be able to stand as long as we have stamina, boldness, and strength. When we are faced with pressure, the stresses of life, and the intense shakings that are beginning to be part of our everyday lives, the structures we depend on—usually our own strength, thoughts, and power—will begin to crumble.

Many of us have received good instruction about prayer and the ways of the Lord, but are still depending on human strength and reasoning. We may have built an altar to the Lord, but are not maintaining it through daily time with Him in His Word or His presence. The strength of our altars, and our faith and dependency on God, are tested and proven when we reach the breaking point during those difficult moments in our lives.

> The strength of our altars, and our faith and dependency on God, are tested and proven when we reach the breaking point during those difficult moments in our lives.

Every one of us has a breaking point where we say, "I know the right thing to do, but I can't because..." Most of the time we can't see a way out of the situation.

Many times we don't have the strength to do what we know is right. Often, we make compromising decisions about what we are going to do because we don't trust God to protect us, provide for us, or carry us through the situation. In our own strength, each one of us has a breaking point where we give in or yield to the pressure.

Look at Lot, for example (Gen 19:1-38). This holy man knew right from wrong. He brought up his children in purity of spirit even in the midst of the lifestyle in Sodom. Peter says that Lot was a righteous man (2 Pet 2:7), so we know that he followed God and His ways.

Lot stood against the darkness of Sodom until that moment when all the men of Sodom, from young to old, were pressing against his door, demanding that Lot send out his visitors so they could abuse them sexually. Under pressure, Lot made an offer that was totally against his values. He said, "Behold, I have two daughters who have not known any man. Let me bring them out to you, and do to them as you please. Only do nothing to these men, for they have come under the shelter of my roof." (Gen 19:8). This offer came from a parent who knew better! Under pressure, the only thing he knew to do was totally against his conscience.

> Today, we often do the same thing Lot tried to do: solve spiritual problems with human solutions.

The Bible says that the angels "reached out their hands and brought Lot into the house with them and shut the door. And they struck with blindness the men who were at the entrance of the house, both small and great, so that they wore themselves out groping for the door" (Gen 19:10-11). Lot's offer to the men of Sodom was not God's solution to the problem. Today, we often do the same thing Lot tried to do: solve spiritual problems with human solutions. However, there are situations in the physical realm that have nothing to do with physical solutions. The angels dealt with a problem that was spiritual in nature with a spiritual solution, and in a brief moment the problem was solved.

His Righteousness Had No Impact

After the angels saved Lot, the threat against him was no longer the men of Sodom, but God. The angels told Lot to gather everyone in the city who was connected to him and get them out of the city, "for we are about to destroy this place, because the outcry against its people has become great before the Lord, and the Lord has sent us to destroy it" (Gen 19:13).

"So Lot went out and said to his sons-in-law, who were to marry his daughters, "Up! Get out of this place, for the Lord is about to destroy the city." But he seemed to his sons-in-law to be jesting" (Gen 19:14). Lot's sons-in-law laughed at him. He was not able to save their lives because his warnings had no impact whatsoever on them. The words he was speaking did not carry the weight of truth or anointing.

The angels continued to urge Lot, saying, "'Up! Take your wife and your two daughters who are here, lest you be swept away in the punishment of the city.' But he lingered. So the men seized him and his wife and his two daughters by the hand, the Lord being merciful to him, and they brought him out and set him outside the city" (Gen 19:15-16).

But even though Lot had just experienced a miraculous intervention and was now being urged to flee or else be destroyed, his faith was in his own ability rather than in God's. Lot asked that things be done his way; he asked to be sent into the small town of Zoar rather than to the mountains, where he believed he would perish (Gen 19:18-20).

> Lot depended on his own ability and his own mind. This is a typical human reaction when one has not built a lifestyle of being in the presence of God.

Lot was not depending on God, but on his own ability and what made sense to his own mind. This is a typical human reaction to a difficult situation when one has not built a lifestyle of being in the presence of God.

People who have broken through in prayer do not look at the circumstances and panic. Those who have spent time in the presence of God react to moments when they are beyond themselves by saying, "My God is able." They have a deep assurance and confidence in God's ability. Facing the threat of death in the fiery furnace, Shadrach, Meshach, and Abednego said, "The God we serve is able to save us." They were also so trusting in God that they went on to say that no matter what happened, they would not bow to the circumstance (Daniel 3:17-18). These young men surrendered to the ability of God and did not depend on their own thoughts or abilities.

The difference in outcome between Lot and the three young men who were thrown into the fiery furnace is astounding. The one lost all that he had to sin: friends, wife, daughters, and right standing with God; the other three saw their God save them, as they had known that He would. Lot saw an entire community destroyed; Shadrach, Meshach, and Abednego saw a king, and through him a whole kingdom, come to have faith in the Living God:

> *The people that do know their God shall be strong, and do exploits.*
>
> Daniel 11:32 (KJV)

Human Strength Cannot Stand Against the Wickedness of This Generation

We live in times when no human strength or stamina will stand. The pressures of the systems around us are getting stronger and stronger. Everyone who knows what is right and wrong undergoes constant challenges; and day by day we give up a bit more

ground and compromise a little bit more. We continually surrender territory to the darkness, as we can see happened to Lot.

If we continue to depend on our own human wisdom, reasoning,
and understanding, we will keep backsliding, our moral standards will keep deteriorating, and our nations will continue to
turn away from God. But God is looking for people who will say
"no" to the dictates of society; He is looking for people who will
say, like Shadrach, Meshach, and Abednego, "We choose God's
way."

The only way we can choose God's way is by depending on His
strength rather than our own. We must therefore seek Him. We
won't seek Him so that we can do the right thing; we will seek
Him because we will find Him and He will make us able to do the
right thing. We will be able to "work exploits" because our God
will give us the strength to do so. If we don't seek God and rely on
His strength, without realizing it the spirit of the land will have
an effect on us and change us, as happened to Lot.

Sin Creeps in Unaware

This holy man Lot found himself in the position of offering his
daughters to be raped and sexually abused. He was unaware that
something had crept deep inside him. It went so deep that he
was able to lower his standards to a heartless level during an
impossible situation.

Something similar happened to Lot's wife. Although there was
nothing to save and desire in the ashes of Sodom, she looked
back on the city, even though God had warned them not to, and
she was turned into a pillar of salt (Gen 19:17,26). Something
had gone deep in her heart of which she was totally unaware,
and she disobeyed God and lost her destiny there and then! We
may think the tragic fate of Lot's wife is not fair, but her sin goes
deeper than the simple act of looking back.

Even Jesus mentioned Lot's wife:

Likewise, just as it was in the days of Lot—they were eating and drinking, buying and selling, planting and building, but on the day when Lot went out from Sodom, fire and sulfur rained from heaven and destroyed them all—so will it be on the day when the Son of Man is revealed. On that day, let the one who is on the housetop, with his goods in the house, not come down to take them away, and likewise let the one who is in the field not turn back. Remember Lot's wife. Whoever seeks to preserve his life will lose it, but whoever loses his life will keep it.

Luke 17:28-33

In heaven obedience and trusting God is a big deal. Where is your heart? The Lord who is saving you is saying, "Come to Me. I'm making a way of safety for you. Don't turn back." But Lot's wife's heart was drunk with the things of Sodom and Gomorrah. She turned back and was judged. She had other gods in her life that she had bowed to, which was unacceptable to God.

"You shall have no other gods before me. You shall not make for yourself a carved image...You shall not bow down to them or serve them" (Ex 20:3-5). Lot's wife may not have necessarily bowed down to a physical idol, but anything that is more important than God and His Word is an idol.

What about the daughters who were brought up with good instruction? They ended up living alone with their father in a cave in the mountains, with one convincing the other that they should have sex with him so they could have children (Gen 19:30-38). The story of Lot and his family ends with each daughter impregnated by their father. Lot's descendants are the Moabites and Ammonites, who forevermore remain thorns in the side of Israel.

Is this natural passion? Is this something Lot's daughters learned or saw exhibited? This behavior would have definitely not been permitted in the house of Lot, but it is highly possible that they saw it in Sodom, where the sexual immorality was so abominable that the Lord came down to destroy the city.

The spirit of the land had penetrated unaware into their hearts. Their minds were fine, but their spirits were defiled. One daughter lay with her father and said, "I lay last night with my father. Let us make him drink wine tonight also. Then you go in and lie with him" (Gen 19:34). That is how far their spirits were corrupted.

No soul was redeemed out of Sodom and Gomorrah. Lot lost his marriage, his children, the generations that followed him, his wealth, and his destiny.

What You Do Not Overcome Will Overcome You

Why are our nations and cities in the condition they are in? Why are there closed heavens, no strength to repent, backsliding, unrighteousness, immorality, and so on? Many of us live in nations that were founded on the principles of the Bible, and yet we are living in times when we aren't seeing the reality of God. We don't see Him being glorified or honored the way that He deserves. Why? Because there is spiritual darkness in the land that has not been addressed. There are altars to idols and false gods that need to be torn down.

> We will not have breakthroughs in our cities and nations until we address the unholy altars by revelation and knowledge.

We will not have breakthroughs in our cities and nations until we address these altars by revelation and knowledge. And we must deal adequately with these altars or they will come back to deal with us. We must remember Lot and his wife and determine that we will allow God to use us to cleanse and restore the land. We have to overcome the darkness; otherwise, it will overcome us.

> *And Jesus asked him, "What is your name?" He replied, "My
> name is Legion, for we are many." And he begged him ear-
> nestly not to send them out of the country. Now a great
> herd of pigs was feeding there on the hillside.*
>
> Mark 5:9-11

Jesus had come to the region of the Gerasenes to deal with
strongholds that had never been addressed. They had paralyzed
the city. These demons had also possessed a man and had tortured him terribly. When Jesus cast them out, the demons asked
that Jesus make them leave the man but not leave the area. They
asked to be allowed to go into a herd of pigs that were nearby.

Do you realize that there are demons that have legal authority
over families, communities, and nations? When you become a
Christian and receive deliverance, the demons may come out of
you, but remain in the rest of the family; they are merely moving
their abode. They can say, "We will leave this person, but we will
not leave their community.

They may come out of one location in the country and move to
another. For instance, sometimes we see a negative occurrence
happening in one part of our region. We may pray about it, but
it simply moves to another town. The forces of darkness have
a legal authority in that region, meaning that there are active
unholy altars permitting them to stay in the territory.

Mark 5:13 says that Jesus permitted the demons to go into the
pigs; He allowed them to stay in the area where they were already
present. Why? They had legal authority to stick around. Something more needed to be done to send them out of the region.
The people of the land who had covenanted themselves to the
demons through their active demonic altars were the only ones
who could give them permission to leave.

Why did the demons choose to stay in the area? That is where
Satan had assigned them. That was their seat, their place of

operation. They could inhabit the region because the people had given them permission.

The demons came out of the madman, and he became well and received Jesus Christ as the Messiah. They possessed the pigs and made them run into the sea, where the pigs drowned. When the pigs had perished, the demons had to find another place to inhabit, so they went and possessed the town as a whole.

The result was that the people "began to beg Jesus to depart from their region" (Mark 5:17). The people said what the demons had originally been saying: they pleaded with Jesus to leave the area.

Only one priesthood could inhabit the region: the priesthood of God, represented by Jesus or the priesthood of Satan, represented by the townspeople. Why? Because spirits inhabit by invitation. Sadly, these people chose the demons rather than Christ. If they had not welcomed the demons, they would have been able to invite Jesus to stay.

We must remain aware that what we do not destroy will destroy us. What we allow to stay will fight against us. This can escalate until we find ourselves, like the people in the region of the Gerasenes, following after the ways of demons and pleading with Jesus to leave our area. Or like Lot, offering up our children to darkness, and losing them and ourselves in the process. What we do not overcome will overcome us.

> We must remain aware that what we do not destroy will destroy us. What we allow to stay will fight against us. What we do not overcome will overcome us.

The Land Is Taken by Force

Abraham lived a lifestyle of the altar. He also brought his children to the altar. We know from Isaac's questions to his father

("Where is the sacrifice?") that Isaac was not a stranger to the altar; he knew the elements that go with the altar (Gen 22:7). There was a generational transfer of knowledge and activity from father to son.

However, there is no evidence in the Scriptures that Lot practiced the lifestyle of the altar. As much as he had holy teachings with his daughters, because it is testified in the Scriptures (Gen 19:8), we don't see any mention of the altar in Lot's life.

The forces of the land affected both Abraham and Lot, but their children experienced completely different outcomes. Isaac could have missed destiny. He was on the verge of going into Egypt during the famine, but because of his relationship with God, he was led to stay in the land. God told him, "Don't go. I will bless you" (Gen 26:1-5). But the children of Lot were completely corrupted, committing incest with their father in order to conceive children by him (Gen 19:30-38).

Isaac, a young man whose father was out of the picture, still had a strong relationship with God, and God protected him and guided his way. However, when Lot's daughters, who had a holy upbringing but no semblance of an altar, came under pressure, there was nothing in their hearts other than their own human reasoning.

When we build an altar to the Lord, we have the potential to draw the influence of either the kingdom of God or the kingdom of darkness by our lifestyle. God is commanding us to "Arise, walk through the length and the breadth of the land" (Gen 13:17) and break the powers therein. We are supposed to take the land for the Lord, but the land can't be taken by mere words and preaching.

> We are supposed to take the land for the Lord, but the land can't be taken by mere words and preaching.

In chapter 10 of the Book of Daniel, you find Daniel in a time of deeply seeking the Lord. The pagan nation Babylon was not full of prayer altars, so Daniel had built his own altar to the Lord. He fasted and maintained a state of desperate prayer for 3 weeks, but no answer came.

In the third week of Daniel's fast, an angel appeared and said, "O Daniel, man greatly loved...from the first day that you set your heart to understand and humbled yourself before your God, your words were heard, and I have come because of your words" (Dan 10:11-12). The angel went on to say that he had brought Daniel the answer to his prayers, but had been delayed for 21 days by the prince of Persia (Dan 10:13). It is like the angel was saying, "I have been fighting all this time. It is good you did not stop praying; if you had stopped, I would not have come through. I have only gotten here now because the angel Michael came and helped free me from the power that had been detaining me."

There is something the Lord wants to teach us in this passage (Dan 10:11-13). The land that every one of us lives in has principalities and strongmen over it. For example, the whole of Uganda or Sudan or East Africa as a region has a ruling principality. Then that principality or strongman has smaller minions under him; they rule over the various regions. They also have smaller ones under them that rule over counties. Each county has a strongman, as does each town or village. This hierarchy goes on until there is even one strongman over each tribe and then over each family.

If all of us—each one—including people in business, education, entertainment, even churches, don't rise up to break the power of these strongmen, we will find ourselves submitting to them and having mindsets shaped by them. This results in many terrible things, but one of the worst is that Christians will not be able to operate in the power of God. They cannot have a breakthrough for God to do wonders, and they cannot really take the land for God. They will pray, but sin will continue in the land because the strongman over their land has not been captured.

The land is taken by force through spiritual warfare. As we raise prayer altars we begin to penetrate the spiritual realm and contend with the powers of darkness. Jesus said in Matthew 12:29, "How can someone enter a strong man's house and plunder his goods, unless he first binds the strong man? Then indeed he may plunder his house." The strongman overtook Lot and robbed his house, but this would not have happened if Lot had been maintaining a strong altar to the Lord.

> As we raise prayer altars we begin to penetrate the spiritual realm and contend with the powers of darkness.

Begin to set up prayer altars to fight the strongman and tear down the strongholds in your life and region. Do not keep silent or get tired until God brings complete change in the territory. When you keep your altar alive with your prayers and devotions, you will draw the presence of God to rule over your family, clan, tribe, region, and even nation.

SECTION 4
HOW TO ESTABLISH
AN ALTAR

Section 4
Introduction

We have been looking at why altars are important and how they affect the spiritual environment by pushing back darkness over a territory. We have seen that it was God's strategy to claim and establish the land of Israel by having Abraham build prayer altars all around the promised land, and that the priesthood that prevails in the land will determine the direction the nation will go, both spiritually and physically.

We spent time looking at how to draw the presence of God by ministering to the Lord, hallowing His name, and letting our focus and heart's attention be drawn to Him. We also looked at how putting the Word of God as the centerpiece of our lives draws us into God's wisdom, thinking, and counsel, into the truth and will of God. We looked at how the lifestyle of yielding and surrendering ourselves to the leading and guiding of God's Spirit and His Word, and laying our lives on the altar develops a lifestyle of abiding in the presence of God.

Now that we understand the importance of the altar, in this section we will look at the practical aspects of how to build altars in our personal life, family, church or city, and workplace. We will define each type of altar and answer several questions: What does it mean to have a personal or family altar? What is the difference between a church altar and a marketplace altar? How do regional or national prayer altars work, and what do they look like? We will also discuss the practical aspects of what it takes to build and establish a prayer altar and to keep it going. Finally, we will paint a picture of what each type of altar looks like, and then share testimonies of the altar from different nations of the world.

One of the keys to a successful altar is seeking the presence of God. This is more than just a discipline, method, or formula. As we lay out the practical aspects of building an altar, we must emphasize this again and again because it is so easy to reduce the time we spend with God to a mere discipline or formula. As we crystallize in our thinking that the altar is a place of communion where we come into contact with the presence of God—that it is a spiritual gateway between the physical and spiritual realms—we will begin to understand that as we are seeking God's presence, He will use His presence to take us deeper into His purposes and His will. Under certain circumstances, He may also withdraw His presence to cause us to seek after Him.

> One of the keys to a successful altar is seeking the presence of God. This is more than just a discipline, method, or formula.

When we are building the prayer altar and notice something hindering the presence of God drawing near and abiding with us, we must humble ourselves and seek Him. Through that seeking, God will begin to show us hindrances that we did not even know were in the way and to which we were blind. He will also show us adjustments we need to make to rise to a new level of anointing or to go into deeper communion with Him. We will see that He is calling us into a deeper place of consecration and deeper into His purposes, and that there is a stronger need to abandon ourselves so we can experience breakthroughs in those areas.

It is therefore very important that we do not allow the altar to go into autopilot, where we are just going through the motions of worshiping the Lord, reading Scriptures, and hallowing His name, but not noticing that something is hindering the work of God and the presence of God in our personal or family altar.

—— John Mulinde and Mark Daniel ——

Another key to a successful altar is to constantly be aware that we will encounter warfare at the altar. As we seek to establish an altar or go into a new or deeper level, the enemy will always oppose us, trying to shut things down. There must be a certainty in us that God intended for us to live in communion with Him. We must rise up in perseverance and faith to believe that we were meant to be in the presence of God, so that as opposition comes while we are at the altar, whether it is a family altar, a corporate altar, a marketplace altar, or even the altar of our own heart, we press through in faith, believing that God desires us to be in His presence. We must also understand that as the warfare comes, God will give us the keys that unlock those doors and the understanding needed so we can experience a breakthrough.

It is important to note that we have seen breakthroughs at the altar at the personal, family, corporate, regional, state, and national levels, but there was always great warfare before those breakthroughs came. Therefore, as we face opposition, do not get discouraged, afraid, or intimidated. Remember that as you seek a higher level of breakthrough, the enemy will oppose, but Jesus Christ has already won the victory (1 Cor 15:57). He came to destroy the works of the devil (1 John 3:8), and there is no weapon formed against us that shall prosper (Is 54:17, NKJV). We are more than conquerors through Christ Jesus (Rom 8:37). As we seek Him, He will unlock these areas so we can see breakthroughs at the altar we are building.

CHAPTER 14.
ESTABLISHING A
PERSONAL ALTAR

*Let my prayer be counted as incense before you, and the
lifting up of my hands as the evening sacrifice!*
Psalm 141:2

Building a personal altar does not mean that you are setting
up stones in your house or just having a quiet time in a certain portion of your day. A personal altar is the altar that is built
in your heart. The fire of God's presence must be kept burning
on this altar so that your communion with God is maintained.
You keep that fire strong and your heart open, responsive, and
yielded to the Lord.

Understanding that your heart is your personal altar causes you
to pay close attention keep a careful and attentive watch over
the state of your heart. When you think of an altar as a time or
a place, rather than a lifestyle, then you will believe you are finished communing with God when the time you have set aside
for prayer is over. But when you understand that your heart is
the altar and that you can live in a state of unbroken communion
with God, you will keep watch over it all through the day. You will
become sensitive to the fire weakening as you engage in certain
conversations or behaviors or expose yourself to certain things,
and you will sense attacks coming against your heart. You will
know you need to go spend time before the Lord, allowing that
fire to be rekindled, protected, and strengthened.

To prepare to build your personal altar, take a few days to fast and pray, spending as much time as you can in prayer and the Word to surrender and dedicate yourself to building the altar. Ask the Holy Spirit to guide you to set a time and place for your altar, as well as to give you direction for how to build and establish your altar.

Ask God to pull down unholy altars you have raised to idols; this calls for personal examination and sincerity between you and God. Allow the Holy Spirit to prepare your heart and help you deal with areas where idols may be keeping you from full surrender so that you can give yourself to God on your altar as a pure and holy, living sacrifice to the Lord. The Lord will prepare and adjust your inner being (heart) and your external environment so that it is an atmosphere that draws His presence.

Practical Elements of Establishing a Personal Prayer Altar

Prioritize. One of the first practical steps to building a personal altar is to prioritize and to be intentional. You need to set a specific time and place where you are going to spend time with God, seek Him, draw Him, and come into His presence. If you do not set aside a time and place where you can regularly do that, you will never build the spiritual momentum needed to make the prayer altar a vital part of your life, and you will not be able to fight the spiritual warfare coming against you that is trying to keep you from starting the altar and developing this lifestyle of prayer and abiding in communion with God.

Distractions, diversions, discouragements, and many other things will come against you as you build the altar. One of the first battles you may face will be to set aside the time and place for your altar. You are not just trying to find a brief time to set aside for a quick moment with God, to just have a short quiet time, you are seeking to spend extended time with Him and to truly commune with Him.

The location of your altar is important. It will be your meeting place with God. God says that in the place He allows His name to be honored, there He will come to bless you. It is important that you keep the place as undefiled as possible. The atmosphere of a place is impacted by the activities, conversations, and other sorts of material you allow there. Avoid allowing a radio or TV to spew out ungodly information; let that place be set apart to God. Even if it is your living room or a certain room in a home or other building, the place must be dedicated. Rather than having all kinds of music playing there, try to maintain the atmosphere in a way that will attract the presence of God. This is important whether you are setting up an altar in your home, business, church, or community.

The Spirit of God thrives in the presence of God. Born again believers have the Spirit of God within us, so we require deep communion with Christ if we are going to thrive as believers. This makes it necessary for us to spend at least an hour or two with God every day. This will give us time to seek Him with all of our hearts, respond to Him, and allow our souls to be saturated in Him.

Many people find that they do not develop any depth in the presence of God. This is because they spend short periods of time at their altar. They never really experience that spiritual gateway opening up so that the flow of life can come in to soften their hearts, leading them to a place of yieldedness and surrender before Him so they can abide in His presence.

> One of the first battles is to step across that line of commitment where you say, "Lord, there will be an altar in my heart, and the fire on that altar will not go out."

Therefore, when you first start your altar, remember that one of the first battles is to step across that line of commitment where you say, "Lord, there will be an altar in my heart, and the fire on that altar will not go out. I am going to seek You, I am going to push back the darkness, and I am going to learn how to draw Your presence and live in communion with You. I will set a specific time and place to begin."

The Word. Another practical area to look at is the Word. We need to allow the Word of God to return to being the centerpiece of our lives. To do that, we need to determine that we are going to read the whole Bible. We read the Bible with a desire to see the whole story of God. We don't want to just have a little knowledge of the Bible or be able to quote a few verses that we like because they encourage us. We want to know the whole story, the whole revelation that God has given us through His Word.

God saw fit to give us the whole Bible, and we need to value and treasure it. Because we know some verses that tell us one thing or another but we don't have the whole context, most of us are missing the depth of meaning that comes from the Bible.

When you read a verse like Hebrews 4:16, which says, "Let us then with confidence draw near to the throne of grace, that we may receive mercy and find grace to help in time of need," you might respond by saying, "Lord, I need mercy." But when you consider the wholeness of the Scriptures, you recall how God is rich in mercy (Eph 2:4), that He is full of mercy (James 3:17), that He gave mercy even to Ahab who was the most wicked king ever (1 King 21:29), that whenever anybody humbled themselves before Him, He never turned away from giving them mercy. When you have the whole context of God's mercy illustrated in the entire Bible inside of you, whenever you read Scripture, God's words will have much more depth and meaning.

People often find it difficult to find meaning in the genealogies, yet when you read the genealogies in the context of the entire Scripture, you realize that God had purpose and intent for every single one of those generations. If you look at how He wove His plans and purposes from one generation to the next, you begin to praise Him for how purposeful He is, how full of intent He is, how He has purpose and destiny for your children and grandchildren, just as He did for those whose names you are now reading. You grasp those kinds of things and they start to stir a greater richness in your understanding of who God is and what He can accomplish.

Reading through the whole Bible is vital. If you read 10 or 15 chapters a day, spending 45 minutes to an hour a day reading the Bible, within 1 year you will have read through the entire Bible about four times. In a few years, you will have read through the Bible so many times that the whole of the Bible will be within you. As you read the Bible, you will have the whole scope of the Word of God in your heart and be able to see His hand, how He moves and operates, what is important to Him, what He values, and what He likes or dislikes.

People often say, "But I want to study. If I am spending time reading the Word, why can't I study?" There is a time to study the Word, but we are emphasizing here that there must be a time for reading the Word at the altar so that your soul can be saturated in the wisdom, truth, and counsel of God. As you are reading, there will be times when God will point out a theme in the Bible and then show you where the same theme appears all throughout the Scriptures. Jot these down and take note of these references so that you can go back and study them at another time.

I (Mark Daniel) remember when God started showing me references to the Day of the Lord in the Bible. I had no concept of the Day of the Lord. I did not have any depth of teaching or understanding about it, but I started noticing how God referred to it throughout both the Old and New Testament. I realized that it was the climactic event toward which God is building, and I started writing out every verse where God was speaking about that Day, that season of time He calls the last days, and what He was going to do. I kept track of these Scriptures for several weeks. One day, I realized I had a list of 40 to 50 verses, and I started studying.

The magnitude of these verses broke out over my life. I saw so much more depth than I had ever noticed or identified when I had studied a few of these verses during a quiet time.

We encourage you to not just read the Bible to find a quick fix to a problem or a bit of encouragement, comfort, or direction, but to read the whole Bible. Whether you are having a good day or a bad day, keep reading. Even when the enemy tries to convince you that "This part is no good. This is a boring part," or other similar things, just keep reading, esteeming the Word of God, and knowing that it never returns void.

As you keep reading and saturating in the Word, it will grow deeper in your soul. You won't realize how much it is sinking into you, until one day while praying, speaking, sharing, or even in a time of warfare, the words of God will begin to come out of you. It will be like a reservoir erupting and coming forth with great power.

> As you keep reading and saturating in the Word, it will grow deeper in your soul. One day the words of God will begin to come out of you. It will be like a reservoir erupting and coming forth with great power.

When you first start the discipline of saturating in the Word, the enemy will try to keep the Word from becoming the centerpiece of your life. Your mind will wander; you might start to feel sleepy or to lose your focus. Some people read out loud so their mind stays engaged. Some use phone or tablet apps that read the Word out loud. The app reads a chapter while they read along; this helps keep the momentum going in their hearts.

We encourage you to not give up. As you break through the things the enemy is using to keep you from making saturating in the Word a priority in your life, you will have breakthrough. The Word of God will then be solidly positioned in you and become strong and consistent in your life.

—— JOHN MULINDE AND MARK DANIEL ——

Praise and Worship. Ministering to the Lord is not something we just do for 5 or 10 minutes at the beginning of prayer. It is something we stay in a spirit of—an attitude of—throughout our entire altar time. We draw our focus and attention to the Lord, then continue in an attitude of worship and praise. We do this until we break through whatever is trying to steal our focus and our hearts become fixed on Christ.

The more we remain in an atmosphere of praise during a prayer time, the more the depth of our prayer will increase. Even our intercession will be deeper. Instead of it coming from a deep place where we are crying out because we see God's heart desire, it will now come from an even deeper place of faith and trust that God will answer our prayers because we are standing in His presence, confident in who He is, what He has spoken, and what He has promised.

Remember that your heart is the altar. If you spend time in prayer and being before God, praising Him and saturating yourself in His Word and His presence, you will find your faith high, your focus clear, and your heart set on Him. However, if you go through your day without monitoring the fire on the altar of your heart, you will feel the presence of the Lord decreasing. You may notice yourself speaking out negative words of fear, discouragement, or criticism; becoming self-focused; becoming easily offended; and doing other things you normally wouldn't do. These negative attitudes and behavior are rising up because the fire of the altar of your heart is diminishing and changing the atmosphere around you. A practical way to avoid this is to keep your altar burning and to maintain an attitude of praise throughout the day.

> Your heart is the altar. If you spend time in prayer and being before God, praising Him and saturating yourself in His Word and His presence, you will find your faith high, your focus clear, and your heart set on Him.

People have different ways of praising and worshiping the Lord. Some people use music, some sing songs, and some hallow His name. No matter which is used, the primary goal is to come to a place where their heart is released to God so that they trust Him, believe He is who He says He is, and trust that He will do what He says He will do. Their hearts find rest in Him, and they surrender themselves to Him. They don't hold themselves back, and aren't giving only a part of themselves to Him. They are releasing the sum total of who they are because they know there is no one good but Him. They know there is nothing greater than Him, nothing that can stop Him, and that He loves them with an everlasting, steadfast love.

As you are in His presence, your heart comes deeper into that place of real trust and rest in the Lord. You are trusting God in the fullness of who He bound Himself in covenant to be, and you are giving yourself fully to Him. The more you pray into that place of release and trust to the Lord, the more your heart stays in a position of surrender, and the more you stay focused on God. Instead of taking 20 minutes to get in His presence in prayer, you can sense His presence within a moment because your heart stays in that soft position before Him.

When you are starting to praise and worship, it sometimes takes more time to draw God's presence. This is because we have lived lives focused on so many other things, but the more you continue to minister to the Lord day by day, the more your heart readily comes into His presence and begins to exalt Him and glorify Him.

One of the things we have found very helpful is following practical advice found in the Bible: to fix our eyes on Christ (Heb 12:1-3). The enemy tries to get us to fix our eyes on anything but Christ. Many times, the reason praise is needed to saturate the whole atmosphere is because the enemy is throwing fear, circumstances, or self-focused things at us to try to get us to shut down and lose our focus. In fact, as you look at the things the enemy is using to distract you, you will feel yourself pulling away from the

Lord. To pull yourself back, go into praise, worship, and prayer, setting your eyes on Christ. Speak to your soul, to the spiritual realm, and to the Lord, declaring who He is, how great He is, how glorious He is, how magnificent He is, and how there is no one like Him. Continue to speak out those words, fixing your eyes and attention on Him.

Warfare. Another area where we have some practical suggestions is the area of warfare. As you build your personal altar—this spiritual gateway—the spiritual realm will become very real in the physical realm and you will begin to notice an openness between you and God. There will be a flow of life and an ease of access into His very throne room. You will have a heightened sensitivity to His Spirit, to the Word, to prayer, and to worship. You will experience a flow of life that is continuously refreshing and renewing you. However, as time goes by, you will also sense that the enemy is trying to close that opening. You will feel him trying to decrease, tighten up, or shut down that spiritual gateway.

You will have to fight for your altar, contending for the time. Challenges will come against you to try to shorten or disrupt the time, or to cause you to get discouraged and put off your altar time. There will be things that distract you while reading, trying to make you lose interest in the Word, or you may find your mind wandering while trying to read. You might also find yourself spending more time in the Word and very little time in prayer and communion with God.

We have all experienced these kinds of warfare. You must fight what comes against you and your altar. You will need to make choices to keep the altar a priority in your life and you be determined to spend adequate time at the altar. If you notice the Word coming under attack, consider reading both in the morning and in the evening, determined to be before the Lord and going deeper in the Word. If the level of worship and praise has decreased, choose to spend more time in worship and prayer, pouring your heart out before the Lord because you can discern that the enemy is strategically trying to shut down your time of worship and praise.

Remember that your heart is the altar. As you go throughout your day, your heart will come under attack. All types of things, including fear, discouragement, temptations, or offenses will come against you and hit your heart. It will seem like an arrow got through your armor and has caused a stirring or shaking in your heart. Because you know your heart is the altar, you will not wait for your prayer time the next morning to deal with it; you will deal with the issue immediately.

You may pull aside, go before the Lord, and go into repentance because you realize you have allowed something into your heart. You may go for a walk or be in your car and begin to praise the Lord, turning your eyes and your attention to Him. Your praise will push away the darkness that was trying to come in. You may go home after a difficult day and feel your heart desiring to shut down, but you choose to saturate in the Word. After an hour of being before the Lord, you can sense your heart beginning to open back up. Anybody maintaining the fire on the altar of their heart realizes that the time spent in the morning with the Lord is not adequate to keep the fire burning; you must keep watch over your heart all throughout the day so the fire can stay strong.

Finally, we strongly suggest that you also be part of a corporate altar. This could be your family, church, ministry, or workplace. We all need to have a personal altar as well as to be involved in a corporate altar because there are times when our personal altars come under attack. Corporate altars help keep the fire burning in our hearts because the faith of others gives us strength. Their praise opens things over us, and

> Corporate altars help keep the fire burning in our hearts because the faith of others gives us strength.

their focus on God renews our focus on the Lord. Being part of a corporate altar is vital to our spiritual lives.

Recent Testimonies of Personal Prayer Altars

One of the things that has come from the thousands of testimonies we have heard about personal altars is the truth that saturating in the Word of God, praising God, and coming into the presence of God will change people's lives more than anything they will ever do in all of their Christian life. As they have given themself to keeping that fire burning in their heart, it has developed a con-sistency, a depth, and an anchor that carries them through the storms of life. As they fight for that altar to be maintained, even as the gates of hell rise up against them, they find the strength of God to carry on and to fulfill His purposes. The personal altar has helped the purposes of God prevail in their life.

The following testimony of a personal altar is from a young woman from the UK:

> This young woman had gone through a lot of difficulties and traumas in her life. She had tried to take her life twice. She was in a constant state of anxiety, had frequent panic attacks, lived in depression, had trouble sleeping, and was on pain medication. She could not be left on her own because she was having so much difficulty coping. She was not able to keep a job or function in society.

> She had heard the message of surrender that World Trum-pet Mission carries and had seen what it meant to truly give up her life and to take hold of the life Christ offered her. But she still found it difficult to sustain this surrendered life. She didn't know how to not fall back into the prison cells of depression, anxiety, woundedness, and despair, which sur-rounded her and filled her with condemnation.

> As this young woman began to build her personal altar, she started to see God breaking the grip of darkness over her life and filling her life with His presence. She came to the altar

daily and saturated in the Word of God, allowing it to wash her soul day by day. Her soul became more and more aware of how great, awesome, powerful, glorious, and beautiful God was. Instead of being self-focused, self-centered, and filled with a negative view of herself, her focus began to turn more and more toward God. She became consumed with who God is and what He can do, how awesome and glorious and fierce He is.

Even though she was not an extremely expressive person, she learned how to express her adoration and exaltation to Him. Her heart began to open up and the chains began to come off. In her personal altar, she started to encounter the presence of God. She experienced His love, beauty, and sweetness, and this began to change her whole personality. Her heart opened up so that life, love, peace, and joy could flow inside of her.

This young woman then started to care for the purposes of God, and longed to see them prevail in her land. She gave herself to training, even wanting to be a missionary and carry the message of transforming revival into her nation. God began to use her, opening opportunities to her, and making ways for her life to be productive for the kingdom of God.

As her personal altar went deeper and further, this young lady continued to grow spiritually and emotionally. Every time we saw her, we could see that she had grown even more. She was experiencing more liberty and coming into more of the things of God. She has become a beautiful woman of God.

This young woman, who had never—not even one day in her life—considered having her own family, is now married, has a child, and is serving as a missionary for World Trumpet Mission. All this came about through the personal altar she built, which God used to rebuild and refashion her life to become productive for His kingdom.

—— JOHN MULINDE AND MARK DANIEL ——

Some of the most amazing testimonies we hear are from Taiwan. The Taiwanese are resistant to Christ. They believe that if they give their life to Christ they will no longer be able to honor their ancestors, which is very, very deep-rooted in their traditions. Of the hundreds of testimonies we have heard from Taiwan of people who have started personal prayer altars, every one of them has led somebody in their family to Christ. As these believers drew the presence of God in their prayer altars, their families, friends, and neighbors began to be led to Christ.

One woman shared a testimony about her mother-in-law:
This woman's in-laws did not like her and did not want her in their family. They didn't even want her around, so they never came to visit her and they never let her come to visit them. During the Chinese New Year, families in Taiwan usually get together for 2 weeks of the year. But for this woman, every Chinese New Year, she would send the children off with her husband to go to her in-laws' house while she stayed home alone. This went on for 12 or 13 years.

She began to establish an altar of prayer, seeking to draw the presence of God into her home. As the presence of God drew near, He began to deal with the woundedness, bitterness, and resentments that were in her heart. This began to change things. Even her faith began to rise up.

A few months after the woman started her personal altar, her husband and children went to visit her in-laws for the Chinese New Year. When they came home, they brought food that her mother-in-law had sent back for her. Her husband said, "My mother wants you to have this." "Are you sure it is for me? " she asked. "Yes," he said. "It's for you." Incredulous, she asked again, "Are you sure she said to give this to me?" "Yes!" And she was thinking, "Wow, God!"

A few weeks later her mother-in-law came to visit. She had never visited in those 12 or 13 years. The lady's mother-in-law said, "Next Chinese New Year you need to come with your family to our house." The mother-in-law came by again and again, and the woman started to share her testimony of what Christ had done in her life. Before long, the woman led her mother-in-law to the Lord.

Practical Look at a Personal Altar

Everywhere in the world, spending time with God at the altar looks different to everyone, but there are some common denominators. Many people get up early in the morning so they have a significant amount of time to spend with God (90 minutes to 2 hours). They may start by saturating in the Word of God for an hour, just reading the Scriptures. They might read 10 chapters of the Bible, then allow the Word of God to wash over them. They are reading with the desire to know God more. They are looking for the God of the Bible to be revealed to them. When they are finished reading for the day, they bookmark where they finished reading so they can pick up from that point tomorrow. Their goal is to know God and His ways by reading straight through the whole Bible so they can know the story of God.

After they finish their Bible reading, they spend time hallowing the name of the Lord. They have just spent time reading the Word, looking for how the Word reveals God and His character, and now they spend time meditating on what they learned about God and praising Him, acknowledging His power, sovereignty, authority, greatness, and beauty. They soak in the truth of who God is, going deeper in that, allowing the atmosphere of the room and their heart to become full of the knowledge, wonder, and beauty of who God is.

Many times, worship will continue with singing and music, and the person will allow his heart to be swept away in the atmosphere of worshiping and praising God. In that atmosphere, His presence becomes stronger as the focus is no longer distracted by the challenges of the day or they circumstances he may be facing. He can now allow himself to be led by the Spirit in prayer to take his petitions to God, interceding for concerns he may have. As he goes deeper in the Lord, he starts sensing God's heart for his family, his city, even things in his life that are not aligned with God's way. His prayers come out of that high place in God's presence.

For this to happen, we must make sure we have an extended time of 90 minutes to an hour with the Lord so prayer is not rushed and we are not constantly looking at our clock. We must allow enough time for the Spirit to take prayer where He wants, for Him to take it deeper and further.

The more we come into God's presence on a daily basis, the more His presence changes the atmosphere and we can tell when His presence is being hindered. We can keep the fire of the altar going through prayer, continually being in His presence. As we are in intercession, He will reveal His heart to us, show us ways darkness is trying to push against us, give us prophetic insight into the ways to advance His purposes, and unfold the things of His kingdom before us as we abide in His presence throughout our day.

The Bible tells of people who were walking personal altars, living sacrifices, to the Lord. These people had great impact whenever they entered a territory. King David practiced living in the presence of God. By the time he was brought before King Saul for the purpose of soothing him with music, he was literally casting demons out each time he played his harp (1 Sam 16:14-23). He was a moving altar, so when he played the harp, the manifest presence of God came down, and no demon can withstand that presence.

The apostle Peter's shadow healed people wherever he walked (Acts 5:15-16), and even while in prison the apostle Paul would pray over handkerchiefs or other clothing and they would carry the anointing to heal (Acts 19:11-12). Why? Because both these men spent time in the presence of God and followed God's agenda for each season.

Jesus Christ remains the ultimate example of a personal altar. In the account of the madman of the Gerasenes in Mark 5:1-13, the Bible tells us that this man was so strongly possessed by a legion of demons that nothing could hold him down. He was naked and lived among the tombs, cutting himself with stones. The local people would chain him to stop him from hurting himself, but he would break those chains as though they were pieces of straw. However, the demons had a strong reaction to Jesus.

Jesus, the most powerful personal altar, did not say a word, yet the demons in the man were fearful of being tormented. They asked Jesus to let them go into the pigs rather than be totally cast out of the area. That is how powerful the presence of Jesus Christ, the Son of Man, was; He simply showed up, then demons exposed themselves to Him and left the people they had possessed. This level of spiritual authority is attained through relationship and fellowship with God.

> In the presence of Jesus, demons exposed themselves and left the people they had possessed. This level of spiritual authority is attained through relationship and fellowship with God.

I (John Mulinde) have had this experience many times in ministry. I have been to places that have been very "hard ground" for other people, yet the Lord opened doors for me in a very special way. I had influence and gained spiritual authority in territories that other people prefer not to deal with, especially in Western Europe, where people call themselves "post-Christian" and are very resistant to the Word of God.

One person dependent on the Holy Spirit is the "majority" in any given place or time. I can testify to that over and over again in my own life, and have encountered many others who can testify to this truth as well.

CHAPTER 15.
ESTABLISHING A
FAMILY ALTAR

A family altar is established when the people in the home come together to seek, draw, and worship the presence of God so He can tangibly affect and change the atmosphere in their home. Their family becomes more God-centered, and the presence of God begins to affect their relationships and the things they do in the home. It even protects the home from the forces of darkness that desire to attack the people who live there.

When we started the family altars in Uganda, we saw many breakthroughs come into our nation. God was telling us that, "Every Christian home should be a prayer altar." How much more powerful would the effect of such a large number of Christians be if all the families came before God every evening and/or every morning and called on the name of the Living God on behalf of themselves and their communities? There would be chaos in the kingdom of darkness!

What Does the Family Altar Look Like?

The family altar is different for every family and even in different cultures across the world. However, every family altar has some components that are similar: a time for reading the Word; a time to worship, hallow the name of the Lord, and minister to the Lord; and a time to go to Him in prayer.

The family may read the Word together for 20 or 30 minutes, perhaps taking turns reading the chapters. They then worship God as He was revealed to them through the Scriptures, hallowing His name and exalting Him. They sing praises to Him and lift up His name, inviting His presence into their home. As they worship Him and spend time seeking Him, the atmosphere in the house begins to change; the presence of God is drawing near. They may intercede for their family's needs, following the leading of the Holy Spirit.

Many families spend about an hour together at the altar. Some families have an altar once a week, some have an altar every day, and others have their altar two or three time a week. No matter how frequently a family has an altar, the main idea is to establish an atmosphere in the home where the tangible presence of God is touching every area of life in the home. God's presence is affecting the conversations and attitudes, helping resolve conflicts, and changing the way family members relate to one another. It affects the family's values, mindsets, and how they spend their time.

> The main idea of a family altar is to establish an atmosphere in the home where the tangible presence of God is touching every area of life in the home.

The presence of God can be seen tangibly touching other people as they visit the home, no matter whether they are extended family members or friends of the family. The whole family begins to see that the presence of God is changing the way they live, talk, and think, and it will provide a protection to the family members from the darkness that is desiring to come in.

Many families report children confessing things they used to hide. They are finding that their communications have become clearer, their hearts have become softer and more open, and the ways they choose to entertain themselves or spend their money have changed.

The altar is not just having a time where we have prayer, read the Bible, and worship, it is a time where we are seeking as a family to come before the Lord and draw His presence. Allow the members of your family to have various roles. For example, selecting the music, choosing the Scriptures, or taking turns reading.

Even if some members of your family do not want to come to the altar, don't give up. Maintain the time and keep the altar going. The altar does not just impact those sitting in the room while it is going on. Because the presence of God is being drawn into the house, the atmosphere is changing, so even if other family members are not participating, the presence of God in your home will minister to them, working on their hearts and stirring their spirits.

The Marriage Altar
The marriage altar is a very powerful foundation for a strong and godly family.

The Unbelieving Spouse. If your spouse is not a believer and will not join you in your altar, stand by faith on his or her behalf, praying and bringing the needs of your marriage before the Lord. Prophetically proclaim that you will both serve God and will fulfill the redemptive purpose God has for the two of you as one. Also proclaim prophetically that your marriage will be a shining example to many others whom God has allowed to be around you, both at home and in your community, church, or workplaces.

> The marriage altar is a very powerful foundation for a strong and godly family.

Bring your spouse's weaknesses and strengths before the Lord and prophesy the godly changes you desire to see in your spouse. Also ask the Lord to continually reveal ways you may be pushing your spouse away and not reflecting a Christ-like nature.

The Believing Couple. As a couple, you may desire to have an altar with just you and your spouse. If you do, ensure that you have a designated time and place for your time of prayer where you can share various issues and challenges that you may not be able to bring to the wider setting of the family altar.

At the marriage altar you can
- Pray for the salvation of your spouse
- Pray for deliverance from various bondages and wrong soul ties
- Bring repentance for generational bondages that are present in your families as a first step of removing legal ground from the enemy. Remember that you do not have legal authority to carry out spiritual warfare over your spouse's generational bondages; they have to be broken by your spouse or by a blood relative (Ex 20:5, Lev 26:40-42)
- Bring repentance for the weaknesses and failings of your spouse and yourself
- Bring repentance for the failings in your relationship before God
- Bring repentance for any breakdown in relating to your relatives and friends on both sides of the relationship
- Ask for the desires of your heart concerning your relationship with your spouse and children or other relatives
- Ask for unity of purpose in your marriage and in both your families
- Present your petitions for your own and your children's future and redemptive purpose
- Call forth the giftings, calling, destiny, and godly character in yourselves and your children and families
- Contend with forces of darkness that want to bring confusion in your relationships, business, and ministry
- Get spiritual nourishment, refreshment, and rejuvenation of the love you have for your spouse

Children and the Family Altar
Train up a child in the way he should go; even when he is old he will not depart from it.

Proverbs 22:6

God wants us to fellowship and pray corporately as a family. Your children are the pastors, prophets, and presidents of tomorrow. They are the ministers, national and spiritual leaders, and policy-makers of the future.

Many people ask us what to do with their children when they are having their family altar. We encourage you to let everyone in the family come to the altar. It is fine if the younger children sleep at the altar; they are being raised up in the presence of God, in a family that is seeking God. The children may sometimes play with a small toy or disturb you a bit during the family altar; do not let that be a hindrance. The devil wants to get those children when they are small, so make sure you also get them for God when they are very, very young. As time goes on month after month and year after year, they will put away their toys and join the family in prayer.

Teach your children the Word of God and His promises. Teach them to repent and to ask God to not let judgment come upon their nation. Also ask them to pray always that all the children in their nation would grow strong in the Lord. They may not understand exactly what you are saying; nevertheless, let them cry out and ask, "God, please send your Holy Spirit to our home. Send the Holy Spirit to our city and cover our nation with the Blood of Jesus Christ." You will be surprised how much children can receive from the Holy Spirit and how much they can see in the Spirit.

When the Lord spoke to us in Uganda when we cried out under the scourge of AIDS, He said, "Stop praying about problems and pray for My purposes. Fill the land with prayer. Teach My people to seek My presence. Don't do it in churches only. Teach people to take prayer back home and raise prayer altars at home."

"Bring your children to the family altar. Stop praying sugar-coated prayers with your children when you lay them in bed and then come to Me and bare yourself in private saying, 'God I need Your help.' Come with your children before Me. Let them hear you cry before Me and plead your case before Me. Let them see you express your trust and confidence in Me. When you are frustrated and have no hope, let them see that frustration. Don't act strong before the children and lay them in bed with a one-minute prayer, then come and break down before Me. Let them see you before Me."

God went on and said to us, "When you are not there and circumstances become overwhelming for them, when they are being tempted to turn away from Me and are discouraged, fearful, or anxious, they will remember how much their parents depended on Me and how faithful I proved to be."

It is not useful for your child to come to you and say, "Mom, I have a desperate need," and you cover them with a short prayer, send them on their way, and then break down in desperate prayer, saying, "God, You know how broke I am. You know I have no means. I am desperate. I need help." You may spend hours interceding until breakthrough happens and you come out in faith knowing He will be faithful to bring your petitions to pass. When you come home the next day, somehow God has intervened and filled that need for your child. But they will never know how much God helped you unless you model your life of prayer. When they hear you cry until your spirit touches the heart of God and see the travailing that takes place, then they will know that it is not an instant thing.

Don't let your prayers with your children stop with petitioning or with expressing desires and needs; let them also include seeking the presence of God. Every time you pray and worship, staying before the Lord and pressing in, not only looking for answers but for the God who gives answers, when His presence comes into the prayer room you know a breakthrough has happened, and your children will learn about the Living God and approaching His throne of grace.

—— JOHN MULINDE AND MARK DANIEL ——

In Jeremiah 9:20-21, God asked Jeremiah to call out the wailing women who were to teach their children to wail and stay the destruction and judgment that were coming to the land.

Let your children learn how to woo the presence of God. Take them with you to the altar and let them learn the sweetness of His presence, the aroma of His presence, and how to tread softly in His presence so that in their own time, when you are not there, they will hunger after God's presence and not settle for less.

When they think they have done everything enjoyable, they will come home and yearn for that sweet aroma of God. Nothing else will satisfy them. No drugs or sexual immorality—nothing the world offers them—will quench their deep yearning for the real presence of God. All this is done at the family altar.

When the family altar is strong, it will have an influence over the family for generations to come. Just as Jacob, who lied to his father, usurped his brother's inheritance, and had no fear of God, was eventually called back by the altar that Abraham had raised more than 100 years before, your children, too, will be called back to the family altar you build. A strong family altar will call the children back to order. When you have trained up your children in the way of the Lord, and you see them go astray, go back and tap into the power of your family altar.

> When the family altar is strong, it will have an influence over the family for generations to come.

Practical Elements of Establishing a Family Prayer Altar

Start With Anyone Who Will Join You. Starting the altar with everyone in the family is difficult for many because not everyone in the home wants to participate. Many people have started a prayer altar by first confessing, "We have not been doing this as a family. We didn't even know we needed to do this. I want to repent before you and ask for your forgiveness because I have not helped raise up this family the way I need to."

Some people try to legislate the altar, forcing people to attend. This creates a bad spiritual atmosphere because some people will come in with a hard heart and will be shut down to the others at the altar. It is better to start a family altar in repentance and humility.

If you start an altar and only one or two people in your family want to join you, do not be discouraged. Even if no one in your family starts the altar with you, if you humbly continue to go before the Lord, worshiping Him, reading His Word, and even repenting for how your family has not made room for God, the atmosphere in your home will begin to change. Start with anyone who is willing, then keep the altar going. The others will be drawn in over time.

In many homes, one person started the family altar. Within a period of time, one person would join, then another, and then another. Before long, because the atmosphere was changing in that home, the majority of the family, if not all of them, were coming to the altar.

Spiritually Prepare for Establishing a Family Altar. The first thing to do when building a family altar is to prepare. Before you even take the idea to the others in your family, pray and seek the Lord, repenting for anything that God shows you. You may even consider having a time of fasting to seek the Lord before you make this proposal to your family.

As you pray, God will show you a good way to present this to your family members. Come to them with a humble heart, knowing that you may have slow beginnings. Share with your family that yours is a Christian home and that you want the presence of God to dwell there with you. You want an altar to the Lord established in your home so it is filled with His presence.

—— John Mulinde and Mark Daniel ——

Set a Time and a Place. As you go through the spiritual preparation, you may want to set a time and place in your home when
most people can be present. Even if everyone cannot be there
at that time or some family members attend inconsistently, you
have the altar at the time you set and keep it going.

Begin by worshiping God and reading the Scriptures. Do this
with an attitude of truly seeking God, not putting on a show for
the people in your family. Just come to the altar time with the
attitude that you are approaching the Lord on behalf of your
family, seeking to draw His presence into your home. You desire
His presence to be felt all throughout the house; you are inviting
Him in and welcoming Him into that place. Come with an attitude of humility and love. Let there be no judgment, anger, or
haughty spirit; let there only be an attitude of love.

Do not grow weary when you start your family altar. Not many
people will want to join you at first. However, God is faithful; per-
severe, do not give up or shrink back, and believe Him for the
victory.

Warfare. As with any altar, there is going to be warfare. The
enemy is going to try to oppose your altar. Don't be discouraged.
One form of opposition comes from family members who refuse
to take part in the altar, as we've already discussed. Keep the
altar going because you know it will have impact. Even hearing
the others pray and worship as they sit in their room will touch
their hearts.

We heard of a husband who had not wanted to come to the altar,
but because his wife and children were worshiping God, the altar
began to minister to him, even to the point where he broke down
in tears in the other room. Another man with a mental illness
would not attend the family altar, but his wife and two children
continued to have the altar day after day. The altar began to stabilize the man's mental abilities and his whole personality began
to change.

Don't underestimate the power of the presence of God. Don't underestimate what God's presence is doing in your home. Even when you see family members rebelling against the altar, do not focus on them; keep your eyes fixed on the Lord and trust that He is our Redeemer, our Salvation, and our ever-present Help.

When the atmosphere in the home comes under attack, or there is conflict, fear, or financial challenges in the family, take these to the altar. Saturate in the Word, worship God, draw deep into His presence as a family, and then take the battles before the Lord and watch Him break through.

Many families have been amazed as they brought their issues to God at the family altar and watched Him provide miraculous solutions, change circumstances, and bring breakthroughs. As they saw God move, even the children began to experience how real and tangible God is.

You might experience times when you sense the family altar is getting weaker. When this happens, seek the Lord for insight, asking, "God, what is hindering Your presence from coming? From moving in our home?" He may show you that you need to strengthen your personal altar. Or He may want to take your family altar to a new level. There may be things in your family that God wants to address; if this is so, humble yourselves and seek God. He will show these to you and you will see Him cleanse the house of darkness and take your family into a deeper reality of His presence.

One of the greatest types of warfare that will come against the family altar involves schedules. Even if your family has developed a good rhythm of altar times, something may come up that will tempt you to change the schedule. Don't let this discourage you. Keep the schedule going even if one member can't come as regularly as they had before. Be determined to keep your rhythm going, and begin to pray; maybe the Lord will lead you to add another altar time that your family member will be able to attend.

—— John Mulinde and Mark Daniel ——

There may be times you are required to make an adjustment in your altar time; this change may make it possible for everyone to take part in the altar. Whatever the case, don't allow the altar to be taken away. The enemy loves to come and steal that time; we must contend for it.

Testimonies of Family Prayer Altars

Choosing which testimonies to share about family altars is very difficult because we have literally heard hundreds, even thousands of testimonies of families that have changed because they started building an altar together. People in nations known for prayer, but who weren't having a family altar, heard the testimonies coming out of nations that were beginning to do this, and it would inspire them to begin to build family altars. In Asia, Africa, and other parts of the world, thousands and thousands of family members and neighbors have come to Christ because of a family altar.

In all the nations where we have shared about establishing altars and drawing the presence of God—creating a spiritual atmosphere in which He will work—as families have established altars, they have found their children being drawn back to God. In the Far East, we have heard amazing testimonies of people getting saved as Christians started prayer altars in their homes. This started happening in every home that had an altar. Buddhists would come to their homes and give their lives to Christ. People would come to visit and begin to confess their sin, their needs, and their struggles, and the Christians would have an opportunity to lead them to Christ. As they drew the presence of God, even when in-laws and extended family came to visit their homes, God would begin to work on their hearts and they would have opportunities to lead their family members to Christ.

In Taiwan, there are numerous testimonies of family members who had rejected Christ for decades coming to Christ within a few months of a family building an altar in their home and drawing the presence of God. People with mental illnesses, in major rebellion, or even in adultery have been saved as an altar was built that began to break the darkness in their family. Many children's lives, more than we can count, were ignited for God because of their family altar. In fact, many young people were indifferent toward God even though they and their families went to church, but when they saw their parents seeking after God and coming together to draw God's presence in their home, to read the Word of God, and to praise Him, those children began to change, catch fire, and pursue God.

One testimony of the power of the family prayer altar is from the Far East and involves a married woman with two children:

The woman's husband had a mental illness that caused him to be very erratic in his behavior. Many times he had thrown things out of the house and destroyed them. The woman was a schoolteacher; sometimes as she prepared her work during the night, he would destroy all the work she had prepared for the next day. He caused a lot of disruption in the house.

This woman said that in many ways it was worse than being a single parent because not only did she have to take care of everything herself, she was the only one in the home earning money, raising the children, and keeping up the house. She also had to cope with her husband. Because of his mental illness, he caused so many disruptions that she felt like someone was constantly working against her.

Their family was in a very bad situation. There was a lot of pain and woundedness. There seemed to be no way for the circumstance to change, and medication was not helping the situation. The woman was desperate for help.

She began to hear the testimonies of prayer altars. She didn't even think there was hope of starting one in her home because her children were young, about 8 and 10 years old. She wondered if the prayers of a few people could really change such a home situation. But the more she heard the testimonies of the prayer altars, which were spreading across her nation, the more she was compelled to start one in her home. The woman and her children began reading the Word of God together, and then they began to pray and invite Him into their home so His presence would come and change the atmosphere around them.

Many times when you ask God to draw near, He starts to show you things that grieve Him and hinder His presence from coming. The woman began to see a lot of bitterness, resentments, and wounds she had in her heart toward her husband. She brought her heart issues to the altar of the Lord, allowing Him to cleanse and heal all those things in her heart. There were times at the altar when she would just weep and weep, and her children would be watching her as she was going before the Lord. God was healing and cleansing, and even allowing the children to receive some healing and cleansing.

As this continued, the atmosphere in the home started to change. Within a short period of time, the woman noticed that her husband was becoming much less disruptive and not doing as many things to cause damage to the family. They continued their altar; they continued to read the Word, worship, and pray, and they experienced God coming and meeting with them, dealing with their hearts and giving them a way to move forward.

As they walked out what the Lord showed them, God's presence worked more and more on the husband's life. He started to join the family more, contributing to the family life and their well-being. He even began to attend church, which he had never been willing to do before.

As the family continued to build their altar, God began to change them. The husband became calm, the mental illness began to stabilize, and he started to contribute and give himself to his family. Within a period of time, this man had become active in the church; he even joined a small group. You could see Christ molding, shaping, and changing his life. The family came to have a completely different atmosphere in their home.

One of the amazing things about this family is that as their testimony was shared by video across the nation, many other people who had battles with depression, anxiety, and other mental disorders in their families started to believe that if they built a family altar, there would be nothing too difficult for God to deal with in their families also.

The family altar is a powerful witness of what can happen when a family comes together to seek the Lord. Below are testimonies of the impact the family altar has had in the lives of a few families.

One testimony of a family prayer altar is from a married couple in the UK:

Neither of these people had ever had a personal altar. They also never had a time when they came together in prayer as a family. At one of our meetings in the UK, they heard the Lord say, "Surrender your lives to Me and I will show you what I can do with them." They decided to commit before God and each other that they were going to get up early each morning, read the Scriptures together, then begin to worship the Lord. They would get up and spend an hour reading the Bible alone, just saturating in the Word of God. Then they would begin to praise the Lord together and share some of the Scriptures they had just read.

They said that at first it felt awkward to praise God. They were not accustomed to doing that even individually, let alone with someone else. But they continued to praise the Lord together, and the more they read the Bible, the more praise started welling up inside of them. The more the reality of who God was in Scripture began to grow deeper and deeper in their own hearts, the more praise they began to have.

—— John Mulinde and Mark Daniel ——

After a few weeks, they lost some of their self-consciousness and worrying about how they sounded or how the praise was coming out. Their time became more and more about God. Within 3 to 4 weeks, they started experiencing their prayers beginning to push something. They said, "It was like there was a covering over us and over our house. The more we prayed, the more we started to feel it giving way until one day, we felt something tear and open up over us."

The presence of God came rushing in. They said, "We just started crying and worshiping Him and just releasing our hearts in abandonment and surrender to Him. And as we experienced that opening up over our house, our time with the Lord grew stronger and stronger. There were many times when we could sense that darkness was trying to shut us down, to put that covering back on. We just kept coming to the altar, day after day, week after week, saturating in the Word, and worshiping God. When one of us was struggling the other just kept on going, and vice versa. The Lord was teaching us how to fight to see that opening stay there."

"There are many times that God took us into intercession. He had us crying out for our nation and crying out for His purposes, things we never even knew how to do. He even led us into spiritual warfare. We had never even been trained in those things, but God taught us how to do this as we spent time at the altar. He equipped us to fight for His purposes and has given us a heart for our nation, which we never had before. We now believe for revival because we have experienced it in our own hearts and lives."

Another testimony is from Cleveland, Ohio:
Four young men living in a house together in the inner city wanted to see whether drawing the presence of God to their home would change the atmosphere of the neighborhood they lived in. Their desire was to not just affect their home, but also to affect the street they lived on. They lived on a

street where drugs were sold. There was even a crack house on their street. The police were often called to their neighborhood because of domestic violence. Many young people were uncared for and living rebellious, destructive lives.

These four young men decided to start a family altar. They would get up early in the morning to spend an hour reading the Word of God together before they left for work for the day. When they came home from work, they would eat dinner, read the Word a little bit more, and then begin to worship and praise God. They did this day after day. They had a morning time and an evening time each day. They began to see the presence of God coming, and their hearts became more abandoned and surrendered to the Lord.

Within about a month, young people began to be drawn to the house. One or two young boys would come near the house as they were having their evening time of worship and praising God. Then these young people began to be drawn closer to the house and came to stand on the porch. Before long, the young men in the house went out to ask the boys on their porch, "Why are you here?" They were being drawn by the presence of God. They realized that the boys were being drawn because God's presence was coming to the house.

Before long, more young people were drawn to their home. They started having cookouts in their back yard, where they led many young people to Christ. Twelve to 15 young people started coming to their house to join their altar, all because the presence of God was being drawn.

The young men's faith increased. They continued getting up in the morning to saturate in the Word of God for an hour, then came home in the evenings and praised, worshiped, and glorified God for an hour or more. They declared God's purposes as His presence started moving in their home, and they started seeing God's heart. They started crying out for their street and then seeing God's will and His desire for the people there.

Before long, the drug dealers abandoned the drug house and it closed down. No more drugs were being sold on the street. The family that called the police all the time for domestic violence began asking the young guys to give them counsel on how to deal with their relational conflicts and difficulty. (And none of them were married!) They began to see domestic violence in their neighborhood decrease.

And all these young men began to catch fire for God. They were bold to evangelize, witness, and testify on their street. They even shared with others how to build prayer altars in their homes. They realized that as they were seeking to draw God's presence to their home, their family altar had impacted a whole street in their inner-city urban neighborhood.

In Uganda, there are many testimonies of families drawing the presence of God at their altar. Their home would be so filled with God's presence that people who lived near the house would be drawn to the home. As those people were drawn to that house, they experienced the presence of God, and then confess their sin, ask for prayer, or even ask how to be saved.

There are stories of children in the homes waking up in the middle of the night and worshiping God because His presence was so strong there. God's presence would cleanse the house of deception and darkness, and the children's lives would begin to be oriented around God. They were being raised in God's presence instead of in the culture or the darkness of the world, and their hearts would be bent toward God instead of toward the world.

CHAPTER 16.

HOW TO ESTABLISH A CORPORATE ALTAR

For where two or three are gathered in my name, there am I among them.

Matthew 18:20

A corporate altar is where a body of believers comes together to seek to push back the darkness over a territory and see the presence of God come. This altar can involve people from a church, city, business, region, or nation, and its purpose is to build an altar that will affect the entire territory. The larger the territory, the more people needed to be a part of the altar.

You can often go deeper in a corporate altar than you can at your own personal altar. You can go deeper in prayer, worship, and intercession, and experiencing the presence of God moving in greater ways.

Every prayer altar needs to be connected to a wider altar, such as a prayer vigil, church altar, and the like. In Uganda we have family, church, citywide, and even nationwide altars, when the nation comes together to pray for particular things.

Once you have established yourself as a personal altar to the Lord, any other altar you involve yourself in automatically becomes a corporate altar. This means an altar that has more than one person. Once there are two or more people coming together in fellowship, a corporate altar has been raised.

What are some of the advantages of the corporate altar? When the kingdom of darkness sees you increase in authority, the opposition against you is increased. This means you must increase your legal spiritual authority, which can be done by coming into fellowship with others. The Lord usually draws you to like-minded people, or at least to people you can raise up to form that corporate authority in the spiritual realm that is so vital as you grow spiritually.

This is why corporate altars become very vital in your life as a child of God. Many exploits can be achieved through such altars. The Bible says one can chase 1,000, but two can chase 10,000 (Deut 32:30).

Corporate Altars Give Greater Spiritual Authority

In Uganda, God led us to start family altars. These in turn come together in a church altar, which consists of different families coming together. From every level of society that we come, we enter greater levels of legal authority in the spiritual realm.

Once we come together, a corporate anointing comes upon us to reach a greater level of legal authority. There are certain forces of darkness we can contend with as a family, especially those that fight against us from our family lineage. However, as a single-family unit, we cannot come against a spirit ruling over a village territory unless we are united with other families or members of the neighborhood.

Corporate Prayer Gives Opportunity for God to Give Strategy

Many people have asked, "Do we only have to pray? Is that all that we need to do?" No, it is not. But if you don't pray, God will have little to do in your nation. The destiny of the nation is in your hands, but the strategy to win it is in God's hands. You can only access it through prayer and communing with Him at the corporate level.

Everything you see in the physical realm is a manifestation of what has happened in the spiritual realm. If immorality, demonic activity, and the kingdom of darkness are overcoming the physical realm around you, then you know who is prevailing in the spiritual realm over the land. The destiny of your family and your nation is in your hands. It must first be won in the heavenly realm before it can be manifested in the physical realm.

> The destiny of your family and your nation is in your hands. It must first be won in the heavenly realm before it can be manifested in the physical realm.

Prayer is the only way of communicating from the physical realm into the spiritual realm. From there, God, through His Holy Spirit, will always give us ideas and strategies of how we can work practically at bringing transforming change in our situation.

After prayer has broken through, then people will have an opening to push for physical agendas in the nation. Otherwise, the world is full of human strategies, and many of the nations from which these strategies are emerging are moving further and further away from God and His purposes.

Practical Elements of Starting a Corporate Prayer Altar

Getting Started. When you build a corporate altar, one of the first things to do is find and create a time when the congregation or the members of the Body of Christ can gather together to press into the Lord. You will need to begin casting vision to the congregation about the need for holy altars and how whichever altar prevails in the land will steer the direction of the land. You will also need to identify a common place and time when you can start to gather the people to seek the presence of God and push back the darkness.

Once you have determined the time and place of the corporate altar, covenant and dedicate them and the people who will lead the altar to God. If possible invite your leaders to come witness the raising of your altar. This may be your cell group leader, your pastor, or another leader whom the Lord has laid on your heart. Take building the corporate altar seriously and God will take you seriously.

If possible, write down the prayers of dedication so you can remind yourself and others of the vision for raising that altar. Remember that vision "leaks"; unless it is kept constantly in our focus, we are in danger of losing sight of it and becoming side-tracked. It is always good to rededicate the altar over and over again. Continually renew your covenant with the Lord, and as much as you are able, take Holy Communion on the altar.

Over the years, most corporate altars diminish because those identified as leaders do not attend the corporate gathering. Many delegate prayer to others in their Body; however, as much as possible, let the leadership be part of the corporate altar. When leaders delegate this to someone else, they are sending the message that they do not need prayer or that prayer is not important.

I (John Mulinde) have made this mistake before and I know from experience that it is not a very healthy precedent. If the leader does not need prayer, then the congregation will surely not see the need for prayer. Research shows that church leaders especially are the people who pray the least; they have assigned the duty to intercessory groups. They do not have personal or corporate times of prayer. I have learned that if the leadership is not actively involved in the ministry of the altar, it will not work. It shows that they do not put much value to it.

Many times when people join a corporate altar, they will look for a common culture or a common way to approach God because they are used to having a certain format for prayer gatherings. Because of this, you may want to begin with teachings about the altar using videos about the Word, hallowing the Name, or even worship. You can use those teachings in the beginning of the gathering, with shorter prayer times. When you start to have common ground to stand on, you will be able to come together and seek God in a similar way.

There also need to be designated prayer and worship leaders. One of the mistakes we all tend to make is that we have people who lead us in Bible studies and people who lead us in worship, but we don't have people who lead us in prayer. This causes the prayer time to have no direction, so it just wanders around. Having trained prayer leaders is crucial to seeing the prayer altar make advancements.

Someone needs to be responsible for seeking the Lord in advance to discern what the group is coming up against. The prayer leader can do this as well as help give direction during the prayer time. For example, they can lead the group into deeper praise if they sense that people need to break through or they can ask them to pray together in small groups so their prayers can build momentum. The prayer leader is constantly seeking to stay sensitive to the Holy Spirit's leading so they can know how to lead the people forward.

Your corporate altar must also have a clear purpose. For instance, when we raised the 24-hour prayer altar at our ministry center and Prayer Mountain for All Nations in Kampala, God had made a very clear statement to us: "I am giving you the nation of Uganda." The role of that altar was to take the nation of Uganda at every level. This was not a one-time call; the vision was to take the nation. Once that had been achieved at a very basic level, the Lord expanded the role of the altar. It was now an altar that represented many other nations. As we were faithful with each mission of that altar, the Lord continued to expand our influence and legal authority in the spiritual realm. He began to require that we take up assignments to take other nations and territories. Our prayer focus was not general; it was very specific.

It is important that as many people as possible who attend the corporate prayer altar have started their own personal as well as family prayer altars. These people will have experienced breakthrough in God's presence, pushing back the darkness that was holding them back. They will also have experienced this in their homes. Therefore, when they come to a corporate prayer time, there is a sense of authority and deep faith. They know that the darkness can be pushed back over this territory and that we can corporately experience His presence together.

At the Corporate Altar. Every corporate altar is different, but each one of them makes room for the Word, prayer, worship, and praise. Testimonies will sometimes be shared to help the fire of the altar continue to be fed. Testimonies from family altars or congregational altars can help stir the faith of the people in the group. As you begin to use these different elements in a variety of ways, you will find that the altar stays fresh, alive, and vibrant.

There may be times when you begin the altar time with reading the Scriptures. For example, you may read the Bible for about 45 or 50 minutes by having different people reading one chapter at a time. As you do this, you will notice the atmosphere in that corporate setting become filled with a sense of reverence and awe for God.

There are times in our mission bases when we read a whole book of the Bible during our corporate altar time. As we go through the book, we can sense the presence of God thickening as we read chapter after chapter. After we finish reading and go into prayer and worship, the people's hearts are eager to engage with God.

At the corporate altar, we also will need extended times in worship to just press into God. This allows time to worship Him so that the people's hearts can begin to be released and their focus can be set only on Him; they are holding nothing back and desire to give all they are and all they have to Him. Too many times we go into intercession or prayer before we have come into God's presence and become captivated by Him.

Many times we have extended periods of worship with live worship leaders, then we go into hallowing the name of the Lord, just praising Him and letting our words and hearts flow toward Him. Everybody prays at the same time, just hallowing God's name, letting our hearts be filled with praise and honor and glory to Him.

At other times, as the praising is going on, the prayer leader will take us into intercession, leading us toward those things we want to target in prayer. Sometimes this happens in small groups of three or four people as we pray about various topics. Other times we just continue praying as a large group. As the leader prays, the other people also pray on that designated topic, doing warfare and making intercession before God. After intercession for that particular topic is done, the prayer leader brings us back into praising the Lord for a while longer. This strengthens our faith and draws our attention back to the Lord. Depending on what the prayer leader is sensing, we may then be taken into another area of intercession, another target of prayer.

One of the most important things we have discovered at the corporate altar is that we can feel the darkness pressing against us. We can sense the things that keep the prayer from taking off, opening up, and really beginning to flow. We use worship, praise, and the Word to impregnate the atmosphere so much with the presence of God that it breaks through that darkness. When that happens, we can sense people's hearts and lives being able to release and go into intercession.

If we have 2 hours to pray and it takes us 90 minutes to break through the darkness, that is the time we will take. We use however much time it takes to really break through. Otherwise, we are not drawing the presence of God and people are unable to have breakthroughs. A key objective of the corporate prayer altar is to break through so that people can touch and encounter the presence of God.

Warfare. There is also warfare at the corporate altar. Repentance is key to warfare. Most of your warfare is done when you repent; it removes the enemy's legal ground, allowing God to begin to work.

If we are having difficulty in our corporate altar, it is often because our private times with the Lord are drying out. Just as the corporate altar can help fan the flame of our personal altar, helping to expand it and open it up, many times when the corporate altar is having difficulty, we need to spend

> A key objective of the corporate prayer altar is to break through so that people can touch and encounter the presence of God.

time teaching on, strengthening, solidifying, and helping people build their personal altars. We need to ensure that people know that the corporate altar does not take the place of their own personal altar and that we all have to keep the fire of the personal altar going.

There are also times in a corporate altar when dark forces will come against the group. The prayer altar will not be progressing or taking the territory, and it will be difficult to break into God's presence. At these times, we have to humble ourselves, spend time before the Lord, and ask Him what is coming against the altar and why we are not experiencing breakthroughs. Often times, as the group fights for God to advance in the land, we will sense the darkness of the land beginning to provoke the darkness that is in us. As we are praying for a breakthrough, we realize that the reason our prayers are being pushed back is because there is a level of repentance that we need to go into ourselves. This causes us to humble ourselves and seek God. We don't want any of the darkness that is in the land in us, and a cry, an abandonment, a willingness to do whatever God wants us to do rises up within us. He begins to cleanse us of that darkness and we see it broken in our lives.

> Often, as we fight for God to advance in the land, we will sense the darkness of the land beginning to provoke the darkness in us. As we pray for a breakthrough, we realize that the reason our prayers are being pushed back is because there is a level of repentance we need to go into ourselves. This causes us to humble ourselves and seek God.

There are also times when God may show us that what we are coming up against needs repentance or that we need to go deeper in the Lord. This calls for spending longer times in worship and in hallowing His name. We then become more and more saturated in God's presence, putting our focus on Him and drawing Him deeper into the atmosphere.

It is important in the corporate altar to not be casual or passive. There is something in us that wants to follow a program or a formula, or just to get through the time, but there are times when we will sense that we need more of the Word, we need to dig deeper into lifting up the name of the Lord, or we need more time to worship. We sense that there are adjustments we need to make in order to see a breakthrough. Sometimes we will notice the people getting weary, so even though we are gathering for prayer, we may need to do some training to help strengthen the people and keep the altar strong.

We must have prayer and worship leaders who are very sensitive to the Holy Spirit. They are not performing or just leading a prayer time; they are focused on the need to break through into the spiritual atmosphere. They are very sensitive and can follow and make adjustments according to the leading of the Holy Spirit. These people need to have effective and powerful personal and family altars themselves. The only way they become effective at seeing how to break through darkness and seeing the presence of God come is that they have been doing it personally and in their family. Without that reality of the lifestyle of that altar, they don't have confidence to deal with the spiritual forces they will encounter when a number of people in the territory come together.

Testimonies of Corporate Prayer Altars

With our God all things are possible. We need to win battles in the spiritual realm so the physical realm will manifest our success.

As the family altars in Uganda were set up and the network of prayer began to take shape, villages started experiencing transformation. One of our WTM missionaries gave the following testimony:

> Our town is 17 miles from Kampala. As you enter the town, there are two mosques on each end that act like entrances to the town. Muslims would wake up every morning to pray. They did that every morning until one day, the Holy Spirit brought up spiritual anger in us and we declared, "This will not happen while we are here."

> When we came to the church altar, I shared with my brothers and sisters what was on my heart. I said, "We have to come against this spirit. We will wake up at 5:00am and call on our God in our families and He will bring turbulence in the spiritual realm, so that when they call on their god, they will find that the firmament is already taken up by godly principalities."

> We went to our family altars and repented of the covenants and sacrifices made to the forces of darkness in the town. In the family altar, we have no legal authority to contend with the warfare over the town, but we are able to repent at any level.

When we came together as a church, we started to come against that spirit. We now had legal ground to attack it because of the families who came to the corporate altar from the different parts of the town. Within one week their speakers stopped making the morning call to prayer.

A few weeks later a Maalim, a teacher of Islam, came to the Sunday service. We wondered, "What has he come for? A fight?" As we welcomed the visitors to the service, we asked him to greet us. He said, "I have come here not as a visitor. I have come to stay."

We knew we had done something in the spiritual realm, but we did not stop there. Once a week we resist that spirit and continue to pray for sustained victory. Muslims are coming to Christ, not because we have gone to preach to them, but because the strongman in the town has been overcome.

Another testimony of the corporate altar is from Taiwan, where the Lord has used us to help build prayer altars all over the nation:

In Taiwan, there is one corporate altar that is the foundation of all of the corporate altars in the nation. The National Prayer Network gathers together four or five pastors and leaders from each of the 17 counties for about 2 days every month. There are usually approximately 120 people in attendance, mostly leaders, who gather from around the nation. These days are a time of prayer and fasting, prolonged periods of worship, and a time of hallowing the name of the Lord and crying out to God. Each month, these leaders seek to just go deeper and deeper into God's presence. They spend time in teachings related to revival and how to see a move of God within their nation, and also have times of fellowship.

They fellowship some, spend time in worship and prayer, and then give direction on how to carry the work forward throughout the nation. This altar has been ongoing for over

3.5 years. It has built a sense of continuity across the nation and a sense of unity for the work to be carried forward. In many ways, it has been a driving force for building altars across the nation.

As we go forward to carry out the work of God, He is going to build these different corporate altars, at both the regional and city level. The frequency of the times they meet will depend on God's leading, but He will build the corporate altars, which will then bring a covering to a village, city, region, or nation.

The Marketplace/School Altar

Definition. A marketplace or school altar is a gathering together of people from the same workplace or school to seek the presence of God, to push back the darkness, and to see the presence of God come in deeper and deeper ways so that there are greater manifestations of the kingdom of God in their workplace or school and they see the purposes of God advance. Each type of altar (personal, family, church, workplace, school, etc) plays a role in the darkness being broken over the land.

In many workplaces, as people have begun to build the marketplace altar, they begin to see God moving, saving souls, and transforming their industry. The industry and society become godlier, and the influence the industry has begins to advance the kingdom of God. The environment in the workplace changes, and the presence of God creates a life-giving atmosphere in that work place.

Corporate Altars Penetrate
Where Pastors Cannot

There are some places where pastors have no access, but others do because that is their place of work. You are the pastor and missionary in that place. As the priest in that place, pray for an altar to be built in your workplace or school; with time, God will honor your prayers and your workplace.

Wherever you are stationed, you are an ambassador. You are not there only to obtain money or have a position. In that place, God does not identify you by your job description. He identifies you by the ministry He has placed on you in that position.

If He has called you as the prophetic voice in your office—or the pastor, teacher, or priest in that place—then whatever position He has placed you in is how God sees you. He wants you to be a good and faithful steward. Seek God for what He wants you to be and to do in that place where He has stationed you in life.

> *The two angels came to Sodom in the evening, and Lot was sitting in the gate of Sodom.*
> Genesis 19:1

Do not be like Lot in the Bible. In Biblical terms, "sitting at the gate" implied being a man of authority, with decision-making capacity. He was an elder in the city. However, Lot was not known to anyone by any other description except that he was a man of influence there. When it came to matters of righteousness, he was quiet about the wickedness of the city. Even when he began to speak about judgment, everyone found him quite ridiculous.

If you are in a business or company, office, etc, God has placed you as a leader there. Start instituting a marketplace prayer altar and ask God to raise up others to join you. God wants to visit your shop or business and to bring His transforming power there.

Practical Elements of Starting a Marketplace/ School Prayer Altar

As you seek to establish a marketplace or school altar, one of the first and most crucial things you need to do is prepare. You must have already established your personal altar as well as a family altar. This will help you experience what it means to break through the darkness and to have the presence of God becoming more tangible and real, and opening up over your life. You will have a confidence that darkness can be pushed back and that you can draw the presence of God. You also will have the faith that rises up and does not grow weary.

Prepare to start a marketplace prayer altar by fasting and praying. You will want to prepare yourself spiritually before you approach anyone to ask him or her to join you at the altar. As you pray in preparation for the altar, you will receive specific guidance and instruction from God about the time and place for the altar, which people to approach, and how to share with them about the altar. Spend enough time with the Lord so that the ground and atmosphere will be ready as you begin to build your altar.

Secure a place where the altar will be held at your workplace or school, then begin to gather testimonies about workplace altars you can share with people about why you want to have a prayer altar and how you think it will benefit the people who become involved.

As you begin the altar, do not become discouraged. If only a few join you in the beginning, don't worry. Remember that you are trying to start something that has never been done before. Most people have never been involved in this kind of thing before, and that it isn't a common thing to do. In some cultures, this will be very easy to do, while in others, it will be very uncommon and difficult. Therefore, don't get discouraged if you have a small beginning. It will help to keep in mind that the desired end is to see darkness over your workplace pushed back and the presence of God coming in tangible ways.

Many people hold their prayer altar before the workday begins so there are no complications with the boss or problems from other coworkers. Some altars are held on Monday morning and Friday morning; this is to cover the beginning of the week and the end of the week. Some altars meet three times a week. Have your altar meet often enough that it begins to impact your workplace.

Every workplace altar is going to be different, but it needs to include the Word, worship, and prayer. More importantly, you need to respond to what the Holy Spirit is showing you about the altar. You may be led to have a time where the group reads the Bible together, allowing the Word of God to come into that place and be held up and honored there.

You will also want to have the freedom to worship. Don't hide your love for Jesus. He said that as we exalt Him, men will be drawn to Him, so as we lift Him up in our prayer altars, men will be drawn to Him. Too often we become afraid and hide our faith in the workplace instead of allowing ourselves to be bold and showing ourselves to be Christians. In your worship times you will want to praise Him and hallow His name. People will be drawn to you as you are unapologetic and not afraid of revealing your Christianity.

As you are worshiping the Lord, hallowing His name, and praising and exalting Him, His presence will become more tangible and He will show you ways to intercede for your workplace or school and the atmosphere that is presently there. He will even show you things that are hindering His presence from coming. He will show you how to take the kingdom of God forward. Be sure to respond to these leadings of the Holy Spirit.

In many workplace or school prayer altars, God gave the group insight. As they obeyed what He said, He would open more doors. The altar would start to have greater impact, even changing the way the company and its employees did business. This is what we want to see: the industry being changed to become more God-centered instead of self-centered.

Warfare. There are many things that will oppose a workplace or school prayer altar. People will tell you that prayer or meetings not related to the business or school aren't allowed. There are people who will openly oppose you. However, don't be afraid.

*Blessed are those who are persecuted for righteousness'
sake, for theirs is the kingdom of heaven. Blessed are you
when others revile you and persecute you and utter all
kinds of evil against you falsely on my account.*

Matthew 5:10-11

Jesus told us that if they persecuted Him, they would persecute
us (John 15:20). Some people in society are against Christ, but
we are His servants, so we do not allow them to intimidate us
from going forward and seeing the altar of the Lord drawing His
presence in all aspects of society.

Do not back down. Do not be afraid even if ridicule comes against
you. Realize that as you stand, people are going to be drawn to
Christ.

As they begin to establish prayer altars, many workplaces and
schools start to face hindrances. Challenges may come against
them that they don't understand. They may ask, "Why are we
having these problems? Why is
the presence of God not coming?"
As they humble themselves and
cry out to God, "What is hindering
Your presence from coming to this
place?" He will begin to show
them the hindrances, such as
unethical practices that are repulsive to Him or quenching His
presence from drawing near.

> If you see a hindrance to
> God's presence coming,
> humble yourself and seek
> Him. He will show you
> what to cleanse out of your
> workplace; as you do, you
> will see greater and greater
> manifestations of His kingdom.

There are many testimonies of
lies, deception, and unethical or
dishonoring activities that were happening in the workplaces
that were exposed during a prayer altar. As the people repented
of those impure ways, to cleanse them and stop doing them,
God's presence would come in tangible ways. Therefore, if you
see a hindrance to God's presence coming, be willing to humble

yourself and seek Him. He will show you what to cleanse out of your workplace; as you do, you will see greater and greater manifestations of His kingdom.

Testimonies From Marketplace Altars

One of the most exciting things in the work of transforming revival is the testimonies about prayer altars in the marketplace. They are changing the fabric of society.

One time, while we were ministering in Taiwan, there were about 800 business leaders gathered together from all types of industries: medical, educational, retail, manufacturing, civic, media, etc. They began to stand and share testimonies about how the presence of God was coming into their industry and changing the way they did business. The altars they had established in their workplaces were changing the way they treated their employees, their clients, and even their patients. These changes were affecting their workplaces and helping them become witnesses with influence and impact.

As we heard testimony after testimony, we could see how the fabric of society was changing. I (Mark Daniel) remember weeping and weeping because I realized that all kinds of workplaces and industries were represented there, and the people were seeking to draw the presence of God. I thought, "If they keep this up, if they keep going deeper and further with this, it's going to change the course of this nation." Those testimonies were so powerful. And we continue to hear them every time we return to Taiwan.

Impact in the Manufacturing Industry. One of the first testimonies we heard of a marketplace altar was from a gentleman who works for a company in Taiwan that manufactures electronics:

> He was head of a department of about 100 or more people and had experienced the prayer altar in his personal life and in his family. He had been so transformed from those altars

that he had the faith and passion to want to take this into his workplace, so he began to fast and pray, looking for a way to begin this altar. Soon there were three or four people who said they would join him to build an altar in their department.

They held their altar on Monday morning and Friday morning because they wanted to begin and end the week with prayer. They would spend about an hour of time with the Lord, reading Scriptures, then going into praising and worshiping God. This would lead them into intercession. Their desire was to draw His presence, not just have a devotional time. They realized that there were Buddhists and people who followed other religions at their workplace who were drawing dark spiritual forces, and they wanted to see the presence of God come so the One True Living God could reign faithfully and fully in that place.

As they began to meet for prayer and worship, they noticed that they were having a hard time drawing the presence of the Lord. This man knew he had experienced God's presence much more deeply in his personal life and in his home, so he started asking God, "What's wrong? Why is Your presence not coming here? What is hindering You from working in this place?" As these people prayed into that, God began to make it clear to him that there were things they did in his company and in his department that were unethical, against God's heart and His desires.

There were several things they were doing that weren't totally ethical or honest. They lied to vendors. They manipulated numbers and reports. Faced with what the Lord was showing them, this man knew he had to make a choice. Was he going to go to his boss and tell him "I'm not going to do these things anymore"? Or was he going to give up the prayer altar?

This man decided to go to his boss. He said, "I can't do some of what you have asked me to do anymore. They offend my God." And his boss said, "Get somebody else to do them then. You don't have to be the one who does them." The man said, "You don't understand. They offend my God. I can't tell anyone else to do them." His boss got frustrated with him, but said, "Okay, okay. You don't have to do them anymore."

As the man adjusted the way his department functioned to align with the ways of God, the presence of God began to come. It got stronger and stronger, and they knew that God was leading and guiding them. They started to change the way they treated people, they changed the way they did things in their department, and more people were drawn to the altar.

By then, the altar had grown to about 15 people. People were coming to Christ, and the man was buying Bibles for them so they could read the Bible together. The altar was beginning to have a real impact in their workplace. The department went from about 3% Christian to about 15% Christian, and the changes began to have real impact in the workplace. There was less absenteeism, less complaints, and even greater productivity.

One day, as they were praying at the altar, God put a conviction on this man's heart that the work hours were so long that these people didn't have time to go home and build family altars. God directed him to declare that there would be no more overtime in the factory so that everyone could go home to build altars with their families.

This was a very radical move. The man knew if they did not meet productivity he would be immediately fired, but he felt so clearly this was God that he decided to obey the Lord without question. He knew that the purpose of the altar was not just to have prayer, but also to see God's presence come so that He could begin to bring a greater and greater manifestation of His kingdom.

As the people in the department obeyed the Lord, more and more of them went home to build altars in their homes. Many testimonies of God moving were rising up, and families in this man's department were beginning to change, to experience healing, and to become whole. The people were becoming more full of life, happiness, and joy.

These changes began to have such an affect in that company that the man's boss came to him one day and said, "Your department has fewer complaints, less absenteeism, less HR problems, and higher productivity than any other department. In everything we measure, your department is doing better than anybody else. I'm going to call all the executives and managers of departments together, and I want you to tell them what you are doing so that all the top people of this factory can understand." He gave this man 1 hour with the top executives and all the department heads.

He came to the meeting with five Power Point slides. The first slide said, "The fear of God is the beginning of wisdom," and he shared how reverence for God is necessary to begin to know His heart and mind. His last slide said, "Jesus Christ is the answer for any problem you face." He shared with them what he had been doing and how that had changed the atmosphere in his department. The people in that company didn't understand it all because most of them were Buddhist, but they said, "Whatever you are doing is productive. We are going to build prayer altars in the other departments so we can get the same results all throughout the company."

Impact in the Retail Industry. Another testimony was from a shop owner in the retail industry:

In the Far East, counterfeiting products is something that is somewhat acceptable to do. You can copy people's inventions and designs, and then sell the merchandise like it is an authentic product rather than a counterfeit. These retail people were buying counterfeit products because they were cheaper and then selling them as the name brand. They had placed an order for a large shipment, but at the same time they were building a prayer altar in their shop.

They began hearing the testimonies from around Taiwan about the marketplace prayer altars and what God was doing, but they had no sense of God's presence moving in their industry. So they started asking "Why?" and humbling themselves and seeking God. God showed them that what they were doing was stealing. They genuinely panicked, and prayed, "But God, if we buy the true product and our competitors are selling counterfeit, they will get all the business. We are going to lose business."

And they struggled and struggled with these different questions. "What are we going to do with the product we already ordered? Do we sell it to someone else?" They kept seeking the Lord and finally decided to obey Him. God then began to give them a strategy and a way to do their business. Today, their business is thriving and successful. The Lord led them to give up all the counterfeit goods they were going to buy, even though they would lose money, and He began to lead their business forward. They found that as they started doing things God's way, their business continued to make a profit.

The presence of God came into their store and they were shocked. In fact, they had a few employees they had invited to church in the past, but who had never been interested in Christ. These employees began coming to the prayer altar, and as they did, they touched the presence of God. All their employees became Christians, one after the other. The atmosphere in their shop changed and they testify that it has been the presence of God in their shop that has helped them succeed in business.

—— JOHN MULINDE AND MARK DANIEL ——

Testimony From Florida. Another prayer altar testimony is from a man who works at Kennedy Space Center in Florida (USA):

> This man was digging ditches to help lay electrical wiring, and he started thinking, "This is my work place." So he started inviting the guys who were digging the ditches with him to come together twice a week to read the Scriptures, worship God, and invite the presence of God into the ditches with them. As they did this, those he thought would be the most resistant—the people who were the most profane and the most un-Christian in their behavior—were the most open people. As God's presence came, they were changed.

Testimonies From Uganda That Affected the Nation

> In Uganda, our ministry began to teach people about praying in their workplaces, schools, and other areas where there was more than one believer. We taught people how to pray for the specifics of their workplace and to raise the nation of Uganda before the Lord.
>
> AIDS was affecting employers and employees. Many people were sick. The challenges in the nation could be brought down to the specifics of each place, whether in families, offices, or schools. The prolonged civil unrest and violence in the nation had affected all these places.
>
> As people prayed in these areas, something began to happen. Transformation began to take place, and God raised God-fearing men and women into positions of prominence in the various government and private sectors.
>
> For example, the most corrupt government organization was the Uganda Revenue Authority. For many years, people knew that the taxation system in Uganda did not work. Anyone could get waivers through bribing the revenue officers at

every level. However, prayers were being made by people in very lowly positions in these offices. For example, Christian messengers, tea-servers, and cleaners who worked there prayed together, as well as Christian clerks and managers in other departments. The Lord soon raised up a God-fearing Commissioner in the revenue authority. The lady cleaned up the system so effectively, that the URA became one of the most effectively and efficiently run organizations in the nation. They have beaten every government deadline given to them under the watch of this commissioner.

The banking system in Uganda was also in a bind. The Uganda shilling had become quite worthless; and the banking sector had suffered one of its lowest points when the Governor of Uganda Central Bank was assassinated by Idi Amin. As Christians began to pray in the sector, God brought recovery not only in the banking sector but also in the nation's economy. The banks had one of the strongest interbank fellowships. Many banks were opened up in the nation. The struggling ones began to expand into the rest of the nation; services were improved and today the banking sector in Uganda rivals any other on the continent of Africa.

Corporate altars in Uganda have become commonplace, and God has used them in wonderful ways in the marketplace as well as on a government level. It has been very exciting to see what God can do when we invite His presence into our workplaces and schools.

In Closing

In Uganda, God told us, "Get every Christian family to become an altar. Let the families come together and pray together because I want to meet My people there."

You find that as you begin, God will deal with issues that affect you individually. As you meet in the family context, God reveals and deals with issues at the family level. This also happens at the church, community, and national levels as each group meets often. Soon individuals, families, workplaces, churches, communities, and the nation will be impacted as you win spiritual battles and things start to manifest in the physical realm as answers to prayer.

We decided to put the Abrahamic Strategy into practice in Uganda. It was very tough, and we were very few and very unknown. As the Body of Christ came together and people built prayer altars all over the land in their hearts, homes, workplaces, schools, villages, and larger communities, the Lord began to reveal more strategies on how to help prevent the different problems that were plaguing the nation, AIDS being one of them.

As the Body of Christ prayed, the government was being touched. God released wisdom on how to mobilize the nation to fight the pandemic. The World Health Organization later reported that Uganda prevalence levels of AIDS had dropped to around 7%, from the highest rate of 36%. Many other great things began to happen in the nation. In the past few decades, the face of the nation has changed in many ways due to the continuing prayer.

It does not end with prayer. It begins with a dedicated personal altar and then grows to entire territories experiencing the power of God. As people come into the presence of God in prayer, God also releases strategies of how to solve the many other problems they are facing in a practical way. Today in Uganda, it is very easy to pray, not because we are powerful, but because we have humbly repaired the altar of the Lord all across the nation and are living a lifestyle of effective holy priests.

As the net of prayer was spreading over the nation of Uganda, a number of things happened, which God opened our eyes see to after about 10 years of their development. In 1997, when the president of Uganda came for the repentance and reconciliation conference, he did something miraculous. After speaking, he got the national flag and handed it over to the intercessors. He said, "I hand over this nation to you intercessors. You are the ones who can bring change. We have tried here and there, but without success. Now Uganda is in your hands."

What prompted that? A network of prayer altars, which began in individuals and grew into families and cell groups and churches and whole communities.

Also in 1998, he sent the Ugandan Vice President to AfriCamp with a signed document for the launching of the African Missionary Initiative, saying "In the name of the government of Uganda, we send missionaries all over the world. Go and be a light." Then they brought a light and handed it to the missionaries. This means that our missionaries do not go out of the nation alone; we stand under a mandate released by the President and Government of Uganda.

There are certain things that take effect even if the leader of a nation is not saved. Leaders already have a kingly anointing over their lives. They have an authority to open up the nation to godly or ungodly influences. They stand in the gap as leaders and can declare things into the spiritual realm, whether knowingly or unknowingly. Even when he does not recognize it, the President has a kingly anointing that comes with his position, and by giving us the seal of approval, it is conferred on us. We must steer their decisions and declarations through fervent prayer for them (1 Tim 2:1-2).

Today we have a number of Christian radio stations and TV stations. Every morning at 5:00am we have pastors leading prayers in various corporate prayer altars set up over the nation's airwaves.

We got those radio stations after prayer, because the national radio had refused to announce anything to do with born again Christians. The Minister of Information was not interested in promoting anything of the born again Christians, so we went into prayer, from family altars to the national prayer altars, and cried out, "God, do something about the airwaves of Uganda." If you have 1 million homes putting on the radio in the morning and praying for the same thing corporately, you have corporate anointing. On seeing that, the government said, "Please give them free airtime on Uganda TV to preach the gospel." After that, the national radio even gave them free airtime. We now have Christian programing on TV and radio, and much of it is free.

The transforming revival in Uganda began with this instruction: "Draw My presence into your homes in such a way that people will walk in and sense My presence and My peace. Guests who sleep in your homes will wake up and begin to open their hearts to you. When you worship Me, I will come down and manifest Myself to you."

Drawing the presence of God to the nation of Uganda began with building altars all over the land, where we did not just say prayers, but sought to draw the presence of God, to worship and minister to Him, and to draw His presence all across the land. God was teaching us to create an atmosphere all across the nation that would attract His presence, and He was saying, "In that environment, I will begin to reveal Myself and My mission. I will begin to give direction and move in the lives of people. You are opening a gateway over this nation that will allow Me to impact the physical world."

God taught us that it is not just seeking, talking, and walking with Him that creates change; the spiritual atmosphere in which all these things happen means everything. If we seek to push back darkness and draw the presence of God, we will see Him do great things—open doors, move hearts, change circumstances—that we could never do on our own.

We have taken this same strategy that God deployed in Uganda into other parts of Africa, and we have seen it change lives. The testimonies from thousands of families have been remarkable. We have watched the establishment of altars change the church, affect and change society, and even impact the marketplace.

Building and repairing altars of the Lord in other parts of the world is producing a unity of purpose to see the power of darkness broken, the presence of God being drawn, and the kingdom of God rather than the kingdom of darkness reigning on the earth.

In Asia, as one nation began to build altars and raise up a great testimony, that nation's spiritual atmosphere changed so much that all the nations around it began to ask how to build prayer altars. They want to learn how to do this, too. Even the secular newspapers have commented on how the atmosphere in the nation has changed. The church as a whole began to function at much higher levels of effectiveness than they ever had before.

—— JOHN MULINDE AND MARK DANIEL ——

Building and repairing altars of the Lord in other parts of the world, such as North America and Eastern Europe, is producing a unity of purpose to see the power of darkness broken, the presence of God being drawn, and the kingdom of God rather than the kingdom of darkness reigning on the earth.

Our prayer and hope is that this book has not only changed your life, your family, and the ministry you are involved in, and that you will begin to experience revival in your life, but also that it will help the Body of Christ in your territory come together to work as one to see the darkness over the territory broken. We also pray that we will see the end-time global harvest spoken of in the books of Joel and Haggai as the church begins to make itself ready by repairing the altar of the Lord.